TRAILBLAZER

TRAILBLAZER

TRAILBLAZER

AN INTIMATE BIOGRAPHY OF SARAH PALIN

LORENZO BENET

POCKET BOOKS

NEW YORK   LONDON   TORONTO   SYDNEY

Pocket Books
A Division of Simon & Schuster, Inc.
1230 Avenue of the Americas
New York, NY 10020

Copyright © 2009 by Lorenzo Benet

All rights reserved, including the right to reproduce this book or portions thereof in any form whatsoever. For information address Pocket Books Subsidiary Rights Department, 1230 Avenue of the Americas, New York, NY 10020

First Pocket Books paperback edition July 2010

POCKET BOOKS and colophon are trademarks of Simon & Schuster, Inc.

For information about special discounts for bulk purchases, please contact Simon & Schuster Special Sales at 1-866-506-1949 or business@simonandschuster.com

The Simon & Schuster Speakers Bureau can bring authors to your live event. For more information or to book an event contact the Simon & Schuster Speakers Bureau at 1-866-248-3049 or visit our website at www.simonspeakers.com.

Cover design by Ariana Grabec-Dingman

Manufactured in the United States of America

10 9 8 7 6 5 4 3 2 1

ISBN 978-1-4391-8758-6
ISBN 978-1-4391-5555-4 (ebook)

For Aimee, Hannah, and L.J.

Thank you for all your love
and support;

and for my father, Pete;

and in memory of Mary, Gil,
and Shaun.

ACKNOWLEDGMENTS

I want to give a heartfelt thanks to everyone who contributed to this book.

Literary agent Jarred Weisfeld of Objective Entertainment; Threshold senior editor Kathy Sagan; researcher Alondra Hernandez; proofreader and apprentice editor Angela Velez; journalist Vicki Naegele; and vice president and deputy publisher of Pocket Books Anthony Ziccardi.

With special gratitude, thanks to the members of the Heath and Palin families; to Heather Bruce for her insights into her sister Sarah and beautiful photographs; to Chuck and Sally Heath—while fielding a hundred calls a day from media they managed to find time for me; and to Jim Palin.

Special thanks to *People* magazine editors Larry Hackett, Betsy Gleick, Rob Howe, Nancy Jeffrey, and Elizabeth Leonard.

I also want to recognize the people who cooperated extensively for *Trailblazer* with their thoughtful words and/or photo contributions: Judy Patrick, Nick Carney, Laura Chase, Jessica Steele, Warren McCorkell, Don and Deby Teeguarden, Paul and Helen Riley, Vicki Naegele, Christine Garner, Kay Fyfe, Anne Kilkenny, Katie Johnson, Berkley Todd, Jerry Kramer, Lauren Maxwell, Roger Nelles, Steve MacDonald, Tom Whitstine Jr., Paul, Barbara, and David Moore, Dwight Probasco, Melissa and Jim Keen, Scott Davis, and Cheryl Welch.

Finally, to some of the finest journalists on the planet who provided inspiration throughout the project: Michael Arkush, Howard Breuer, Vickie Bane, Johnny Dodd, Oliver Jones, Champ Clark, Frank Swertlow, Tom Cunneff, and Lyndon Stambler. As always, a special shout-out to my family, John, Edwin, Maria, Sarah, Pia, Jonna, Ron, and Roberta; and dear family friends, Victoria and Dan Wang; and buddy Marlon Stepteau.

In a project like this, the work of journalists at newspapers and periodicals is paramount. I want to give a special nod to the reporters who covered Sarah Palin before and after her rise to fame. There were many contributors, but I especially want to recognize the groundbreaking work by the *Anchorage Daily News*, the *Mat-Su Valley Frontiersman*, the *Washington Post*, the Associated Press, and the *New York Times*.

CONTENTS

FOREWORD

Six months before Sarah Palin resigned as governor of Alaska, I had my second face-to-face meeting with the first woman to be nominated for vice president by the Republican Party. We had met seven months earlier, just weeks after the April 2008 birth of son Trig. Now, I was standing in the Hotel Captain Cook ballroom in Anchorage approaching Sarah for *People* magazine to discuss the birth of her first grandchild, Tripp, whom daughter Bristol had delivered just days earlier on December 27.

Life had changed notably—for Sarah. At one time she eschewed security, now two plainclothesmen cloaked in black trench coats escorted her everywhere that day. After speaking about Alaska's fiftieth anniversary for statehood, she was mobbed by crowds. Interviewers are generally given time to speak with subjects in inverse proportion to their celebrity, so my access was limited— just a couple of questions. Then she sat down at a table next to Alaska Senator Lisa Murkowski and several former governors and signed autographs and posed for pictures for two hours, creating a logjam at the table. I'm not sure if Sarah could defeat Murkowski in a Senate race now, but on that day, judging by the enthusiasm of the crowd, Sarah would have been the hands-down winner.

Perhaps it's an impossible task for any politician to keep up that kind of momentum, even in their home state. Nationally, Sarah absorbed hard hits in the media over the McCain campaign's purchase of $150,000 in designer clothes for herself and her family, but she returned the outfits to the Republican National Committee and they quietly donated the goods to "undisclosed charities," according to a RNC spokesman. Back in Juneau, Sarah endured a winter of discontent marked by tense budget battles with lawmakers as the state's primary revenue source—oil profits—dwindled and forced program cuts. Like one of those polar bears trapped on a melting ice flow, Sarah searched for new territory, in the Lower Forty-eight. She spoke at friendly events and even campaigned for other politicians, but was harshly criticized back home for ignoring state affairs. Detached and distracted by everyone from Levi Johnston to David Letterman, maybe there was another trail for Sarah to blaze to get where she wanted to go.

Palin watchers waited, convinced she was preparing to announce that she would complete her gubernatorial term but not run for reelection in 2010, but Sarah shocked them again. Announcing her resignation on the back lawn of her home, she said, "I'm doing what's best for Alaska. You can effect change from the outside, and I can too." Levi, the jilted son-in-law-to-be, weighed in on this, too. He had split with Bristol Palin months earlier, and surmised that her mother had quit to make more money and reduce the stress in her life. Sarah had plenty of things to keep her worried, including $600,000 in personal legal bills to fend off a constant stream of ethics complaints, some of which were dismissed outright. Other complaints she resolved herself, such as reimbursing the state $8,100 for expenses incurred by her children when they traveled with her on business. "If you're not in office they can't file ethics complaints against you," reasoned her father-in-law, Jim Palin.

Since leaving the governorship on July 26, Sarah spent the rest of the summer completing her memoir, in the warmer climate of San Diego. She worked with a collaborator and sometimes called on her father, Chuck Heath, to help with fact checking. Husband Todd traveled back and forth, as Alaskan websites openly doubted the stability of their marriage. "Nonsense," says Jim, while Sarah's own rep called the rumors "lies and fabrications."

The children also attracted attention wherever they went. "The kids were with Sarah and Todd throughout the summer," said Jim. Bristol, now the most famous single teen mom in the country, kept her promise and graduated with her high school class in June 2009. She was named a teen ambassador for The Candie's Foundation public awareness campaign for teen pregnancy prevention. She also got an office job in Anchorage and was expected to enroll in college this fall. She was spotted at the Alaska state fair with friends, pushing son Tripp around in a stroller. "I'm really impressed with Bristol," said a relative. "She does a great job with Tripp. She's very passionate about being a mother." The younger kids, Trig, Piper, and Willow, spent part of the summer in Dillingham, helping Todd run his commercial fishing operation in Bristol Bay. Piper, now eight, still eats up the attention. "That girl is used to living a life of glamour," a family friend says. "I saw her at a wedding and she loves native food. Someone offered her berry *agutuk* [Eskimo ice cream] and salmon smoke strips, and she said, 'No thank you, I've had my fill. I've outdone myself again.'"

Her mother has a history of that, too, politically speaking. Even with the surprise resignation, Sarah is hard to count out. She has left public office before—from the Alaska Oil and Gas Conservation Commission—and three years later, in 2006, she made a successful run for governor by campaigning for ethics reform. All indications are Sarah will run for public office again, though nothing formal has been announced. In the meantime, there's family. Last September, Sarah wrapped up her memoir in time to celebrate Track's return home from his army tour of duty in Iraq. "We're thrilled to have him back," Jim said. Todd also became a full-time caretaker-snow machine racer. On September 18, 2009, he officially resigned from his position with British Petroleum, ending his twenty-year tenure with the oil company. Now there was time for him to do a little moose hunting before training began for the 2010 Iron Dog snow machine marathon. In February, Todd would shoot for his fifth title with partner Scott Davis. "We're signed up and that's the plan," Davis said. The Palin family was also coping with Todd's half-sister, Diana Palin, who was indicted by a grand jury on burglary and theft charges in April 2009. A family friend said she had been battling a substance abuse problem for years but she was getting help. "She's in rehab. We hope she gets better."

Sarah also embarked on what is expected to be a lucrative public speaking career, making a September stop in Hong Kong to address a prominent group of financial fund investors, for which she reportedly received a fee in the low six figures. Though reporters were barred from the speech, reportedly she spoke about dropping capital gains and estate taxes but mystified listeners when she called the collapse of the U.S. financial markets a government failure and dismissed any need for new regulation, which seems to contradict even the most boisterous advocates of a free market. Still, she provided a glimpse of the political trail she hopes to blaze in the coming years, one that will take her to the corridors of the beltway, even if she has yet to draw up a precise map. But there's plenty of time for that. Tom Whitstine Jr., a Wasilla resident who has known the family for years and counts himself as a conservative who doesn't support Palin, said he believes Sarah has a shot at the White House for one simple reason: "Because Sarah is convinced she's presidential material," he explained. "She will spend the time honing her message and if she can figure out a way to attract moderates, she might have a pretty good chance."

INTRODUCTION

I met Sarah Palin on June 2, 2008, while on assignment for *People* magazine. No, we didn't have advance word that she would be named to the GOP ticket later in the summer. And politics wasn't the primary focus of the story. At the time, Alaska's youngest and first female governor was making news for giving birth to her fifth child, Trig Paxton Van Palin, making her only the second sitting governor to have a baby in office. (Having given birth to twins in 2001, Massachusetts acting governor Jane Swift was the first.) What's more, the results from an amniocentesis Sarah took thirteen weeks into her pregnancy showed Trig was afflicted with the developmental disorder Down syndrome, which she kept secret from everyone except her husband, Todd, right up to the time Sarah gave birth on April 18.

The story was held for more than two months, not an uncommon occurrence at a weekly magazine for a profile without a timely peg. Then on the morning of August 29 (Sarah and Todd's twentieth wedding anniversary), John McCain provided the bump we needed to run our story by naming Sarah Palin his running mate. *People* magazine garnered the first interview with Palin moments after she was picked. "*Absolutely*, yup, yup," she replied when asked if she was prepared to serve a heartbeat away from the White House.

As the only national journalist in the country who had spent significant time with Palin in the weeks preceding her selection, I was awakened by my editor asking me to prepare a story for the Web site, People.com. In the story, "Five Things You Didn't Know about Sarah Palin," I quoted Sarah and her husband and touched on a few details of the governor's life: competing in beauty pageants to pay for college; her penchant for designer sunglasses and shoes; her secret pregnancy; eldest son Track's imminent deployment to Iraq; and Todd's Yu'pik Eskimo lineage. There is more to her story, much more, which is why I decided to write this book.

It was pretty clear from the first moment I met Sarah that she wasn't your typical gubernatorial executive. I remember covering a ribbon-cutting event in California not long after Arnold Schwarzenegger took office and was stunned by the amount of security and the Secret Service–type planning that went into his appearances.

Palin went about her business without a security detail, which is how she likes it. Few connect with voters with the grace and charm of the Alaskan governor, despite all the drama swirling around her. She has taken a lot of heat for being a policy lightweight and sometimes answering questions in what critics call "Palin gibberish," but her people skills are downright Reaganesque. I don't care who you are, you have her undivided attention when you speak. And when you meet her again, she's likely to remember something about you and the last time you met. Undoubtedly, McCain erred in not letting Palin be herself on the campaign and restricting her access to media.

While I was researching the book, I had a conversation with Sarah's sister Heather Bruce. Heather was upset over another terrible headline about her sister and was near tears when she confided in her husband, Kurt. "How is Sarah dealing with all this?" she said. Kurt knew just what to say to help his wife regain her composure. "Heather, remember, it's Sarah; she can handle it."

She was in full multitask mode the day I arrived to interview her at her Anchorage office. She walked through the door a little after 9 a.m., armed with a large cup of coffee and two BlackBerrys, one red, one black. I was immediately struck by her aw-shucks style and friendly manner. That day, she was going to sign a bill, do an interview with *People* and CNN, and lead a staff meeting on the natural-gas pipeline proposal. A special session in Juneau was to begin the next day dealing specifically with the gas-line project that Sarah hopes someday will pump natural gas from Prudhoe Bay to the Lower Forty-eight.

The other side to Sarah is her private life, which people don't often get to see. After work, Sarah drives herself to Wasilla in a black SUV, occasionally picking up a pizza for dinner. She arrives home to a family on the go. The house is usually filled with children, friends of Piper and Willow, or cousins. If they're shooting baskets in the driveway, Sarah joins in for a game of Horse or a little one-on-one contest with Willow. At mealtime, Sarah might discuss a business trip to Juneau while Todd briefs everyone on his plans for a midnight training run to prepare for the Iron Dog snowmobile race. Later, Sarah keeps an eye on Piper, who plays with baby Trig like he's one of her dolls. The ribbing is nonstop and sometimes the Governor is the punching bag; jokes fly about Sarah's weight gain during her pregnancy with Trig, Willow's inability to beat her mother at basketball, and Bristol's nonchalance about her mom's meteoric rise in national politics. The governor takes all the needling in good humor.

For Sarah and her family, 2008 was an adventure

through uncharted territory, and 2009 and beyond promises to be just as challenging. In accepting McCain's invitation, Sarah took a leap of faith. But as her past shows, it's not an unfamiliar course. In *Trailblazer: An Intimate Biography of Sarah Palin*, friends, relatives, and Sarah herself recount her improbable journey from small-town Wasilla to the power centers of Washington, D.C., and how her drive and perseverance were shaped by a demanding father with an insatiable curiosity and wanderlust and a soft-spoken mother, a faith in God, and the ability to leap forward where others step gingerly. She's the tomboy who became a beauty queen, the shy, quiet student who became a broadcast journalist, the young, apolitical mother with the blue-collar husband who became a controversial mayor, then a regional GOP star who defied the party hierarchy and outlasted all her political enemies to become governor of Alaska, the youngest in the state's fifty-year history. Her journey, no doubt, inspired John McCain to name Sarah his running mate for the 2008 presidential election. That is the story *Trailblazer* tells.

ONE

THE FRONTIER BECKONS

On the day the Beatles invaded the United States with their first live appearance in concert, in Washington, D.C., Sarah Palin was born in Sandpoint, Idaho, the third of four children to Chuck and Sally Heath. The date was February 11, 1964, and she was greeted by a family of teachers and runners. Her father, Chuck, taught science and ran in the Boston Marathon. Her mother, Sally, caught the running bug, too, later competing in Anchorage's Mayor's Marathon.

Sarah's mother, the former Sally Sheeran, was raised in Richland, Washington, part of the Tri-Cities area of southeast Washington State. Sally's parents, Clem and Helen Sheeran, had moved there from Salt Lake City in 1943, three years after Sally's birth. The United States was in the throes of World War II and in a race with Germany to develop the nuclear bomb. The Hanford Site in Washington, sixty miles up the Columbia River from Richland, was a centerpiece of the Manhattan Project, producing the plutonium needed to manufacture the weapon. Clem, a veteran IRS administrator, was recruited by Hanford as a labor relations manager for a workforce numbering in the thousands. Hanford scientists were at the forefront of their field, but the facility's woeful waste-disposal systems eventually left the site a toxic disaster. Today, the site is a decommissioned nuclear production complex. Shut down after the Cold War, it now is home to one of the largest environmental clean-ups in the country.

While the Washington-born Clem worked at Hanford, his Wisconsin-born wife, the former Helen Gower, was a do-it-all homemaker and whiz with the sewing machine, making clothes, window drapes, and furniture upholstery. They had six children in all, including Sally. The practical skills Sally learned from her mother were later passed on to her own children. "She taught me to be self-sufficient," Sarah told *People* magazine about her mother. A recreational swimmer and tennis player, Sally was a 1958 graduate of Columbia High School, which has since been renamed Richland High. From the start, the Sheerans were a family that valued hard work, education, religion, and community service. Helen volunteered at local nursing homes. Sarah Palin's late uncle, Pat Sheeran, received a doctorate from Gonzaga University and served as a District One judge. After the war, Clem returned to civilian life and went on to a career in arbitration, specializing in workplace issues. Clem and Helen were steadfast churchgoers and had all the Sheeran kids baptized as Catholics. Clem also introduced the kids to tennis, golf, and swimming. "My father was an athlete," Sarah's mother remembered. "I think he wished we all excelled at sports, but we had fun with it."

Sally Heath's Pacific Northwest childhood was never far from her heart, and she and her husband, Chuck Heath, made annual family trips back to Washington with their kids even after they moved to Alaska. Sally's sister, Katie Johnson, recalled an active, little, doe-eyed Sarah who loved to swim in a public pool across the street from her grandparents' house in Richland. "The girls and Chuck Jr. would come to Richland, and Mom and Dad would give them pool passes and they'd stay there all day; that was a big deal for a kid from Alaska," Katie said. When Sarah attended college in Idaho in the mid-1980s, Richland was her second home. During school holidays, Sarah and Chuck Jr., who was also attending college in Idaho, made the 150-mile trek from Moscow, where they were enrolled at the University of Idaho. "Everything she's ever done she's excelled at," said Sarah's uncle, Ron Jones.

The trait of excellence ran on both sides of the family. Sarah's father, Charles R. Heath, who went by Chuck to his friends, was born in March 1938 in Los Angeles to a sports photographer father, Charlie, and a schoolteacher mother, the former Nellie "Marie" Brandt. His father photographed many of the legendary fighters and wrestlers of the day and even entertained many of the greats at his Los Angeles home.

"My mother taught school in North Hollywood, and Dad covered boxing and wrestling matches at the Olympic Auditorium. I have pictures of me with boxers Joe Louis and James J. Jeffries," said Heath. "One of my earliest memories is finding a rat caught in a trap at the Olympic Auditorium." Decades later, Heath would work for Alaska's department of agriculture and develop an expertise for exterminating nuisance rat infestations devastating native bird populations.

His family moved to Hope, Idaho, in 1948 when Heath was ten. "My parents wanted to get away from L.A.," Chuck Heath said. "Mom came to Hope and taught school, and Dad worked as a freelance photographer and drove a school bus."

Heath's only sibling, a sister two years his senior named Carol, died of cancer at age forty-two.

The move to Hope, Idaho, exposed young Heath to the great outdoors, as he took up hunting and fishing.

His father was so into fishing that he handcrafted lures and started a small lure company. Heath attended high school ten miles away in Sandpoint, where he earned his diploma in 1956 and played football under legendary high school coach Cotton Barlow. Heath, a running back, had the privilege of having his path through the defense cleared by Green Bay Packers legend Jerry Kramer. "He made me look good," Heath said. Kramer, a big Sarah Palin fan, said he was "hooked" by the Alaska governor when her candidacy was announced. "How can I not like a girl from Sandpoint?"

But Kramer also knows what can happen when a quarterback enters a game too early in his career. After Sarah was selected to run with McCain, he predicted that she might get roughed up on the campaign trail. "She appeared from the bushes to save McCain, save the Republican Party, and save the world. . . . I'm just afraid they're putting too much of a burden on her," he said. "But you like her character and the qualities she brings."

On the job, Sarah often wears gold earrings in the shape of the state of Alaska, but Idaho claims her as one of its own. After high school, her father, Chuck, enrolled at Columbia Basin College in Pasco, a few miles from the Sheerans' Richland, Washington, home. He played football, studied science, and met his future wife, who was interested in a career as a dental assistant. "We were in a biology lab together, and Chuck picked me as his partner to do a blood test," Sally said. "He thought it would be fun to prick each other's fingers."

On their first date, they went to a drive-in movie, which Chuck paid for with a sock full of coins. "To this day he does not walk past a penny on the ground without picking it up," she said. "He is a great saver."

Katie recalled meeting Chuck for the first time after Sally brought him back to the Richland house to meet their parents. "I remember Sally bringing Chuck home on a date, and when he wasn't paying attention, she giggled, 'Isn't he cute?' " The introduction was a success. Clem, a football and basketball referee and an avid tennis player and golfer, approved of his daughter's choice. "Dad liked Chuck because Chuck was into sports," said Katie.

In 1959, the year President Eisenhower signed the declaration making Alaska the forty-ninth state of the Union, Chuck transferred to Eastern Washington University in Cheney to finish up his college degree. Sally followed, taking a job as a dental assistant in nearby Spokane. Before graduation, Chuck landed a teaching job back in Sandpoint and returned to work, finishing up his college degree at night school. In the summer of 1961, Chuck and Sally applied for a marriage license and wed at St. Joseph's Roman Catholic Church in Sandpoint. Sally gave birth to a quick succession of children—Chuck Jr. arrived on February 7, 1962; Heather was born on January 28, 1963, followed by Sarah a year later. Their fourth child, Molly, was born two years after Sarah on November 26, 1966, after the family had relocated to Skagway, Alaska.

Old Sandpoint neighbor Loralee Gray, an artist, recalled the Heaths as a young and active family. Chuck coached basketball to ninth graders and spent his leisure time hunting and fishing with pal Bill Adams, a teacher whose wife befriended Sally, a stay-at-home mom.

"Chuck took me under his wing," Adams said. "I was a small-town kid from Montana, and [Chuck] said, 'We're going to teach you the Idaho way.'"

But like his father before him, Chuck aspired to something greater for himself and his family. He was stretched financially with three new mouths to feed, and there was only one place that could satisfy his wanderlust and ambition—the Alaskan frontier. By the time Sarah was born in February 1964, he had already mailed out job applications to cities throughout Alaska. "The call of the wild got to him," Adams said. In addition, he was lured by the forty-ninth state's growing service industry. "We had a great little neighborhood there in Sandpoint," said Gray, who lived in the house behind the Heaths' rental home. "But schoolteachers in Idaho weren't making much. Wages were abysmal."

Not in Alaska. With the oil boom just around the bend, the state was recruiting good teachers from the Lower Forty-eight, and the pay difference was substantial. The region had another draw for the outdoorsman in Heath; it had the best hunting anywhere. "The talk was that it was the best place to go for that," said Katie. "He talked Sally into it by promising, 'Let's try it for one year and see what happens,' and they loved it."

Looking back, Sally reflected, "I didn't think it would be for forty-five years." She chuckled. "When I married him I knew I was in for an adventure and had to be ready for his crazy ideas."

Chuck was a popular science teacher and coach in Sandpoint, but the wilderness beckoned. "I applied all over Alaska but took the job in Skagway," he told the *Anchorage Daily News* in 2007. Undeterred by the colossal March 27, 1964, Anchorage earthquake that registered 8.4 on the Richter scale, Chuck wrapped up his teaching duties, packed up the family, and headed for the last frontier in June 1964. He drove the family station wagon alone to British Columbia, where he caught a ferry for a two-day cruise to Skagway, which wasn't accessible by car at the time. Sally, joined by her mother, flew in by plane with the kids after Chuck found a place to live. "Chuck was the pied piper of Sandpoint; he led an exodus of locals to Alaska," said Gray.

When he arrived, "I had a fishing pole in one hand and a gun in the other," Chuck said. "I guess I still haven't put them down."

They first settled in a duplex at the White Pass tank farm that was once an old military complex and then rented a second home before moving into a larger turn-of-the-century, three-bedroom home on the south side of town known in Skagway as the Elmer Rasmuson house.

When Sarah visited the town in 2007, the memories came rushing back: porcupines hiding under the house, hikes along the Chilkoot trail, the wooden sidewalks leading to town, catechism classes at a nearby Catholic church, and basketball games coached by her father. "I used to walk around by myself," she told the *Skagway News*.

The tiny city of Skagway was situated on the scenic Chilkoot Inlet, one hundred miles north of the capital city of Juneau on the southeastern peninsula of Alaska. A tourist attraction for the cruise liners and ferries, the town needed educators for the service industry population. They had offered Chuck a grade-school teaching position at the Skagway City Schools, which operated a kindergarten-through-twelve program out of a two-story building near the center of town. The school yearbook showed a burly young Chuck Heath with a receding hairline and wearing a pressed white short-sleeved shirt and black tie. In his four years at the school, he taught grades five through seven and coached the high school basketball team. Students recalled a "tough" teacher—when he visited Skagway with his governor daughter in 2007, Chuck bumped into an old student and reminded him he owed him a book report. The student apparently had been caught using comic books as a source for his paper, and Chuck remembered.

The school didn't have cooking appliances to prepare hot food, so kids went home for lunch, except when the temperature outside dipped down to ten degrees below zero, not uncommon in the winter because of the windy conditions. "On those days the kids took a sack lunch," said Barbara Moore, a Heath family friend whose husband, Paul Moore, taught with Chuck.

Though nowhere near the oil fields on the state's North Slope, Skagway was still remote. This tiny old mining town was nestled on a flat riverbed amid seven-thousand-foot snow-capped peaks. The local inlet waters teemed with king and silver salmon while the surrounding mountains were filled with wild game, bears, mountain goats, and Dall sheep. It was hard living for the local population. Basic services and information were difficult to come by. There was no direct television signal because the state didn't have a satellite, so television shows were taped and shipped in for rebroadcast. A single radio station and the region's sole major daily newspaper were based in Juneau, a six-hour ferry ride down the inlet, and also a scenic glacier field that draws tourists from around the world.

Skagway had a single paved road, State Street, an improvement residents actually fought against because they felt it impinged on the city's rustic appeal. The winters were cold and windy, and an early spring thaw sometimes flooded the streets and forced residents to head for high ground during high tide. But the tradeoff was a wilderness unmatched for its natural, rugged beauty.

On a map, Skagway is located near the southern edge of the Klondike Gold Rush National Historical Park, a favorite hiking destination for the Heaths. In the late nineteenth century, when the Alaska gold rush was at its height, the town's population surged past ten thousand. It has a very basic layout—buildings and streets on one side and the railroad, marina, and airport on the other, nearest the water. During World War II, the economy was robust as the railroad passed through town and funneled supplies and workers building the Alaska Highway to the north. "Chuck worked for the railroad in the summertime," said Sally. "He was a gandy dancer, and he loved it. They'd take the tracks up into the mountains and tap ties into place." During tourist season, both Chuck and Sally drove taxicabs. On Sundays, Sally walked the kids to church at St. Therese of the Child Jesus parish while Chuck worked or went hunting with a friend. He also organized family hikes in the mountains in search of artifacts left behind by the miners of the Klondike gold rush. "He got into the hunting," recalled Sally. "Not many residents did, so he and his buddies had the mountains to themselves. At that time you could hunt seals. He would go out in a small dinghy and wait for a seal to poke its head through the water. We kept the hides, but there was a local family that loved the meat, and we shared it with them."

Skagway in the mid-1960s was scrambling to increase basic services for its then eight hundred residents, who could get by without a laundromat but worried after the local hospital closed and the only doctor in town retired. For a couple of years, a nurse-midwife was the sole medical practitioner in town. Families had to wait for dentists, eye doctors, and physicians from Haines to make periodic visits, or if there was an emergency, they had to rush to them—by sea or by air, since the only highway leading into Skagway wasn't built until the 1970s. "If you needed to see a doctor or a dentist, you had to fly to Juneau, or fly or take the ferry forty-five minutes to Haines twelve miles down the Chilkoot Inlet," said Paul Moore, a business teacher. During an official visit to Skagway in 2007, Governor Palin herself remembered when her brother, Chuck Jr., burned his foot terribly running through a fire and Sally had to take him all the way to Juneau by ferry to get proper medical treatment at a hospital. "All these years later, that's still what people have to rely on here in some instances," Sarah recently told a reporter. There is still no direct road to Juneau, and residents remain split on whether one should ever be built.

In the Skagway years, the Moores and the Heaths became good friends, and they remain in touch today. "Chuck used to borrow my eighteen-foot Reinell boat to take the kids to the dentist," said Paul Moore. "There were no [life-threatening] emergencies I can think of; our families were blessed by guardian angels."

Chuck Heath also took up fur trapping, inspired by a neighbor who used to show off his pelts, said Moore. "I remember a veteran trapper in Skagway telling Chuck not to bother trying to trap wolverines; they're too smart, and you'll be wasting your time. So what does Chuck do? He goes and traps not one but two wolverines. I believe Chuck has hunted just about everything there is to hunt in Alaska. Before the Marine Mammal Act went into effect, we hunted seals and sea lions and sold the hides. We sold our bear hides, too."

But the annual moose hunt was the highlight of the year. Licensed hunters in Alaska today are allowed to take one moose per annum, but only one in three hunters who try is successful. To get a moose, Heath and Moore would fly twenty minutes to Yakutat, a small fishing village located on Monti Bay. After shooting the moose, the legs are severed and the head removed, and the carcass is quartered on the field and hauled out in backpacks on foot, not too far from the source of transportation, usually a boat or an ATV. It takes more than one trip to remove the meat from a seven-hundred-pound moose, so hunters have to be on the lookout for bears. Once Chuck and Paul returned to Yakutat, they transported the meat by plane back to Skagway, where the wives and kids were ready to go to work. "It's an assembly-line operation," said Moore. "We'd grind the meat into hamburger, roasts, and stew. The kids packed up the meat and put it in the freezer. We had this great commercial meat grinder, and one night we ground four hundred pounds of moose meat. A couple of moose could last you the winter depending on how large your family was."

The wild game sustained families like the Moores, who had thirteen mouths to feed, including their own, and the Heaths. "Skagway had no beauty parlor, no barber shop, and if your car broke, you fixed it yourself; if your washer broke, you fixed it," Moore said. "You wore many hats: carpenter, plumber, electrician, and boat mechanic; you did all your own stuff. We had just two grocery stores in town—there was no fresh milk, and the produce ship came twice a month. Banana skins are yellow, but our kids grew up thinking they were black, so we ate a lot of banana bread. We ordered clothes from catalogs—and in those days they sent the clothes first and then you paid, just in case things didn't fit. They don't do that anymore."

Moore also noticed that Chuck was a bit of a pack rat and never wanted to part with anything. He mounted trophies of his kills in his home—caribou, moose, bears, Dall sheep, and mountain goats—and they lined the walls of his home like natural history museum pieces. Pelts were laid over chairs and couches, and skulls and jars of fishing lures also found their way into the nooks and crannies of the Heath household. "All that business started in Skagway," Moore recalled. "Chuck didn't like to part with anything he might have use for. Chuck was blessed with an inquisitive mind and interested in anything that was outdoors. It wouldn't surprise me if he were hunting right now. The wild game and fish—that's food and not just a hobby."

It's a philosophy inherited by his daughter Sarah, who has said Alaskans are raised on local sources of protein and prefer wild game to grocery-store meat if they can help it. There is an old photo of young Sarah as a mere toddler, standing in a blue jumper in a Skagway yard dangling two shrimp from her tiny hands. Her clothes are soaked, and her pearl skin is filthy, her brown hair tousled. "That was Sarah for you," Moore said. "She wasn't your typical little girly-girl."

While Sally took the kids to church every Sunday at St. Therese's, "Chuck was his own keeper," Moore said. "There were just three churches here at the time, and on Christmas Eve and Thanksgiving we'd have interfaith celebrations," said Barbara Moore. "I don't know why Sally changed churches later in Alaska, but sometimes you go where there is a church, and if you get out into a place where there are just a few, the choices you have are dependent upon what's available."

Sally and Barbara became good friends, and they co-starred in a community theater production, a melo-drama called *Love Rides the Rails*. They performed for a group of teachers during a conference. "She was a good actress," Barbara said. "I played a mother, and she played a heroine, and then she switched parts since we both had memorized each other's lines."

Barbara got to know Sally well because she relied on the Heaths' washer for backup when hers broke down, a frequent occurrence, since she was washing clothes for a family of thirteen. "It was the neighborly thing to do and a good excuse to catch up over snacks and a cup of tea. I'd bring my laundry over; we'd make a day of it," said Barbara. "We'd sit and talk, and the kids played. Everyone got along just fine. We didn't worry too much about deco-rating; it was more like whether we had enough money to keep our kids in shoes and warm clothes for the winter."

One afternoon, Barbara was folding her last bit of laundry when Sally invited the Moore clan over for dinner. "All of us?" Barbara asked. "We had eleven children, and that was the first time and the last time they invited all thirteen of us." Paul Moore laughed. "But we had a great big spaghetti feed."

David Moore, Paul's son who was close friends with Chuck Jr. and now lives in Anchorage, remembered those boisterous get-togethers, which included fifteen kids in all. "We didn't have a TV so we always went over to the Heaths' to watch TV," he said. But the TV schedule was between 3 p.m. and midnight. "TV didn't play a role in their lives or ours," David Moore said. "The nice thing about living in Skagway was that when it came to hunting and fishing, it was all right there."

Sarah bonded with Moore's younger sister, Mary, and most days were spent outdoors, hiking in the woods, playing cowboys and Indians in the summer, cross-country skiing in the winter. After dinner, the families would huddle around the Heaths' wood stove, and Paul and Chuck would break out the boxing gloves and referee matches between the kids. "Sarah boxed with Mary and the older boys," he said. "She was a tough little girl." Years later, Chuck would describe his daughter as both tough and stubborn. "She was strong-willed," he said. "From an early age she thought she was always right, and she usually was." He chuckled. "If I needed something done, I could bend the other kids one way or another, but Sarah was strong-willed, and it was hard to change her mind. That's still her."

In 1969, the Moores watched the moon landing on tape delay at the Heath house. It wasn't long after that Chuck and Sally packed up the brood and moved to Anchorage, where they stayed with relatives of old football buddy Jerry Kramer, who was starting his last season in the NFL. There were now four kids to move, with the addition of the Heaths' third daughter, Molly, who arrived the day after Thanksgiving in 1966. At that time, Barbara Moore said, a doctor from Haines was flying in when the pregnant women went into labor, and babies were born at the local clinic.

"Chuck saw the growth potential in south-central Alaska," said Paul Moore, who later retired back to Sandpoint with his wife after their children were grown. "Chuck and Sally were just down here two years ago having supper and regaling us with stories of trapping rats off St. George's Island in Alaska and chasing ducks and seagulls off the runway at small airports along the coast. Chuck Heath is a character, blessed with an inquisitive mind, and interested in anything that moves."

TWO
REFRESHING THE SOUL

On June 2008, when Sarah Palin gave an interview to *People* magazine about the April 2008 birth of her youngest child, Trig, she was reminded of a story her father had shared with her about diversity in the classroom. If five decades of teaching taught Chuck Heath anything, it was that it was impossible to define a "normal" child.

"What is normal?" her father used to ask. At seventy, he still serves as a substitute teacher at Wasilla Middle School, bringing in his collections to illustrate his lessons on the life sciences—animal skulls, bones, and deer antlers. The kids marvel at the artifacts, and Chuck, in turn, is inspired by the menagerie of shapes, colors, and sizes occupying his classroom, where every child is a special ingredient.

His appreciation for diversity helped Palin cope with

the circumstances besetting her own son, who has Down syndrome, a disorder that causes developmental delays requiring speech and physical therapy. Palin also has a nephew who has autism. Days before Trig was born, she thought of her father's words as she sat down to write a letter to friends and family about Trig's condition, which she was keeping a secret. "This new person in your life," she wrote and later shared in a *People* magazine interview, "can help put things in perspective and bind us together, and get everyone focused on what really matters. . . . Those who love him will think less about self and focus less on what the world tells us is 'normal' and 'perfect.' "

Once the Heaths left Skagway, the lessons Chuck and Sally imparted to their children during adolescence shaped the core of their youth. The future governor of Alaska and Republican vice-presidential candidate would develop the patience and skill to be a hunter, the faith to accept Jesus as her savior, and the competitiveness and work ethic to lead her basketball team to a state title and also win local beauty pageants.

In 1969, after briefly staying in Anchorage with the Kramer relatives, Chuck found a teaching job in Eagle River, about fifteen miles north of Anchorage. They lived there two years before moving to Wasilla, about forty miles northeast of Alaska's largest city. Though it was founded in 1917 as a railroad staging area for mining ventures in Talkeetna and Mount McKinley, Wasilla didn't incorporate until 1973 and listed a population of just four hundred people when the Heaths moved into their home on Lucille Street. In the 1930s, during the Depression, the government encouraged homesteaders to farm in Wasilla, drawing two hundred families to the area. From Skagway, Chuck believed the region's growth potential and proximity to Anchorage would make it a great place to raise a family and ensure a secure future, even if the round trip to Anchorage was a daylong affair, since the main highway was gravel part of the way. In time, Wasilla emerged as a bedroom community and the hub of the Matanuska-Susitna (Mat-Su) Borough, which now supports a population of 80,000 and is roughly the size of West Virginia.

Wasilla itself now ranks as Alaska's fourth largest city, with more than seven thousand residents, and is blessed with classic frontier diversions—two lakes and pockets of thick woods with forests of birch and spruce. Once home to the first leg of the state's famous Iditarod sled-dog race, Wasilla is nestled between the snow-capped Chugach Mountains to the south and east and the Talkeetna Mountains to the north. The Talkeetnas, the gateway to Denali National Park, is home to Hatcher Pass, an expanse of scenic tundra where families can hike, camp, and pick berries. Chuck would lead his kids through the meadows and woods, pointing out flora, fauna, and fossils etched in stones, and then quizzing his children on their discoveries. Those mountains were filled with wildlife—grizzly and black bears, moose, caribou, wolves, and Dall sheep. In the spring, the mountains burst with wildflowers; their colors shifting and moving with the sun, evoking a natural canopy of yellow, violet, and rose.

The Heaths first took up residence in a small wood-frame house on Lucille Street that is now a commercial building in the center of town. When they moved in, a birch forest with winding dirt trails that linked the Heath kids to other homes with children surrounded it. The girls shared an unheated attic bedroom that was bearable thanks to the wood stove downstairs. When the temperatures dipped into the teens and a pile of blankets and quilts failed to fend off the chill, the girls would jump into a single bed and use body heat to keep warm.

Heather Bruce remembered, "When we first moved, all four of us were there, and Mom converted a small sewing room downstairs for Chuckie. We shared the room for several years until Dad built an addition, which had a bedroom for Chuckie and me. We had a code, 'Want to play Sleeping Beauty?' and that was the signal for all of us to jump into bed together."

"They were typical kids at playtime," Sally said. "They liked to play dress-up, and Sarah didn't have to be the boss of the group to have a good time. Around the house, the kids never complained about chores. Being outside made them happy."

Chuck Heath was moved by education, hard work, and physical prowess, and he insisted that his own children earn their keep around the house. The kids stacked firewood, washed floors, and tended a communal garden. Heather said the girls used to pitch in by washing the dinner dishes together.

"My brother had all the boy chores to do like taking out the trash; I felt sorry for him because he got the short end of the stick," she said. "We never had a dishwasher, so we did the dishes by hand—I washed, Molly rinsed, and Sarah dried and put away. I can remember Sarah sitting on the counter, dangling her feet, and I thought, 'She's got the easy job.' I was bossy—possessive of my stuff, since I was oldest. . . . I learned how to cook and picked up Mom's duties when she went on vacation without the kids, and it seemed like I had to fill in with the motherly duties. Molly was the youngest one, the baby of the family and a sweet little sister. She was bouncy and spunky. Sarah was to me a pest for some years and very determined that she was going to get her way with me. She had a way of using my stuff and wearing my clothes when I wasn't around, and I couldn't borrow hers, but she could use mine. She wasn't loud and obnoxious—she was a quiet, determined little girl. She could get stubborn. She'd work her little butt off to finish a race or an assignment, and if she didn't get what she wanted, she'd cross her arms and stomp her foot. I had many friends, but we did so much together as a family that we had to get along. Mom and Dad used to take us on camping trips, and we'd spend the night in tents. There was a lot of sibling rivalry and fighting, like any family. My mother didn't lose her temper much; our father was the disciplinarian, and Mom was the nurturer. Those were the days where we probably got spanked if we deserved it. I think once Mom got to the end of her rope while we were camping; it was the middle of the night, and she was telling us to be quiet, and she had had enough and warned us that she was going to spank us. I was eleven, and we laughed. I said, 'She can't hurt me.' But when my dad was around, it was expected that we would follow rules; all he had to do was give you a look or a strong word, and Mom would say, 'Wait until your dad comes home,' and we'd straighten up right away."

Warren McCorkell, a neighbor who would later marry one of Sarah Palin's friends, Amy Hansen, grew up around the corner from the Heaths. On his walks into town, he'd pass by the house and usually spot Sarah and her siblings outdoors playing with their German shepherd, Rufus, or chasing their cat, Fifi. "They had an old black-and-white TV, but Chuck didn't like them watching it much. He kept it upstairs in a part of the house that was heated only by a wood stove, so if the kids wanted to watch something, they had to collect the wood and light the stove."

Sarah said the kids were usually too lazy to gather the wood and light the fire to warm the room. "So we never watched much TV," she told the *Anchorage Daily News*.

On Sundays after church, they went hiking or cross-country skiing up at Hatcher Pass, and sometimes they'd bring their guns and hunt ptarmigan, a wild grouse that occupies chilly mountainous regions of Alaska. Sarah learned to shoot at eight and honed her skill by picking off rabbits in the woods near her house and the white ptarmigan in the Talkeetnas.

Hunting trips always carry a risk, and the Heaths' ventures into the wild were no exception. During a trip to Denali National Park, the Heaths had a dangerous run-in with a cranky grizzly bear that literally caught wind of a caribou Chuck had bagged, quartered, and strapped to a rack on top of the family car and on a second rack thirty yards from camp.

"There were no trees or brush to hang the meat," he said. "I suppose it wasn't the smartest thing to do, but we had never had trouble with bears before out there, so I put the meat on two racks to air it out. Sally woke up first and heard the bear outside—it was still kind of light out so we could see pretty good. I see this bear standing on its legs and reaching for the meat on top of the car, like it's at a diner. It was hunting season, and I said to Sally, 'I'm going to shoot the darn thing.' Sally tried to steady a flashlight on the bear so I could take a shot, but she couldn't hold the light steady. But I thought better of it because the kids' tent was nearby, so I let it grab a quarter of caribou and drag it away. That was at midnight, and then it came back two hours later—and I'm like, I'll be darned. But this time it got close to the kids' tent, so I got my rifle and went over to the kids and got them out of bed and put them in the car. We all got in the car, and the bear circled the car and put his nose up to the window and looked in and then tried to pull some more meat off the car top. It was a big male grizzly. It stayed around camp for two hours and finally at four a.m., it wandered away. I got out of the car to make sure it wasn't around, and I went over to our other rack, and it had taken three quarters of the caribou. So we packed up and left quickly. I found out that bear was shot the next day by a ranger. It apparently cornered a ranger in a cabin not far from our camp, and he killed it. It was a twenty-seven-year-old bear, and I think it had a couple of tooth abscesses, so it wasn't very happy."

"We spent the night there, all of us crammed into that car, watching the bear take our meat," Sarah recounted to the *Anchorage Daily News*. Heather remembered the bear encounter well. "I heard Dad yell, 'Get out of the tent and get into the car!' And he hustled us to the car, and we spent the night there. We turned on the headlights and watched the bear eat the caribou meat. He took huge chunks and devoured them. The story was Mom heard the bear first, and Dad was protecting us so we could get to the car. I don't remember being frightened—I felt safe in the car, and Dad had his rifle. Mom and Dad have had close bear encounters before. They once went on a hiking trip, and a grizzly bear tore through their tent, but they got out."

Chuck also used to take the kids bird hunting, which meant 3 a.m. wake-up calls and hunkering down in a canoe as they blasted shotgun pellets at grouse. "The first two hours of daylight and dusk are the best times to go hunting," he said. Usually, there was another hunting party close by in a blind, and the pellets would invariably hit the kids as they fell to earth. "There were pellets splashing in the water around them, and I said, 'Relax, they don't hurt,'" Chuck recalled. "Sarah was a really good shot. I taught her to shoot and taught her how to field dress a moose, to fish and hunt for game," Chuck told the London-based *Sun* newspaper.

Of the kids, he ranks Sarah just behind Chuck Jr. as the most enthusiastic hunter. But she didn't shoot her first caribou until she was in college, and Chuck was with her when Sarah shot two more—once in 1993, with five-year-old Track by her side, and once more three years ago before she was elected governor. Track joined her for that hunt as well. "I have more fun watching my children and grandchildren hunt than I do myself," Chuck said. "We were in a camp off Denali Highway where all these people were coming and going, visiting with us. Caribou are wanderers. We were camped on a ridge and had a view two or three miles in each direction. The caribou were everywhere, and we saw one, two hundred to three hundred yards away from where we were camped. Sarah grabbed her rifle and shot it. The second time, we were on a snow machine and saw one, and she shot one from long distance, and we were able to take it down the mountain to a level spot to field dress it. She is a very good shot—calm, cool, and collected—she shot quite a few rabbits and ptarmigan and got very good doing that. She always used to help me field dress a moose. She would hold the legs when I cut them and then help me pack the meat."

As for taking those caribou, Sarah had no reservations. "That caribou has had a good life," she told *Vogue* magazine. "It's been free out there on the tundra, not caged up on a farm with no place to go."

Heather said her father has quite a sense of humor on

the hunt. "I shot my first moose when I was eighteen. We always accompanied Dad on moose hunts—we never had to go on sheep hunts and goat hunts, since that was tougher hunting in the mountains. I was home from college my freshman year, and we went out together before he had to go to work. That's when I got my moose. He said, 'I'll help you start it.' He had a bone saw, and we quartered it. But he had to go to work, so he left me in the field with his rifle and told me to look out for bears. He promised he'd be back after school. Knowing I'd be out there all day, he also gave me a book about bear attacks in Alaska."

Heather stayed by the kill, listening to gunshots in the distance as hunters tracked their prey. Chuck returned later in the day. By then, Heather had packed up the meat in game bags. They hiked it out through the woods to an open area where Chuck was able to park his truck. "We walked several miles that day," Heather said. "Hunting caribou is a lot easier, and you can usually do it in the winter. It's cleaner in the snow, and there are fewer bugs, and the smell isn't as bad. And usually you can pile the meat on a sled and pull it out."

Sarah helped her father field dress a moose when she was fourteen. It was early, before the first school bell, when Chuck bagged his prey and asked Sarah to help him butcher the moose at once, as is custom. Her father quartered the animal while Sarah assisted, holding the legs and packing the body parts. Ever the science teacher, Chuck liked to take specimens to bring into class, including a set of eyeballs that he tried to hand off to his daughter. She wanted no part of it. "I couldn't do it," she said. Heath was fine with that. There was no shortage of other items to show the kids. "He liked to get us outside doing projects," said former student Sam Gardener, now an Eagle River businessman. "He was an avid hunter and used to bring in hides and horns— he'd fill tables with them and put them on the walls."

Sarah's aunt Katie Johnson described the Heath home as a natural history museum. She was impressed at how well the kids could handle weapons and sharp knives, as if it was second nature. "I was amazed watching those girls gutting fish. No hesitation. I thought, 'They can do whatever boys do.'"

Sally's passions and activities also weren't overlooked. An avid recreational swimmer as a youth, she took the kids for lessons at Lake Wasilla, where the water is so cold it can turn your skin blue, even in the summertime. "I was in Wasilla visiting one spring, and we were driving by the lake," Johnson recalled. "Sarah said, 'Look, Aunt Katie, the ice is melting; we can go swimming soon.' I couldn't believe it. I wouldn't get near that freezing water."

As in Skagway, Sally continued taking the kids to

church. Though the Heath kids were baptized Catholics as babies, they joined the Wasilla Assembly of God, a modest Pentecostal church that urges congregants to establish an individual relationship with Christ and where some congregants speak in tongues. She and the children attended Sunday and Wednesday night services, attended the congregation potlucks, and spent one week each summer at the church's summer Bible camp at Beaver Lake, run by Pastor Paul Riley. If Sarah got her competitiveness and drive from her father, she absorbed her spiritual nature from her mother. "Chuck worships Mother Nature," said family friend Marilyn Lane. "Sally instilled in them that 'the wild game . . . was a gift to have.' "

"Chuck taught them all about the outdoors," said Helen Riley, Pastor Riley's wife, who taught Sunday school at the Assembly of God church. "Being outdoors in God's creation was the same to Chuck as going to church. He's a great teacher and has always been that from day one. In Sarah, I see her mother's mannerisms; she walks in a room and brings the light, happiness, and cheer, just as her mom did."

Sally said the choice to leave the Catholic church was determined more by convenience than any disagreement with the church's philosophy.

"When we moved here," Sally said, "we went to the church nearest our home; we were able to walk to it. It happened to be the Assembly of God, and eventually we asked to be baptized, and we all did it on the same day. We switched denominations as a matter of convenience, and we fit in very nicely there. They had a wonderful youth group and great activities for the children. Church was an important part of our lives—we didn't have all the other activities kids have today, and back then we went to church twice on Sunday and once in the middle of the week. Today, there's too much other stuff to choose from, but for me, Sunday morning was the day to refresh your soul. Sarah still attends church in Wasilla and in Juneau."

The Assembly of God Bible camp at Beaver Lake still has special meaning to Sarah. It was here that Pastor Riley baptized all the Heath kids and Sally, full immersion-style, in the lake's chilly waters. "It sure wakes you up," Sally said, chuckling. Campers would go on picnics, take long walks over trails past fields of wild flowers, and gather for outdoor Bible readings under the shady spruce and birch trees. Bear and moose would sometimes appear at the water's edge, and the kids would pick flowers and craft bouquets. Sarah was twelve when she was baptized with her mother and siblings. Last June, she made an official visit to a religious gathering at the Wasilla Assembly of God Church and gave a speech that was later posted on the Internet. As she happily reminisced about how "cool" it was to grow up in this church and be "saved here," she recalled getting baptized by Pastor Riley in Beaver Lake and how those early years worshipping at the Assembly of God had an indelible effect on her spirituality. She went on to become the president of her high school's Fellowship of Christian Athletes, leading her track and basketball teammates in prayer before competition. She wrote Bible verses in her friends' yearbooks, and under her own candid photo in Wasilla High's 1982 yearbook, she wrote, "He is the light and in the light there is life."

"They were a very neat group of kids that would meet before school and have a Bible reading, and on certain national days of prayer, they would meet at the flagpole before school, and Sarah would lead them in prayer," Helen Riley recalled.

In the biography *Sarah*, author Kaylene Johnson wrote that Sarah felt that the sermons she heard at the Assembly of God were not just being "directed to the general congregation but specifically to her. The music lifted her spirits in a way that nothing else did. And she discovered that when she prayed, she felt the presence of something far greater than herself." Pastor Riley and his wife like to tell the story of how the church's former youth pastor, Theren Horn, would remind his adolescent charges that God has a specific calling for them—teaching, parenting, medicine, or politics. Sarah heard the same command, and Horn's mention of politics stuck in her head. Years later, after Horn had moved to Minnesota and was back in Wasilla for a visit, Sarah, then the city's mayor, reminded him of the lesson and said, "I was called into politics, and that's the direction I took."

"Theren always inspired the kids that God had a plan for each of us personally, and that got Sarah's attention; politics was what she related to the most," Riley said.

By the time Sarah reached eighth grade at Wasilla Middle School, she was still finding her place in the world and experiencing typical adolescent growing pains. She wore a pair of thick glasses, and her hair was styled in an unsophisticated bowl cut parted down the middle. In 2008, when she hit the national stage, bloggers would drool that she was "the hottest governor in all fifty states and my total girl crush." Sarah would try to play down her looks, telling *Vogue* magazine in a 2007 interview that she tried "to be as frumpy as I could by wearing my hair on top of my head and these schoolmarm glasses. I wish they'd stick to the issues instead of discussing my black go-go boots."

Beauty's burdens spared thirteen-year-old Sarah Heath. "She was a little chunky," recalled classmate Cheryl Welch. "She was always pushing the glasses back up her nose; she reminded me of Thelma on *Scooby-Doo*."

As Sarah worked her way through the Wasilla school system, she needed no introduction to teachers and administrators, who knew her parents, especially her father, one of the most popular teachers in Wasilla. Sally worked as a high school secretary, and Sarah also had the good fortune of following in the respected footsteps of two accomplished older siblings, Heather, the captain of the girls varsity basketball team at Wasilla High, and Chuck Jr., a star football and basketball player at Wasilla, who would go on to play football at the University of Idaho. In middle school, Sarah was a good, if not exceptional, student, and classmates said she rarely spoke up in class.

"She worked hard," said Chuck Sr. "I remember her reading the newspaper in the third and fourth grade. I'd grab the sports, and she would read the national section from cover to cover—that's where her interest in politics came from. As a student, she never had any problems—she was in honors—and whatever she took up, she jumped in with all four feet—she always came home and did homework and then went out to play."

Sarah's friends were a tight-knit clique of churchgoing jocks. "She was good friends with my daughter, Jackie," Jerald Conn said, referring to his daughter, now a police detective, who played high school basketball with Sarah. "They were religious and liked sports."

Sarah was friendly and known by everyone—one

of the more popular kids but not necessarily the most popular girl in class. In junior high, that distinction belonged to a pretty blonde named Tammie Dickinson, who had gone out with the eighth grade's most popular boy, Curtis Menard Jr., son of the town dentist by the same name and one of the region's most influential Republican politicians. (Today Curtis Menard Sr. is the mayor of the Mat-Su Borough.) Sarah had a schoolgirl crush on young Menard and sometime off in the distant future, that crush would be returned, but not in 1977–78. In the first month of school, Menard asked another girl to go steady, a new kid in class from far-away Hawaii. She was taller, prettier, and even a better basketball player than Sarah. Her name was Cheryl Welch.

As prominent as Sarah Palin would become, she was not immune to everyday teenage drama. After Palin was picked by the GOP to run with John McCain, Welch wrote an e-mail to friends describing herself as "Sarah Palin's worst eighth grade nightmare."

One day near the start of school, Welch was running laps around the gym when a tall, pale boy with huge eyes and red lips stopped her in her tracks and asked, "Do you want to go with me?" He meant "go" as in "steady," Welch explained. Welch thought that the overture was a bit odd and declined. She really didn't know the boy. As she was getting dressed in the locker room, another girl walked up and asked her what "Curtis" had wanted from her. "He asked me to go with him," she replied.

"Suddenly, from behind me in the front row of lockers, a girl burst into tears," Welch recalled. It was Sarah Heath. As Sarah's friends huddled around to console her, Sarah got up and ran from the locker room. "I found out later Sarah was in love with Curtis and wanted to marry him someday," said Welch, now an English instructor at the University of Arizona. Once Welch got the lowdown on Menard—smart, athletic, and available, as available as a thirteen-year-old can be—she understood Sarah's interest and took a longer look at Menard herself. She changed her mind and accepted his offer, and they became steadies for the rest of the school year, much to Sarah's chagrin.

"When I look back on it now, we should have been friends, but it was never going to happen," Welch said of Sarah. "I tried to be nice, and generally, she was nice in return, but I could tell it was eating her up. I couldn't relate to wanting anything that badly—to be first, to get the guy, to get the highest score, that you could be sick with it," Welch wrote in her e-mail.

Welch felt Sarah's envy. She was Menard's girlfriend, and her GPA was higher than Sarah's. When they got back tests, Welch said Sarah always tried to peek at her score. For their nicknames, Menard and Welch chose their GPAs: "We called each other '3.95,' " Welch said.

"Sarah's grades were good but not that high," Welch said.

The rivalry continued on the basketball court, where Welch and Sarah played on the middle school team. "She ran around like a rabid little thing," Welch recalled. "She did not like to lose and sometimes cried after losses. She was very petulant and formidable—there was no stopping her. We'd be practicing and drilling—she wanted the ball so badly she'd get really red in the face and scratch and claw until you just wanted to say, 'Here, take the ball.' When I heard they nicknamed her Sarah Barracuda after the way she played on the basketball court, I thought, 'Wow, perfect.' "

Welch said that even after she left middle school, her experience with Sarah Heath stayed with her forever. "She struck me as too competitive and didn't strike any balance in her life. What she wanted, she really wanted, and no one was going to tell her no. She acted like she was everyone's favorite."

Sarah wasn't tall, and she wasn't the most gifted athlete. An argument can be made that her energy and hustle compensated for her lack of size and skill. And classmates say Welch was no picnic herself.

But Welch also felt Sarah was on the verge of blossoming. In the years to come, Sarah would repair a chipped front tooth and grow out of her baby fat. Her tomboy sensibilities, apparent to everyone, gradually faded away, replaced by an assertive female who felt there was nothing a man was entitled to that she couldn't have herself. "She was always pretty; she just took longer to figure it out," Welch wrote. "She was a guys' girl. She stayed with the boys instead of hanging with the gals. She had more of a macho thing going rather than wanting to be coquettish."

At the end of the school year, Menard and Welch broke up, and Welch, who was picked to give the eighth-grade graduation speech, moved out of town. A few years later, when young Menard came to California to participate in a mock United Nations conference that Welch also was attending, they caught up on old times. "I jokingly asked if Sarah had got what she wanted, and I learned the puppy love crush on Curtis had faded," Welch recalled. "Curtis said, 'You know, Sarah has become a big deal in high school.' "

"Menard was well liked, and he was a great friend of our family," said Heather. "I wouldn't doubt that Sarah liked him. He was such a great boy. Before Todd Palin came along, I would not put it past me that she had feelings for him."

At Wasilla High, Sarah's circle of friends included fellow jocks Jackie Conn and Kim Ketchum, who runs an Anchorage frame store. There was a clique of intellectuals who liked theater and took AP classes, but Sarah didn't belong. "We were considered the geekier, nerdy kids. We were smarter," Elle Ede, a former classmate and one of the clique, told the *New Republic*.

Chuck Heath remained an enormous presence. Sarah is better known for her basketball prowess, but she was exceptional in two sports coached by her father, cross country and spring track. His assistant was Don Teeguarden, Sarah's varsity basketball coach and now a retired math teacher who still coaches high school girls' basketball in Washington, not far from Sally Heath's hometown.

Teeguarden remembered Chuck recruiting him. "Hey, I'm going to be the track coach, and you can help."

"I don't know anything about coaching track," Teeguarden replied.

"Don't worry," Chuck promised. "I'll get you some film. We'll have a lot of fun."

Fun might not be the operative word here for someone coached by Chuck Heath, who brought his football mentality to track. But his runners did achieve success. "He was a very intense and competitive guy," recalled Teeguarden. "He did a great job as track coach. When he started out, Wasilla High had never won a meet."

That nonsense stopped in Chuck's first season as

coach in 1978. Wasilla won its first dual meet and came in second at the regionals. Then Wasilla won successive regional championships from 1979 to 1981. "His enthusiasm was contagious," said Teeguarden. "He could get the kids performing at their highest levels and was able to recruit the kids he wanted at school."

One of those kids was Sarah, who, thanks to her dad, was already an above-average runner when she enrolled at Wasilla High. Chuck Sr. wasn't the type to stand around with a clipboard and a stopwatch, shouting orders. He was a taskmaster at home and on the job. He ran alongside his athletes and exhorted them to fight through the agony of the workout so they would become stronger and better competitors. Chuck drew on his lessons from famed high school football coach Cotton Barlow, sparing no quarter and inspiring his runners to do better. When they felt pain, he'd shout, "Run through it!" When he got in his daughter's face, Chuck recalled, "She just looked me straight in the eye and didn't talk back or anything. It's a wonder she didn't whack me," Chuck once told a reporter.

Chuck explained that he didn't want to be perceived as playing favorites just because Sarah was his daughter. "I was hard on her—if she was deficient in an area like hurdles, she'd work and work. She started out in the middle of the pack and became my best distance runner by the end of the season. In basketball, she wasn't a God-given talent in dribbling and shooting—but she worked at it. It was like that in whatever she undertook, including politics.

"My old football coach Cotton Barlow said the harder you worked, the better you got; he said if you got hurt, just run it off. I was a 'no pain, no gain' type of coach, and I pushed my daughters and Chuckie harder than the others. I wasn't mean to them. But at the end of every season, the other kids on the team would come up to say to me, 'I'm glad I'm not your daughter.' When I look back—I expected a lot more from them."

Chuck was just as tough on himself. Roger Nelles, the boys basketball coach at Wasilla High, used to cover Chuck Sr. in pick-up basketball games and come home with bumps and bruises. "Chuck loved to win and wouldn't back off for anything," he said. "They say basketball was a noncontact sport, but Chuck was really hard on defense."

Sarah inherited that defensive-minded tenacity and applied it to her basketball game. That fiery style that intimidated the likes of Cheryl Welch was the catalyst for Sarah's famous nickname—Sarah Barracuda.

"I discussed that topic with my [former] assistant coach at Wasilla, and neither of us can remember where that name came from," said Teeguarden, who believes

Sarah's sister, Heather, came up with the epithet after watching Sarah's fierce play at a summer basketball camp. "I remember Sarah as an aggressive defender—probably overly aggressive," he said. "As a freshman and sophomore, we had to teach her how to tone it down, because she'd be on the floor a couple of minutes and find herself in foul trouble. As a coach, I think it's a desirable trait, because you can teach those kids the limits they need to follow to keep themselves in ballgames. If you foul, you sit, and Sarah didn't want to do that. Sarah was intelligent, and she figured that out pretty quick."

Heather, who was co-captain of the varsity girls basketball team the year Sarah was a junior, said Sarah scratched and clawed her way around the basketball court. "Defensively she could eat you up," her sister said. "She'd bend at the knees, grit her teeth, and spread her arms wide. She wasn't a dirty player—just aggressive, with high endurance because of her great conditioning. When I look back, I was not as confident a player as Sarah. Neither one of us was a high scorer. We passed the ball and were the same defensively, but she could barrel through situations where I might stay outside and shoot."

By Sarah's junior year, the Wasilla High girls varsity team was becoming the talk of the region, having reached the state finals the year before. This tiny school of three hundred students was playing on the same level as the larger schools in Anchorage, Fairbanks, and Juneau. Sarah itched to play varsity as a junior, but Teeguarden felt it made more sense for her to get experience on junior varsity rather than sit on the bench behind five seniors. "Sarah wanted to play varsity, but it didn't become a disruption. I told her, 'I hear what you're saying, Sarah, but you have to live with this choice and be ready if the opportunity comes.' She understood."

Sarah wasn't happy about the decision, but it helped that two of her close friends joined her on the JV squad. She got her chance to play varsity at the end of the season when she was promoted to the roster as a reserve for the state tournament.

Usually when the team traveled, it was reminiscent of the lifestyle portrayed in the movie *Hoosiers*. The Warriors players would pack a bus and drive more than six hours to some away games, doing schoolwork and blasting boom boxes during the ride. After the game, they'd roll out their sleeping bags and pillows and bed down in a classroom. In the morning, they'd drive home or to their next road game and repeat the process all over again.

For the state finals, the team got to stay in a hotel in Juneau. Sarah watched from the bench as Wasilla lost in the championship game for the second year in a row. The next morning, Teeguarden was mulling over the loss with his assistant coach during breakfast, when they discovered the girls had abandoned their rooms. Had they gone out the night before and not returned? That seemed out of character, Teeguarden thought. "I was a little worried about how the kids took it," he said. "Then we looked outside and spotted them coming down the street. They were carrying Bibles and were returning from church. Sarah was in the Fellowship of Christian Athletes, as were a lot of our kids. She would have organized that. We had lost one tough game the night before, and I figured they'd be laying around feeling sorry for themselves, but it wasn't in their nature. They got up the next day and went on with their lives."

Coach Teeguarden bid his seniors a farewell and began preparing for the 1982 season. He decided to build a back court with three girls—seniors Sarah and Jackie Conn and junior Michelle Carney. When the time came to select team captains, the honor went to seniors: Sarah and her good friends Jackie and Heyde Kohring. It was another sign that Sarah was coming into her own and transforming into the "big deal" Curtis Menard Jr. had described for Cheryl Welch.

"They earned it," Teeguarden said. "Sarah was really a good competitor and had good leadership qualities: integrity, drive, strength of will. She had a mind of her own, and still does. There was leadership off the floor, too. We had to endure those six- to eight-hour bus rides, play a game, sleep in a school overnight, and drive the next day to play in another game. Nobody ever complained."

In Sarah's senior season, Teeguarden's offense was designed to pound the ball inside to the taller players in the low post. The guards were set up on the perimeter as safety valves for the forwards in case they didn't have a shot. The primary scoring threat was Wanda Strutko, who was nifty around the basket. "We had a conservative offense with a strong post game," Teeguarden recalled. "It was our only chance to win. All our perimeter gals had to take good care of the ball, get it inside and get open to be ready to shoot if the ball was kicked out. There was no three-point line or shot clock, so it was best to play for the high-percentage shots close to the basket."

Sarah and the other guards were not thrilled about their new roles until they gave Teeguarden's system a chance and started winning games. "It didn't happen overnight. These were seventeen-year-old girls with strong wills," he said.

And win they did. The Warriors finished the regular season with an outstanding 26-5 record, with Sarah establishing herself as the starting point guard. Typically, she covered the opposing team's best ball handler, earning herself yet another moniker, "The Pusher," for her ability to force dribblers to one side of the floor.

During the season, she twisted her ankle badly, and when the tournament play began, Teeguarden could tell it was bothering her. "We had to play three nights in a row, and that took its toll, and then after we advanced, we had a few days' rest, and we had to play three nights in a row again. I could see it was affecting her movement, and we iced her ankle after games and taped it up before games, but it was affecting her mobility."

Teeguarden considered shutting her down. But first he decided to consult Chuck Heath. "They were involved in the decision, and Sarah decided to play on," Teeguarden said. "She sensed we had something special this year and wanted to be a part of it."

After beating archrival Palmer in the regional championships, "which to some people in Wasilla meant more than winning the state title," Teeguarden noted, the Warriors advanced to the state finals in Anchorage. Three games were on tap, the first against formidable East Anchorage, the odds-on favorite to win the title. Wasilla wasn't expected to be much of a match. In the last game of the regular season, East smothered the Warriors with a stifling defense and an aggressive offense. "I don't remember the final score," Teeguarden said, forgetting that his team lost by forty points. "But at the half, it was 32–10, and we didn't get any closer."

Instead of being intimidated, Teeguarden remem-

bered, the team had a quiet air of confidence on the bus
ride to Anchorage on the day of the tournament, which
was being hosted by West High. Enrollment at Anchorage schools typically exceeded one thousand. "The kids
were never afraid of them," he said. "Our seniors were
not afraid. As a group, we seemed very businesslike. We
were so small as a school, we never took anyone lightly."

During warm-ups, assistant coach Cordell Randall
noticed a couple of East players wandering into the stands
to talk to friends. East's warm-ups seemed lackadaisical,
players floating in for layups at half speed. "Their heads
were not into the game," he thought to himself. Coach
Teeguarden took it upon himself to post an article published in that day's *Daily News* in which another coach
commented, "East has a cakewalk to the finals."

"East's coach didn't say that, but I showed it to the
girls anyway," he said. It was a nice piece of ammuni-
tion. "We had the small-school chip on our shoulders to
begin with, so it wasn't hard to ignite that."

Wasilla stayed close to East in that first half, and
they pulled it out at the end, winning by two, 50–48.
"There was no margin for error," said Teeguarden. As
time expired, Sarah aggravated her ankle injury. After
the game, she iced down the swollen, blue ankle and told
her coach she was all right. Lathrop High from Fairbanks was up next, and Sarah wrapped her ankle in tape

and played. Wasilla got a small lead and maintained it until the end, winning 62–51. "We won by eleven, but I don't think we were ever comfortable in that game," said Teeguarden. "I could tell Sarah's ankle was still bothering her, but she played on it."

The finals pitted Wasilla against Service High, another sizable Anchorage school with a population of two thousand. Nevertheless, it was Wasilla that had the distinction of boasting teams in the state finals three consecutive years. Teeguarden still didn't have a championship to show for it, and it gnawed at him. He thought about it during the team dinner at a local restaurant and later at a coaches meeting and when he sat with the team to watch the consolation game. In the locker room, Teeguarden went over the X's and O's as Sarah wrapped her ankle tight. Teeguarden had already decided she was going to start, but he would watch her closely. Just before the Warriors took the floor, the team stood in a circle, and the captains led them in a prayer. "Everyone stood in a circle and held hands," Teeguarden said. "If anyone had something to say, they said it. Never did I hear anything about winning—it was always about doing your best, protecting us from injury, being honorable in competition—never did I hear the word 'win.'"

As the Warriors took the floor, more than two thousand fans filled the gym, including a substantial crowd from Wasilla, which had caravanned into Anchorage each night of the tournament. In March, the daylight strains to reclaim the morning and late afternoon hours. While it remained bleak outdoors, Wasilla fans were feeling optimistic about their chances if the team could continue to ride the wave of momentum that carried them in the first two games. Sarah's family was in the stands along with her new boyfriend, Todd Palin, a standout on the Wasilla boys team. He had transferred his senior year from Glennallen, a city 189 miles east of Anchorage. Sarah first heard about him from her father, who told her there was a new boy in town and that he was an excellent basketball player. Coming from a hard-to-please coach like Chuck, that meant something to Sarah. At practice, Sarah got to see him with her own eyes and was impressed. "He was the best basketball player I had ever seen," she told *People* magazine. Todd noticed Sarah as well, telling friends she was easily the best-looking player on the girls team.

As Teeguarden watched the Warriors in layup lines, he surveyed the gym and liked what he saw. "It was an away game, but we had a home crowd with us," Tee-guarden recalled.

Wasilla opened up a lead in the first half, but Sarah was having a difficult time moving laterally and making cuts with her wrapped ankle. Sarah's defense suffered, and Service closed the gap. In the second half, Tee-guarden pulled Sarah from the game and sat her on the bench. "She couldn't move defensively," he said. Tee-guarden could see Sarah was miffed, and he tried to console her, telling her to rest up in case he needed her to go back in. "We're going to need you," he told her. Going into the fourth quarter, Wasilla held a nine-point lead, but Service gradually crept closer.

Assistant Coach Randall noticed the tenor of the game changing. To catch up, Service needed to foul and put Wasilla on the line. But one of the team's best free-throw shooters was still on the bench. Randall was thinking, "We need to get Sarah back in there," just as Teeguarden called Sarah's number. Wasilla's lead was just four. "I needed Sarah's judgment and her good free-throw shooting," he said.

With thirty seconds to go, she was fouled. She needed to make at least one of two shots to give her team a five-point cushion and make it a three-possession game. She stepped to the line and made her first shot. "When she made it, we all exhaled," Teeguarden recalled. "No one scored again." The final score was 58–53, Wasilla. "That was a big deal for Wasilla," said Jerald Conn, the father of Sarah's teammate Jackie Conn. "They didn't win another basketball title for twenty-five years."

"I don't remember a wild celebration," recalled

Teeguarden, though a photo shows a very festive team cheering and jumping up and down as Teeguarden held the championship plaque over his head. "We shook hands with the Service players and gave each other hugs and kisses and went back to the locker room. There were tears. Sarah had not played much on varsity the previous year, and I know she had wanted to play more, and I think it made her a little hungrier."

Sarah scored just nine points in the three-game state tournament, and her ankle was so ravaged she had to sit out the spring track season. A state title made it easier. Years later, after she entered politics, Sarah continually referred to the Warriors' championship season on campaign stops. "I know this sounds hokey," she was fond of saying, "but basketball was a life-changing experience for me. It's all about setting a goal, about discipline, teamwork, and then success."

THREE
A MAN IN CARHARTTS

One day, when Sarah Heath and a friend were talking about what attracted them to men, Sarah made a telling remark. "I like a man in Carhartts," she said.

The bib overalls are popular among blue-collar workers employed with the oil companies drilling on Alaska's North Slope. With their built-in insulation and knee pads, they're perfect for doing chores back home. "Carhartts are what Todd wears around town," said Warren McCorkell, an old family friend. "I'll see him down at the auto shop—he's got his parts, and you got your parts, and he'll be talking a steady stream about a project he's working on. He's a big sports celebrity here in Alaska because he's won the Iron Dog four times. His wife is governor, and some people like that might act like stuffed shirts—but he's not self-promoting at all or too big to talk with you."

Then there's the other side to Todd—the devoted, stay-at-home dad who some years makes less money than his wife and helps raise the children. Around Wasilla, it's well known that Todd is an equal partner, perhaps more, when it comes to running the household and raising the kids. McCorkell recalled a birthday party Sarah and some friends gave for a girlfriend; Sarah, with her political star on the rise, was surrounded the moment she entered the room. "Sarah has this big crowd around her," McCorkell recalled. "Then I see Todd off to the side holding one of the kids. I said, 'Todd, how do you deal with all these people fawning over your wife?' He's so laid back; he shrugs his shoulders and says, 'She's being Sarah, keeping everyone happy, and I'm Mr. Mom.' "

Mr. Mom was born on September 6, 1964, in Kanakanak Hospital by Nushagak Bay near Dillingham, a small fishing village. In the early nineteenth century, it was a Russian trading post, and by 1900, there were eleven canneries in the region. It's an isolated community of 2,400, accessible only by boat or air. Prices are high—gasoline is more than six dollars a gallon—and a premium is attached to most goods, since they're carried in and out by barge.

The economy in the region is centered on Bristol Bay, the murky body of water Todd and Sarah chose to name their eldest daughter after. Describing her husband to *People* magazine, Sarah said, "There's that saying, 'Still waters run deep.' That's Todd." She could have been describing Bristol Bay in summertime. The link to the Wood and Nushagak rivers supports one of the largest red salmon populations in the world. Each June and July during the salmon run, those waters teem with life.

Todd was born into a family of commercial set-net fishermen, said Jim Palin, Todd's father. One month each summer, Todd fishes from a designated section off Coffee Point beach using a technique called set-netting. He owns a limited entry set-net permit to fish the site. During high tide, set-netters cast the nets out into the water, secure them over fixed underwater posts, and then retrieve their catch using aluminum skiffs—twenty-seven-foot boats rigged with outboard motors supporting up to several thousand pounds of fish. It's hard and dangerous work done in all types of extreme conditions. When the catch is pulled aboard, each salmon has to be plucked through the net by its head—called "picking"—and tossed into a hold to await transfer to a second boat for delivery to the Peter Pan cannery.

When the salmon run, crews work all hours of the day and night and endure rough weather if they must. When it gets busy, several hundred pounds can be caught in an hour. Most of the fishermen pack a lunch or gorge themselves on snacks. Todd's favorite is Spam and crackers. "Sometimes he puts peanut butter on it," family friend Steve Becker told *People*.

Growing up, Todd developed an affinity for the outdoors. He liked to hunt and learned how to drive a snow machine. Todd's mother, Blanche, is one-quarter Yu'pik Eskimo, the product of her late Caucasian father, Freeman Roberts, and Helena Andree, a half-blooded Yu'pik, who today lives in Homer. Helena, eighty-six, is a respected Yu'pik elder with a political past of her own, having years ago served on a state task force for alcohol and drug abuse. In interviews, Sarah has pointed out Todd's native heritage and his grandmother's respected position in the Yu'pik community. Sarah supports the subsistence way of life that has maintained families like Todd's. The fish from the bay and the meat from the wilderness fill Alaskan freezers and enable families to get through the winter.

The Palin family is close to Todd's mother, Blanche, and stepfather, Bob Kallstrom. Blanche and Bob have been married for three decades. They operate Dillingham's only hardware store, a lucrative operation that has rewarded them handsomely. Beyond the usual hammers and saws, "they sell a little bit of everything there," says a Palin family friend. "Furniture, toys, cars, and boats." Friends believe Todd inherited his mother's good looks; with her dark hair and olive skin, she is an older version of her attractive middle child. "She is one of the most beautiful women I've ever seen," said a family friend. "The years have been kind. She has the greenest eyes you've ever seen."

As a boy growing up next to the wilderness of western Alaska, Todd hunted, fished, and played basketball. Blanche and Jim Palin would eventually divorce. Todd and his two siblings stayed with their mother in Dillingham until the late 1970s, when Todd and J.D. moved to Glennallen in Alaska's interior to live with their father, who had remarried to Faye Braun Palin. In 1981, Jim took the general manager's post for a regional electric company, Matanuska Electrical Association, and moved his family, which now included Faye, Todd, and J.D., to Wasilla.

Jim threw himself into civic affairs, joining the Rotary Club and the local chambers of commerce.

Boys varsity basketball coach Roger Nelles was thrilled to have Todd enroll at Wasilla High, but probably not as excited as the young ladies at school. Sarah has told the story about how some classmates wrote "TODD" across their knuckles, and the gossip swirled around the hunky new senior boy who had his own fishing boat and drove his own car. Todd stood apart from his peers—he was a great basketball player, owned his own business, and drove a truck and a car, making the commercial fisherman quite the catch. Watching Todd dive for loose balls on the basketball floor, Sarah became a big fan of his work ethic on the court and the quiet self-confidence he carried off it.

Wasilla's long road trips during basketball season seemed tailor-made for budding romances. A forty-eight-seat school bus ferried the boys and girls varsity and junior varsity teams across the state for games, trips that could take them out of town for up to five days. That year, both the Wasilla boys and girls varsity teams won more than twenty-five games each, and both teams made their respective state tournaments. Since Wasilla High had a smaller enrollment than the bigger schools in nearby Anchorage, schedule makers pitted them against similar-size high schools in outlying regions of the state. On a typical trip, the teams would put their luggage in a separate van and then pile into a bus, two to a seat. They'd leave school on Friday morning and drive six hours to Valdez, play on Friday and Saturday nights, sleep on the floor in a classroom, and then drive and take a ferry to Cordova, play Monday and Tuesday, finally getting back to Wasilla on Wednesday, recalled Nelles. "We missed a lot of school, but that was a given if you played high school sports in Alaska."

The players spent a lot of time together and became good friends. "We had enough coaches and chaperones along so there was no funny business," he said, chuckling. "But kids will be kids; there might have been a few lip locks. But overall, the kids were really focused."

Nelles was thrilled with the arrival of Todd, whom he had known for several years because he was friends with Todd's father, Jim, a well-known high school basketball referee. He earned the starting nod as a ball-control point guard who played hard-nosed defense. Varsity athletes were required to be passing all courses that led to graduation, "but I didn't have to worry about Todd," he said. There were high expectations for the boys team, which won its regional and advanced to the state tournament, held at a different time and place from the girls varsity tournament that Wasilla won. "Todd hurt his ankle in the regional, and he wasn't one hundred percent for state," said Nelles. The boys team lost its first game in the double elimination tournament and finished fourth overall. A week later, Todd was in the stands at West High, watching Sarah help lead the girls team to the state title.

Back home in Wasilla, Todd romanced Sarah aboard a snow machine. On one of their first dates, Todd took her on a snowmobiling trip to Eureka, a valley two hours away from Wasilla known for its deep, powdery snow. Sally joined the young couple and kept busy cross-country skiing while Todd and Sarah raced up and down the hills. Today, it's still a way they keep the romance alive. "They get away from it all," biographer

Kaylene Johnson told *People* magazine. "They go to a friend's cabin, but it's off road, so they have to take snow machines."

Todd helped teach Sarah how to drive, and Sally and Chuck warmed to their daughter's new boyfriend. For the senior prom, Todd escorted Sarah wearing a classic black tux, frilly light blue shirt, and black bow tie. Sarah looked stunning in a red, flowing evening gown supported by spaghetti straps. Still the athlete, she wore her hair short but neat, and a small dark pendant hung around her neck. Coach Roger Nelles recalled that the Wasilla High gym was made over into a dance hall with balloons, streamers, and a deejay blasting dance tunes like Toni Basil's "Mickey" and the Go-Gos' "We Got the Beat." When things slowed down, they could slow dance to Billy Joel's "She's Got a Way" and Kenny Rogers's "Through the Years." That summer after graduation, Sarah joined Todd in Dillingham to fish for the migrating red salmon before they got ready for college.

By the end of her senior year in high school, Sarah had made up her mind to leave home to attend school. She certainly had the résumé to attend a good school. In the 1982 Wasilla High yearbook, *The Chieftain*, she was listed as belonging to numerous clubs. "She was outgoing and one of the more popular girls in the school," said Teresa Modaunt, a classmate now living near Seattle. She belonged to all kinds of clubs: Honor Society, pep band (Sarah played the flute), basketball, cross country, prom committee, student council, student body treasurer, and varsity club. Under a yearbook photo, there was an image America would become familiar with in 2008, showing a doe-eyed, smiling brunette. At the time, her ambition, she wrote, was to "sit up in a press box with Howard Cosell on Monday nights broadcasting Eric, Dave, Todd, and J.D.'s games. Todd was, of course, Todd Palin, her boyfriend; Eric was Waldner, a football player and one of the more popular guys in the school; Dave was Tresham, who also played football; and J.D. was a reference to yet a fourth senior jock.

Sarah and three friends plotted out their college plans together, agreeing to attend a school in a warm-weather state where they could all get accepted. The winner was the University of Hawaii-Hilo, which for Alaskans is truly about as far away as you can get. It was a time for Sarah to strike out on her own and experiment with new relationships and new environments. Sometime during this period, Sarah tried marijuana and didn't like it. "I can't claim a Bill Clinton and say I never inhaled," she told the *Anchorage Daily News*. But she reminded voters that when she tried pot, it was legal under state law, though she would never advocate legalizing it because of the message it would send to her children.

During their college years, many local teenagers get the itch to leave home if they have the means to get out of town. "If you lived in Alaska, you'd understand," said Katie Carney, an old classmate of Sarah's, who remembered her as a "decent" student and one of the more popular kids. At that time, many college-bound kids left the state to continue their education—Carney attended the University of Idaho—because there were few four-year opportunities at home, and many young people were clamoring for a change of pace. "Sure, there's eighteen hours of daylight in June, but in the winter, there's just a few hours of daylight, and it gets cold. Our warmest day this summer was seventy degrees, and in the winter you could go a week at a time at twenty-five below. And when the wind blows, it gets down to sixty below. You go to work in the dark and come home in the dark."

Sarah had an aunt in Oahu she had visited with her family, so she was familiar with the island terrain and the weather—or so she thought. The sunny, warm temperatures appealed to the four gals, but they forgot to do their homework. Hawaiian weather runs the gamut and varies from island to island and from hour to hour. After enrolling at the University of Hawaii in Hilo, on the Big Island, Sarah and her pals were shocked by the amount of rain. For three weeks, it poured and poured. The foursome got so discouraged that they withdrew from the college. Two of the kids were homesick and returned to Wasilla to re-group. For Sarah, who would attend five colleges in the next five years, it was the start of an educational odyssey that took her from Hawaii to Idaho and back to Alaska, with a final return to Idaho to earn her college degree at the University of Idaho in Moscow.

After Hilo, Sarah and best friend Kim Ketchum transferred to Hawaii Pacific on Oahu, where it was drier and warmer. Living in an apartment in Waikiki, they bussed to school, and Sarah took business administration classes. For fun, they hung out on the beach and spied on actor Tom Selleck, whose TV production *Magnum P.I.* was shot around the island. Holidays were spent at the home of Sarah's aunt.

Still, the girls found the whole experience unsatisfying, especially the warm climate and the absence of seasons to mark the passage of time. The friends went home for winter break and, in the spring, enrolled at North Idaho College, a community college set on beautiful Lake Coeur d'Alene and near many Heath relatives living in Sandpoint. Sarah registered as a general studies major and took political science classes. She completed one more term in the fall of 1983. But she already had her eye on a career and the place to help her reach her goal—the University of Idaho, where Chuck Jr. was playing college football.

In 1984, Todd and Sarah's relationship picked up where it had left off. Sarah joined him in Dillingham for part of the fishing season as she plotted her next move. Linda Menard, today one of the Republican movers and shakers in Mat-Su and state politics along with her husband, dentist Curt Menard, ran the local Miss Wasilla beauty pageant. She bumped into Sarah that spring. Sarah was taking a break from college to make a little money working as a receptionist.

"Would you be interested in competing to be Miss Wasilla?" Linda asked. Sarah initially balked at the idea, as Chuck Jr. relentlessly kidded her about the opportunity. "That wasn't her thing," her dad, Chuck, told a reporter. But Linda prevailed.

"Sarah," Linda said, "even if you don't win, it expands the box you live in."

Besides, there was scholarship money to be had, and Sarah was paying her way through college. Sarah worked on the different aspects of the event—walking, posing, and modeling the bathing suit and evening gown. Her mother took her to Anchorage to buy her a competition gown, and Sarah started visiting the tanning salon to add more color to her skin. For the talent portion, Sarah played the flute. Hairdresser Diane Osborne, one of Sarah's sponsors, was concerned that Sarah was too shy and ambivalent to be a factor in the competition. "I kind of worried about how she would do up there onstage," she told the *New York Times*. "You have to have a certain go-get-'em to get up there and stand up for yourself, and she came across as such a shy, sweet girl."

Yet a transformation was taking place. Sarah won the Miss Wasilla pageant, qualifying her for the Miss Alaska event. The *Frontiersman* covered the contest and photographed her wearing a rhinestone tiara and a strapless gown. In the Miss Alaska event, a victory would put Sarah in the Miss America pageant. The old footage of Palin in the bathing suit and talent portions of the competition has been posted online. A blond announcer introduced her as "an accomplished flautist who has been performing for ten years. She will be performing 'The Homecoming,' as written by Nathan Hardy . . ."

When the camera swung over to Palin in her long black dress and flowing white top, she was standing in front of a band, anxiously swaying back and forth as she raised the instrument to her lips and played for more than two minutes, backed by horns, percussion, and woodwinds. There were a couple of rough spots, but she beamed another smile when she was done.

In the bathing suit contest, Sarah wore a red tank suit and modeled the outfit for judges on a darkened stage as a jazz band played soft music that made it seem as if she was gliding across the stage in her heels. The announcer introduced "Sarah Heath" and rattled off her accomplishments in a radio voice: "Sarah says she wants to prepare for a career in television broadcasting by majoring in television communications and political science. It is no wonder that she has also been recognized by 'Who's Who?' since she has displayed her leadership in all areas, from academics to student politics to athletics. . . . Ladies and gentlemen, contestant number eight, Sarah Heath," he said as Sarah gracefully exited the stage. Her competition that night was Maryline Blackburn of Fairbanks, a singer from Atlanta who was raised in Fairbanks. Blackburn said she could tell Sarah was going to be a tough out. "She was a very sweet young lady who everybody liked," she said. "My first impression was, 'Oh my God, she's gorgeous; she'll probably be the one who wins.'" Blackburn also observed Sarah's growing confidence. "She had this look about her, this look in her eyes that tells you she's calculating, figuring it out, 'how am I going to win this competition,'" Blackburn said. "There was determination there." But not a victory—the title went to Blackburn, and she became Alaska's first African-American to represent the state at the Miss America competition. Sarah was named second runner-up and Miss Congeniality for the event.

Todd was on the move, too. After high school, he took classes at Anchorage Community College and the University of Alaska-Anchorage, and continued playing basketball. A coach in the Lower Forty-eight, Dennis Fox, took a head coaching job at Missouri Valley College in Marshall, Missouri, in the summer of 1984 and started recruiting players from Alaska, including Luther Bartholomew from Valdez, who used to play against Todd in high school. Bartholomew and Todd became friends on the summer ball circuit, and when Coach Fox told his new players he was looking for a couple more recruits, Bartholomew recommended Todd. Fox approached him and offered a partial scholarship to join the team at Missouri Valley. Competing in the National Association of Intercollegiate Athletics, the small liberal arts school brought in twenty-four new freshmen to restock its varsity program. The league represented a quantum leap in competition for Todd, but he jumped at the opportunity, even though it meant leaving his beloved Alaska. Tuition at the college was $6,900 annually, and Fox reckoned Todd received $1,000 in aid to play basketball and major in education. Fox, who now coaches at Cardinal Stritch University in Milwaukee, said Todd arrived that August in the middle of a miserable heat wave and moved into a dormitory without air-conditioning. "It was hot and humid, ninety-degree days," Fox remembered. "It wasn't pleasant for anyone and was much hotter than Todd was used to."

While Todd was a gifted player at Wasilla, small-college basketball is a level up in every way. The athletes are bigger and faster, and most, like Todd, were stars of their high school teams. "I was very impressed with him as a person," said Fox. "He was a blue-collar, hard-nosed-type player—I could use him on my team right now—but not gifted athletically. But he grew on me and worked his way up the roster. He was one of those give-it-all-type players, diving for loose balls, taking charges. Unfortunately, he got stuck behind an all-conference point guard and was fourth string. At the end of the academic year, I found out he wasn't returning, and I was very disappointed. Lots of young guys get homesick, but it's usually not being homesick for Mom and Dad but for a girlfriend."

Todd never did earn his degree. The semester Todd went to Missouri, Sarah enrolled at the University of Idaho. Good friend Ketchum had decided to wrap up her schooling at North Idaho, so Sarah was on her own, save for her brother. "She enjoyed watching him play football," a friend said. But Chuck Jr. hurt his shoulder early in the season and was out for the year. Sarah studied broadcast journalism, and a couple of classmates remembered her as a quiet and serious, good-looking girl. The *Idaho Statesman* newspaper found four students and professors who recalled Sarah as a "serious, caring, quiet student who didn't invite men to her single room in Neely Hall." One friend did recall Sarah because she frequently reminded her to set her alarm to wake up for church. Stacia Hagerty, now a real estate agent and lawyer in Coeur d'Alene, said it took her four days to realize the person McCain picked as a running mate was her old friend. "You never felt like she was too good for anything," she told the *Statesman*. "But at the same time, I never saw her get drunk or act stupid or skip class or betray a friend. She was rock solid."

"I don't think Sarah ever wanted to lead," said college friend Lori Ann Perrin, who was surprised when Sarah burst on the national scene. "In a way, she was almost a wallflower type. I'm not sure what happened between then and now, but something must have."

Sarah also completed two TV internships, one in Coeur d'Alene and one in Alaska, which was a pretty good performance, since students were expected to apply for them on their own. "She was a go-getter," said Sarah's academic adviser, Roy Atwood. "She may not have stood out as a brilliant student that people remember well in class, but her record suggests she was a student who went way above and beyond and maintained a sense of drive and initiative that was rare," he told the *Statesman*.

Sarah returned home to make some money in the fall of 1985, taking a few courses at Matanuska-Susitana Community College in Palmer, and then it was back to Idaho to finish her degree, which she completed in the spring of 1987. Todd had yet to land his job at British Petroleum and was splitting his time between Wasilla and Dillingham. One day in 1986, the twenty-two-year-old was drinking with friends and neglected to sober up before getting into his truck. He was pulled over by police and taken to jail briefly. The incident resulted in a DUI conviction on his record. Years later, he was cited for running a red light in Wasilla and fined $210 for driving an off-road vehicle in a state game refuge. "Getting a DUI around here is not a major deal," observed one longtime Dillingham resident. "What's significant, and I mean this in a positive way, is that it didn't happen again."

Friends say Todd is not a heavy drinker. "That happened when he was twenty-two years old," said Christine Garner, who dated Todd's brother, J.D., in the mid-1990s and had a child with him. "You make a lot of mistakes from age eighteen to twenty-five, and getting a DUI is not uncommon around here."

At college graduation in 1987, Sarah earned a bachelor's degree in journalism, with a minor in political science. Returning home, she landed an internship at the

Mat-Su region's local newspaper, the *Frontiersman*, just around the corner from the home she grew up in. Print was nice, but Sarah always had an eye on a television career in sports broadcasting. She wasn't entirely comfortable in front of a camera, but she showed promise. She had credibility as a jock, just five years removed from having led her basketball team to a state title. Her big brown eyes, huge smile, and dark brown hair gave her that girl-next-door appeal, with the added cachet of being a local beauty queen. Having grown up as a tomboy and been treated like one of the guys by her father and friends, she had no qualms about succeeding in a man's world, and television sports was still largely the purview of men, at least on the local level.

After college, she became a sports broadcaster at KTUU NBC in Anchorage. She moved to the city and shared an apartment with Heather. John Hernandez, the sports director there at the time, gave Sarah her first break when he allowed her to be the weekend anchor on the day of the 1988 Super Bowl. "She jumped at the opportunity," he said. "She was a little nervous and stiff, but it was a decent show."

FOUR

TRANSITION GAME

*I*n July 2008 at the Governor's Picnic in Wasilla, Kay Fyfe was walking through the crowd, under the cool sun-splashed skies of the Mat-Su Valley. Hungry, she wandered over to the concessions stand and spotted two familiar faces, Sarah and Todd Palin. The governor was busy—part of her day was spent in a cooking apron under a white canopy, flipping hamburgers and serving hot dogs to friendly picnic goers. Todd was nearby with the kids. They looked great, Fyfe thought. Sarah's hair was different, fashioned in an updo compared with the shoulder-length style she wore when they'd met. Todd—tall, robust, and handsome—hadn't changed a bit. As Fyfe edged closer to the couple, she saw a gap in the admiring crowd and made her move. "Todd," she said, extending her hand to the first gentleman, who was standing nearby as his wife greeted folks and made small talk with friends and strangers. "You don't know me, but I did something very important for you twenty years ago." Todd squinted and studied her face. He said she looked familiar, but he couldn't place her. Fyfe couldn't contain herself any longer. "I married you at the Palmer courthouse!" she blurted out. He broke into a big smile and tried to get his wife's attention; she was surrounded by a sea of supporters. "Come over here, you have to meet this person!" A minute passed, and Sarah made her way over to her husband and his guest. "Honey, I'd like you to meet . . ." Sarah gave Fyfe a quick glance and smiled. "Kay, how are you?" she said. "Where have you been?"

Fyfe, flabbergasted that Sarah had remembered her name, caught them up on her life—she was still clerking at the Palmer courthouse and moonlighting as a professional marriage commissioner, having performed more than two hundred weddings in her career. The Palins were one of her first couples. Sarah laughed as she recalled that special day on August 29, 1988. "You were so nervous," she recalled. "It was one of my first marriages," Fyfe said, tearing up at the memory, just as she had the day the Palins had exchanged vows.

"I remember that Sarah was just out of college working as a broadcaster, and Todd was working as a commercial fisherman," she recalled. "I was just blown away she remembered my name."

On that day in 1988, Sarah and Todd were supposed to meet her sister Heather and some friends at the Alaska State Fair in Palmer. With its amusement-park rides for the kids, exhibits, and food stands spread over a landscaped fairgrounds against the backdrop of the Talkeetna and Chugach Mountains, it was the highlight of the summer. Vendors served fresh river salmon, oysters, and halibut from Prince William Sound and such exotic wild-game delicacies as reindeer sausage. Sarah and Todd met Heather in the morning, and they were supposed to rendezvous later for the ride back to Anchorage, but they were no-shows. Instead, the couple detoured one mile from the fairgrounds and drove to the Palmer courthouse—to elope.

Fyfe worked in a dreary, nondescript two-story building with aluminum siding. "It was small, and we had to go outside to get to the second floor," said Fyfe, who was a court clerk but was also commissioned by the state to preside over weddings. "The people waiting to get married had to wait in the same hallway as the criminals waiting for arraignment. You would see these men in chains standing next to young women in white wedding gowns. We had all these buckets around to catch the water from the leaking roof."

Fyfe doesn't recall what Sarah and Todd were wearing but thinks they were dressed casually. She doesn't remember if they exchanged wedding bands, either. Fyfe has presided over some bizarre weddings in her day—couples have misplaced rings, and once the groomsmen arrived hours late and inebriated, earning a tongue-lashing from the groom. Sarah and Todd's nuptials had one small glitch. As they were filling out the paperwork, they realized they forgot to bring witnesses. "They went next door to the Pioneer nursing home and brought back two people—one was in a wheelchair, and the other was using a walker," recalled Fyfe, who donned a black robe for the ceremony where Todd and Sarah declared that they took each other as man and wife.

"I was surprised," said Heather, who was sharing an apartment with Sarah in Anchorage while she worked as a television sports reporter. Todd lived nearby on a family property and drove snowplows for a living. "I knew they were a solid couple, but they didn't have two dimes to rub together. I was with them part of the day and remember one had cells, so when they didn't meet me at the end of the day, I figured, 'They're big kids, they'll find their way back.' "

When Heather got home just before dinnertime, she checked in with her mom. Sally answered the phone and said, "Sarah and Todd have eloped."

Before they disappeared for the weekend, Sarah and Todd collected two bouquets of wild flowers, one for each set of parents. Sally and Chuck remembered coming home from work that Friday to find the bouquet on their doorstep. Sally opened the card and shuddered for joy as she read the note. "Congratulations to your new son-in-law," Sarah had written. Sally laughed. "It was a big surprise, but we were thankful to have Todd."

Across town, Jim and Faye found a bouquet and a note on the hood of Jim's car, which was parked in front of the house. Jim remembered the day well—it was his wedding anniversary with Faye, and they planned on having a celebratory dinner together that night. The card from Sarah and Todd read, "Happy anniversary. Seemed like a good day to get married, so we got married." Reflecting back on the moment, Jim said wryly, "Just another fine example of how private they are."

In another odd piece of serendipity, August 29 is also John McCain's birthday, and in twenty years, August 29, 2008, would be the day McCain announced that Sarah would join him on the GOP presidential ticket.

The newlyweds returned to Anchorage after the weekend, Heather recalled. "I don't know where they went—they didn't tell me," said Heather, who got married herself within the year.

Though an official wedding ceremony was out of

the question, Chuck and Sally did give the young couple a reception at their home two weeks later. "I fixed up the house and garage, and we had a big celebration," Sally said. "It was potluck; salmon, garden vegetables, wild game, and blueberries and raspberries because they're in season. We had a beautiful cake made by a friend of ours."

During the reception, everyone toasted the new couple, and a neighbor sang "Sunrise, Sunset" from *Fiddler on the Roof*. "I remember the lyrics," Sally said. " 'Is this the little girl I carried . . . ?' "

Despite the rushed nature of the wedding, Sarah had no regrets, at least none that lingered, said Garner, J.D.'s ex-girlfriend. Years later, Sarah did have a piece of advice for her children. "I tell my kids, 'Don't do what I did,' " she said. Todd summed up the quickie nuptials this way: "We had a bad fishing year, so we didn't have any money. So we decided to spend thirty-five dollars and go down to the courthouse."

The old courthouse in Palmer where they tied the knot is still there, but it houses the local public defender's offices, Fyfe said. Last summer, the other half of the building was used as a political campaign office—for Barack Obama.

When they returned to Anchorage, Todd moved in immediately with the Heath sisters and shared a room with Sarah. He had applied for an oil-company job on the North Slope and was waiting for an offer. In the meantime, he drove snow-removal trucks in Anchorage, usually working the red-eye shift. Sarah was pregnant with Track. "I didn't know she was pregnant until she reached four months," Heather said. "She carries small."

Eight months separate the August 29 wedding day from Track's date of birth, April 20, 1989. Todd's dad, Jim Palin, said he never got an explanation for the month gap. As far as he can recall, Track's birth was normal and on time. "He was a healthy baby boy," Jim said.

"It's my understanding," said a family friend, "that they found out right after they were married." The Palins chose an old friend, Curtis Menard Jr., to be Track's godfather.

They chose to name their firstborn after Sarah's favorite spring activity, running track. Springtime in Alaska evokes hope and renewal, as the days grow longer and the mountains fill with wildflowers and animals that have been hibernating since the winter.

"Sarah never had complications during her pregnancies," Heather said. "She stayed active. All of us had good genes for having babies. Easy pregnancies, and the babies were born on time."

Before Track's arrival, Sarah and Todd moved back

to Wasilla and bought a modest condo near the high school. It would be the first of four Wasilla homes that the Palins would buy. Later, they moved to a ranch house in the Mission Hills development outside Wasilla before settling in a waterfront home on Wasilla Lake.

In 1989, Todd was hired by British Petroleum, which drastically changed the couple's lifestyle. On the slope, production operators and technicians work twelve-hour shifts in seven-day or fourteen-day blocks, with commensurate time off when they return home.

Tom Whitstine Jr., a fellow production operator for British Petroleum, described working conditions that included long hours and little downtime between shifts. North Slope crews fly out of regional airports on charter jets and land at Deadhorse Airport near Prudhoe Bay, about one and a half hours from Anchorage. Vans and buses then shuttle the workers five miles to one of several North Slope camps operated by the oil companies. These two-story, hotel-like structures accommodate 500 to 1,000 workers, providing 80 percent of the workforce with individual rooms and a bathroom shared with an adjoining unit. Todd's camp, called the Base Operations Center, holds an indoor swimming pool, a gymnasium for basketball and volleyball play, a movie theater, and several TV areas where employees can play cards, read, or watch television. Everyone eats in a common cafeteria-style dining room, with a dinner menu that typically offers soups, salad, and three entrees—chicken, beef, or fish, unless it's a theme night with Mexican, Italian, or Chinese dishes. About 5 percent of the workforce is female, and meals and transportation costs are free.

Work shifts are from 6 a.m. to 6 p.m. daily, which leaves little time for recreation. Whitstine said the days begin at 4:30 a.m., with breakfast at 5 a.m., where individuals can pack a sack lunch. Then everyone grabs a shuttle to head to the fields. As a worker comes on a shift, someone else is getting off and heading back to camp for a few hours of downtime before going to sleep. Todd worked at a station called Gathering Center Three as a production operator charged with monitoring the engineering equipment that separates oil from gas and water. To picture the scene, Whitstine said, imagine a medium-size shopping mall with three anchor stores and pipes running throughout them. The flow lines separate the water and gas, which are treated and reinjected back into the rock formation underground, while the oil is sent to a reprocessing facility. From there, it is sent south via the Trans Alaskan pipeline from Prudhoe Bay to the ice-free port of Valdez, eight hundred miles away, where supertankers wait to ship the oil to market, typically to the west coast of the United States.

Todd is a union-represented employee, and his day is a combination of checking equipment and pressure valves, shoveling snow off access ways and steps, and charting up to one hundred technical readings of an assortment of pressure gauges and digital equipment. There's a coffee break at 9 a.m., a lunch break at noon, and another break in the afternoon before the changeover meeting about a half-hour before the end of the shift. The highlights of the weekend are the hot lunches prepared at the gathering centers. "At night, everyone has dinner and then works out or watches a movie," said Whitstine. "Most nights, everyone's in his room by nine p.m."

Todd's father, Jim, has visited Todd on the slope on a couple of occasions. "Food's excellent," he said. "You name it, you got it up there."

After having Track, Sarah went back to work at Anchorage's KTVA CBS, where she was in the sports department covering high school sports. Her supervisor at the time was Steve MacDonald, now the news director at KTUU, where Sarah got her start after graduating from Idaho. Her duties included covering high school soccer and football on the weekends and occasional anchoring chores when one of the regulars needed a fill-in. "She was a one-man band," said MacDonald, who said her sports pedigree at Wasilla High was certainly a factor in her ability to do the job. "And probably one of the early female sportscasters working for a metropolitan sports department. She would go out and cover a game, film highlights, and bring it back to produce, and do the voice-over. It was hard work. Anchoring—she was a little inexperienced, and I remember when she first tried that, she was a little nervous, but she didn't embarrass herself. She knew sports, and she knew what sports were important to Alaskans."

Lauren Maxwell, a veteran anchor for KTVA, recalled working with Sarah one weekend. "She had to do everything, because we were cutting back on staff," she said. "But I recall her anchoring on the weekends. She's a very attractive woman, and I recall thinking, 'Oh, she does her makeup nicely for TV; how did she learn to do that?' "

At the beginning, when Sarah landed her internships during and after college, Sally said her daughter "loved" the job, especially filling in as sports anchor. Over time, "she told me it wasn't as easy as she thought it was going to be," Sally recalled. "There was new subject matter to learn all the time. It was a challenge to her to look relaxed and use expression. It took a lot more than she thought it would. And there was that long drive to work every day."

Maxwell also said that Sarah got pregnant during her stint at KTVA and remembered her working part of the time while carrying Bristol. Sarah became pregnant with Bristol in February 1990 and delivered her first daughter on October 18 of that year.

For Sarah, it was another textbook birth. "She was an athlete," said her aunt, Katie Johnson, Sally's sister from Washington. "Those Alaska people are different—they pop them out, and they're just fine."

Aunt Katie recalled getting a call from Heather after she had one of her babies and was struck by her niece's chipper demeanor.

"When did you have him, a couple of days ago?" Johnson asked.

"Two hours ago; I hope the doctors let me go home in twenty-four hours," she replied.

"Oh boy, you gals are tough," Johnson said.

With two small children, Sarah decided the time was coming to devote more time at home. "She wanted to be at home with the young ones," Heather said. MacDonald said he recalled Sarah leaving KTVA to spend more time with her children. Joined by the young children, Sarah continued attending the Assembly of God church with her mother. "Church has always been a big part of her life," Heather said. "It's not something she talks about all the time, but it's a nice ritual we had growing up, and Sarah likes it."

It was about this time that Sarah began training to

compete in local road races. Like her father, who ran in the Boston Marathon, she caught the running bug in a serious way. McCorkell, who worked for the highway department, remembered being out on Parks Highway one morning with a crew filling cracks in the road with tar, when Sarah came jogging by in a dark tracksuit. Even in baggy sweats, she posed a striking figure, McCorkell said. "I'd give her a wave, and my coworkers would perk up and ask, 'Who's that?' I'd say, 'That's Sarah Palin, running off the baby weight.'" Sarah's best friends admired her beauty as much as the guys did. "My wife used to say, 'Sarah has got it going on, just look at her, and she just had a child,'" said McCorkell.

All the Heath gals were serious runners. "I think they get it from their dad. Chuck was amazing; he used to run back and forth to Palmer—that's twenty miles round trip," McCorkell said. Sarah's intensity left a permanent impression. In the summer, Christine Garner and J.D. would stay with Todd and Sarah when they came to town to attend the Alaska State Fair. "It was early in the morning, and we were making coffee when Sarah blazed by in a tracksuit and went bolting out the door," said Garner.

"She used to train for marathons with Todd's stepmother, Faye," Garner recalled. Sarah competed in five-and ten-kilometer races, which sometimes meant training on the road. On a visit to Richland, Washington, to see Sally's family, Sarah told her aunt Katie that she was heading out to visit her cousin. "I'm going to run over there and will be back in a couple of hours."

Johnson assumed it was just a figure of speech. The cousin, after all, lived twelve miles away in Kennewick. "She was out the door, and then a half hour later, I looked outside and saw Sarah's car. I asked my husband, 'Why is Sarah's car still here?' He said, 'Well, she did say she was going to run,'" Johnson recalled him saying. That twenty-mile Wasilla-Palmer route her father used to do? Sarah liked it, too. "When she was training, sometimes she'd go twice a day," Johnson said.

Running wasn't the only form of exercise for Sarah. She started attending aerobics classes three mornings a week at a local fitness club that was run by two friends, Amy Hansen and the late Pam Hackett. Hansen, who was married to McCorkell until a split in 2008, befriended Sarah. They were all athletic and in their late twenties and thirties, with small children and husbands.

They called themselves the "Elite Six" and got so adept at aerobics that Hansen arranged for them to perform as a group at the state fair in exchange for free parking and food. A few of them also competed together in local 5K and 10K races, with Faye Palin and Sarah's sisters, Heather and Molly. Pretty soon, the Elite Six were gathering on birthdays, baby showers, and the annual potluck Christmas party at Warren and Amy's home on a dirt road outside town. Held on the first Friday in December, the event was the highlight of the year. They wore holiday colors and brought casseroles, chips and dip, cakes, and pies. Sarah typically brought a pan of baked brownies. They also exchanged goofy ornaments.

"We didn't talk politics; it was mostly what our kids were doing. There were no husbands—just the girls," said one of the Elites, who asked to remain anonymous. "We had different political points of view. Sarah is pretty tough; you have to be, in politics, but she is a normal small-town girl. You don't have to think like her to be her friend. We were all from different religious and political backgrounds. And we never discussed religion, and she didn't foist her religion on us. That stuff didn't come up."

The Elite Six included Hansen, a private investigator; Patti Ricker, a Lutheran and a respite-care provider who competed in road relays with Sarah; Sandy Hoeft, a Mat-Su Borough paramedic; and Juanita Fuller, an office manager and a Mormon, whose husband, Norm, is a chiropractor and served on the Wasilla City Council when Sarah was mayor. Hackett, the oldest in the group, passed away from cancer in 2005. She was a youth pastor and taught aerobics with Hansen. "It was a tragedy to see her die in the prime of her life," said McCorkell, who attended the funeral with the Elites and their husbands. "It tore chunks out of Amy; she was there with her when she died and shut her eyes. They were best buddies."

How did the group get its name? "There were six of us meeting at six, so it was a joke," Hansen told a reporter. In September 2008, the inner circle appeared on ABC's *Nightline* together to discuss Sarah and their politics. Viewers learned that some of the friends are pro-choice and that Palin is "just like the rest of us except for she's got a lot more energy," Ricker said on the show. Another thing: Sarah is afraid of Hansen's cat. "[She] doesn't like cats," Ricker said.

Sarah's apparent fear of felines has been a running joke for years, said McCorkell. "[Hansen's] cat has two paws on each paw," he said, laughing. "It used to bother Sarah. She would go find cat ornaments for Amy." He still has a lawn ornament Sarah gave his wife a decade ago. He pointed to a wood pile by his front door, gesturing at a faded tin blue and yellow cartoonish-looking cat with a big Cheshire grin, holding a salmon in its paws. The word "Welcome" was emblazoned across the front. Inside, a cartoon is tacked to a bulletin board that Sarah gave Hansen for her thirty-ninth birthday. It shows a female cat owner staring down her guilty-looking kitty after it has knocked over a plant. "I'm going to be so mad when my mood elevators wear off," the caption reads. Sarah signed it, "Happy 39th, Love Sarah." That sense of humor was evident again when Sarah came dressed as a pregnant Jane Fonda for an Elite Six Halloween party.

The Elite Six gatherings usually took place in the evening after work and were typically casual potluck affairs with lots of coffee and no alcohol. That didn't stop the husbands from joking and speculating about what they thought might really be going on. "They were always organizing their get-togethers," said McCorkell. "These weren't real barnburners." After Sarah became mayor, Norm Fuller joked, "The only reason the cops didn't shut you down was because the mayor was there!"

While men were banned from the Elite Six parties, they were welcome at Hansen and Hackett's rigorous aerobics classes. Wasilla mayor John Stein attended with his wife. They were joined by Irl Stambaugh, a former police captain. Stein noticed Sarah's chipper personality and raw energy and mentioned her to Nick Carney, a former state agriculture director who ran a private garbage-hauling business. Carney needed no introduction. His daughter, Katie, had gone to high school with Sarah, and his niece, Michelle, was a teammate of Sarah's on the Warriors '82 championship team.

Carney and Stein belonged to a community group called Watch on Wasilla, which had been organized to create a police force for the city with a proposed two percent sales tax. Jim and Faye Palin were also active in the group. One day after aerobics, Carney and Stein invited Sarah to one of the meetings. Sarah accepted. She loved politics and, with two children nearing school age, cared about Wasilla's future and growth. No doubt, she was reminded of the conversation she had with her old youth pastor from the Assembly of God. "You are called by God for a specific purpose," he had told Sarah. Later, she confided to him, "I was called into politics, and that's the direction I took."

FIVE
TAKING CHARGE

*I*n 1992, Wasilla was experiencing growing pains caused by a population increase and the city's transformation into a bedroom community to Anchorage. In the twenty-one years since Chuck and Sally had moved their family into the small green house on Lucille Street, the population had surged from four hundred to more than four thousand. One of Sarah Palin's early political mentors, Nick Carney, was a young man of fifteen and just one of fifty residents when his family arrived in Wasilla in 1956—when Alaska was still a U.S. territory—and settled on a modest homestead. "I graduated in the top fifth of my high school class; in fact, I was the top fifth," Carney joked. He went on to earn a degree from Dartmouth. After graduation, he worked in Juneau for five years before accepting a position to run the state's Anchorage office for economic development. Later, he was promoted to state agriculture director, commuting to work each day from Wasilla, where he eventually returned to operate a garbage-hauling business.

Carney got to know the Heaths after they arrived from Skagway. "You knew everybody," he said. "Everyone attended the same functions and helped one another out. Everyone hunted and lived on moose meat and river salmon." Carney lives in Utah now, but he still counts Jim and Faye Palin among his closest friends. Like Jim, Carney loved basketball and worked as a referee.

As Wasilla grew, so did its problems. Crime was rare, but it happened, and the Alaska state troopers were responsible for policing the entire Mat-Su region. The budget for the troopers wasn't keeping pace with Wasilla's growth, and nonviolent crimes, like burglaries and shoplifting, didn't get much attention, Carney said. "The state was in a money crunch, and a bunch of us decided we needed a police force and a tax base to pay for it," he said. The group, called Watch on Wasilla, was composed mostly of white businessmen, but Sarah's mother-in-law, Faye Palin, chaired it. They agreed that a two percent sales tax that maxed out at ten dollars per purchase could finance a police department. It also would have the residual benefit of attracting commerce to the city, since business owners would take comfort in knowing that law enforcement would respond to their concerns. John Stein, mayor since 1987, supported the plan, but the tax proponents needed to convince voters with a credible slate of diverse city council candidates for the 1992 election. "We had a lot of business people, and they wanted the sales tax, but we needed someone who could represent the housewives, nonbusiness people, and the younger voters," Carney explained. "This wasn't a partisan position. No one cared if you were Republican or Democrat," he said. "We weren't looking for management skills but someone to communicate with that voting bloc and get them to accept the police force as positive for the community."

The leaders of Watch on Wasilla liked what they saw in Sarah: charisma, enthusiasm, smarts, and great communication skills. At twenty-eight, she was devoting much of her time to her young family and her church, the Wasilla Assembly of God. "Sarah had a college degree, though it was spotty, but we didn't care about her schooling. It was impressive enough that she went out of state to go to school," Carney said.

Sarah took to the idea of entering politics. She had been an officer in the student government at Wasilla High and believed that she'd had a religious calling to serve in politics since she was a teenager. The only thing that might have deterred her from starting a political career was a medical scare. In 1992, she underwent a breast biopsy to test a lesion. But the results were negative, according to her doctor, Cathy Baldwin-Johnson.

With that potential obstacle out of the way, Sarah proceeded to campaign. Carney, who was influential with voters, took her door-to-door to introduce her to residents and ask them for their support. Her mother, Sally, remembered that Sarah did a lot of campaigning on her own. "She'd go door-to-door, pulling Track and Bristol in a wagon," she said. That fall, both Carney and Sarah won council seats, and for the first eighteen months, everything was great, Carney said.

Sarah embraced the plan to create a police force, and she endorsed the sales tax. She immersed herself in local politics, and less than a year after the election, the council approved her aerobics buddy, Irl Stambaugh, as Wasilla's first chief of police in July 1993. Working from city hall, the former Anchorage police captain supervised eight officers and inaugurated a twenty-four-hour operation.

Husband Todd was starting a new venture as well—professional snow-machine racer. In February 1993, he entered his first Iron Dog competition, a race he has gone on to win four times. It is not to be confused with its more famous cousin, the Iditarod, the world's foremost sled-dog race, where a single man or woman guides a team of twelve to sixteen dogs over rigorous terrain in ten to seventeen days. A poster of the first woman to win the Iditarod, Libby Riddles, who won in 1985, graced Sarah's dorm room at Idaho.

In the Iron Dog, the world's longest and toughest snowmobile competition, racers travel 1,971 miles across Alaska, at speeds averaging seventy-five miles per hour through small villages, past windy coastlines, and over frozen rivers and tundra. The race traditionally begins in the Palins' hometown of Wasilla and takes the racers north over the Alaska Range, then west to Nome, and then back across the Koyukuk River to Fairbanks. For an action junkie like Todd, the Iron Dog seemed to be a perfect fit.

The "Dog," as it's referred to in Alaska, dates back to 1984, when competitors used compasses, maps, and intuition to find their way over the trail. "It was feel your way as you go," recalled veteran racer John Faeo, who won the inaugural race and is the winningest racer in the event's history. Today's Iron Dog racers utilize GPS tracking systems and the latest in sled technology. Their clothing, which keeps racers warm in sixty-below temperatures, is superior as well, both lighter and warmer compared to the wool pants and down jackets that Faeo wore on his first race.

Still, it's hard to figure what keeps the best competitors coming back. "It's torture every year," said Faeo, "and it gets harder as you get older." The training is brutal and begins about two months before the race. The teams train and compete together, usually meeting early in the morning to keep training from interfering with family life. The snow machines need to be maintained like race cars; parts have to be ordered and installed, and the engines must be built up. The prize money—around $25,000 for first—is split among the team, so the seasoned racers rely on sponsors, such as Arctic Cat and other snowmobile manufacturers.

It made sense, then, for Todd to go into the business of selling and repairing snow machines. He began laying the groundwork to open his own shop, Valley Polaris, out in Big Lake, twenty miles north of Wasilla. In the winter, the area draws thousands of snowmobile enthusiasts, providing him a perfect customer base. His business partner was Brad Hanson, a Montana-born businessman who grew up in neighboring Palmer.

Brad's family moved to Mat-Su when he was six, and the forty-six-year-old has been a fixture in the community ever since, except for the years he attended college at Northern Arizona University and the University of Alaska, Anchorage, where he earned a bachelor's degree in finance and a master's in business administration, respectively. Brad shares an interest in ice hockey with Todd and even resembles Todd to a degree, with his broad shoulders and square jaw.

Sarah and Brad would also become good friends. They enjoyed politics, and Brad would eventually win a seat on the Palmer City Council. Years later, after Sarah was nominated as a vice-presidential candidate, the *National Enquirer* alleged that they had an affair after Sarah became mayor, an accusation that was vociferously denied by both sides. "Brad Hanson is a good family friend," said Sarah's father, Chuck. "It's not true. I recently saw Brad, and he was laughing about it, as in, 'What's next?' "

In the spring of 1993, Sarah, under the tutelage of Nick Carney and Mayor Stein, got her feet warm in her first term on city council. Heather recalled, "I remember asking her why she was doing this, and Sarah said, 'I have something to offer, and I want to help. I have some great ideas and a lot of community support.' "

Sarah's schedule was ideal for public service. Track and Bristol were attending nursery school, and Sarah occasionally helped out in the classroom. Later, when the kids enrolled in the local elementary school in town, Sarah became an active member of the PTA. "She loved helping coach the kids," Heather said. "Track was starting hockey, and Bristol was getting into soccer and basketball. Her hours were flexible, and we all got to spend a lot of time together during holidays, birthday parties, and vacations. It was a seamless melding of her political career and being a mom at that time. And Todd was never too proud to help out when he was home from working on the North Slope."

When Todd went to Bristol Bay that summer to spend June and July commercial fishing, Sarah and the kids joined him. Christine Garner, J.D. Palin's ex-girlfriend, was also spending the summer there with Todd's brother. She will never forget the day in 1993 when Sarah spent a long day hauling in a catch as wind-swept surf spattered the boat and crew. The hold was full, and Todd summoned a "tender" boat, which weighs and ferries the fish to a nearby cannery after the transfer. The boats have to come side by side, and during the exchange, Sarah accidentally got her hand stuck between the rails, crushing some fingers. "I'll never forget that," Garner re-called. "It was bad. Todd rushed her to shore, but he went right back out there. Sarah got her hand taped up at the hospital, and she was back on the boat the next day, help-ing Todd. She didn't want to disappoint him."

That summer, officials snagged Sarah for a minor fishing violation, which came to light during her 2002 run for lieutenant governor. She had failed to register as a gill-net permit holder and pleaded no contest in Dillingham District Court. Sarah was a Wasilla council member at the time, and she explained that the violation had occurred because she was a crew member on one of the Palin family skiffs, and she had taken over a permit for her sister-in-law, neglecting to change her status from crew member to permit holder. The violation was accidentally entered into the books as a felony, a mistake that would come back to bite Sarah in a future election.

Commercial fishing permits in Dillingham are hard to come by—about one thousand have been issued—and each member of the Palin family has a permit to fish, said Jim Palin, Todd's father. Todd's older sister, Kristi, who lives in Washington State, owns her own skiff and continues to summer in Dillingham, as does Todd's younger brother, J.D., who makes the trip from Wasilla to work his boat. Their mother, Blanche, has fished her whole life and owns a thirty-two-foot drift-net boat of her own; she possesses a coveted drift-net permit considerably more valuable than Todd's onshore permit, because her crew can fish in the open water. Business has been good. In 2007, Todd, who bought his permit from his grandparents in the 1990s, declared $46,265 from his fishing business and typically hauls in around 35,000 to 60,000 pounds of salmon in a season, which runs from mid-June to mid-July. In the past, Sarah has worked on his crew, along with Track. Families can help, too—one summer when Todd had to return to his operations job on the North Slope, Sarah and her father, Chuck, ran the skiff with Todd's crew.

Todd hasn't missed a season since he got his permit. He didn't even take a break the summer after Trig was born, with a pregnant daughter at home and a wife about to be named to the GOP presidential ticket. His passion for commercial fishing is so intense that during his college years, he invited Sarah to work with him on their summer breaks. Out on the water, Todd was a relentless boss, even to the woman he was courting. All of the Palin children have toiled under his watch, learning how to use the set nets once they were old enough to pull aboard a couple hundred pounds of fish. "Sarah was out here fishing with Todd every summer, except the one summer she was pregnant with Willow [Willow was born on July 5, 1994]," Garner said. "And she worked in all kinds of weather— rain storms, windy hurricane-like conditions sometimes."

When Sarah gave birth to Willow, once again the pregnancy had gone smoothly. "Sarah took it easy that summer," Garner said. "It's the only time I can remember that she wasn't out there on the skiff." After giving birth, Sarah returned to Dillingham for some R&R, spending a few weeks with her baby and the kids at her mother-in-law's home. "She just wanted to avoid the telephone and things like that," Garner said.

As Sarah neared the end of her first council term in August 1994, the relationships between the council members became polarized. Sarah began asserting herself in meetings, asking questions and confronting Carney and Stein about the way the city was being run. No longer the shy teenager who agreed with everybody or the college student who sat quietly in class, dutifully taking notes, she had a confrontational style and conservative political bent that were evolving rapidly, and she wasn't afraid to speak her mind publicly. In her first year on the council, she fired off a letter critical of the *Anchorage Daily News*, lambasting its coverage of a scandal involving Republican state senator George Jacko, a key member of the state GOP who had been censured by the legislature for harassing a female legislative aide. Calling the paper "dangerously biased," she wrote, "How can you justify your restraint in slamming the Clintons, Kennedys, Marion Barrys, and other philandering, chauvinistic left-wingers of the world? Your yellow liberal rag is so obvious. I pray we will someday have a choice in newspapers again."

She was dismayed by the inner workings of city hall, a system she would later describe as a "good-old-boys" network that was in place for the benefit of a few and not the many. She told author Kaylene Johnson that "Mayor Stein and Nick Carney told me, 'You'll learn quick, just listen to us.' Well, they didn't know how I was wired."

Sarah is unremitting in the contention that she was bucking Wasilla's good-old-boys network. As recently as October 2008 in the middle of the presidential campaign, Sarah reiterated her position about those early days on Wasilla's city council. "Since my time as a city council member, and now, of course, as governor, I've been an active reformer. Right away, I think I saw that Wasilla's government was a 'good old boys'—and knew we had an opportunity to change and progress this city."

But Carney felt the label was unjustified. There was progress in the city—the sales tax, which everyone had endorsed in 1992, reduced crime and attracted new business and was filling the city coffers at a time when state allocations were declining. "If we were a good-old-boys network, the last thing we would do is get a young person to represent a block of young voters," Carney said. "We could have had just business people in power, and I suppose I was in that category—we were trying to bring Wasilla in a position to handle the growth with a police force and sewer and water systems to keep our lakes from being polluted. I just think this 'good-old-boys' reference made good copy."

The tension between John Stein and Sarah was palpable. One day in 1994, during a break at a council meeting, Carney approached Sarah after a heated exchange and said, somewhat kiddingly, " 'Sounds like you're running for mayor.' And she got really upset, because I figured out what she was doing. But I thought most of the attacks were unwarranted."

Sarah started butting heads with Carney, too, accusing him of trying to ram through a city ordinance that would require homeowners to pay for trash pickup, when he was the co-owner of the sole trash-hauling service in town. "I said no, and I voted no," Palin told author Johnson. "People should have the choice about whether or not to haul their garbage to the dump."

Carney begged to differ. In an interview with the *New Republic*, he said he couldn't have proposed the trash ordinance because he had disqualified himself from the issue. The magazine also reported that council members, nevertheless, sought him out for his expertise and asked him to contribute as an expert, "sharing information, not conspiring over a contract. There was no way that was happening," said former Wasilla councilwoman Laura Chase, who would later manage Sarah's 1996 mayoral campaign but then have a falling-out with her after the election. Chase, a University of Idaho graduate, joined the council in 1994, the same year Sarah easily won reelection to her second term. Chase was a former planning commission member and director of the city's Chamber of Commerce.

Sarah's relationship with Stein and Carney continued to sour. Initially, the sales tax could barely cover the police expenditures, and to make matters worse, the state began cutting back on revenue for roads, libraries, and sewer and water hookups. But business kept coming, Carney said. The owners liked the idea of a local police force that would respond when they called about a shoplifter or a burglary. Revenues increased with the commercial growth, and the discretionary fund grew to a reserve of $4 million. Sarah wanted to rein in spending and hold the line on salaries against Stein's "tax and spend" policies. "John would have all of us believe that every one of us is eager for Wasilla to become a 'mini-Anchorage,' building new facilities, increasing taxes, and restricting our uniquely Alaskan way of life," Sarah said in a speech before the Wasilla Chamber of Commerce.

"There is a colossal difference between John Stein and me," she said. "I'm a conservative, and he's a liberal. A good-old-boy politician."

Then came the first confrontation with Wasilla librarian Mary Ellen Emmons, over whether Palin was attempting to ban a certain book or merely responding to community concerns about the selection of books appropriate for the library. Of interest to Palin was the 1991 children's book *Daddy's Roommate*, the story of a young boy whose divorced father moves in with his gay partner. It is regarded as one of the first children's books to take an affirmative look at gay relationships and consequently was identified by the American Library Association as one of the "most challenged" books by patrons from 1990 to 2000.

Emmons has been mysteriously silent on the issue and has not returned messages from journalists. Chuck Heath, Sarah's father, said that after all was said and done, when Emmons moved away from Wasilla, she and Sarah parted on amicable terms. Sarah has always insisted that she was never trying to ban books but merely asking questions about content and selection, which was her duty. "As people there know, all questions posed to the library director were asked in a context of professionalism, regarding the library policy that was in place," Sarah said. "Before I became mayor, there was conversation in our community about what sorts of books were appropriate for the public library. I asked the librarian about the process for answering that question as a way to familiarize myself with city staff and the issues being discussed in Wasilla at that time. I certainly never advocated banning books. This was a ridiculous, false claim."

Carney said he doesn't have much recollection of the so-called book-ban controversy, since he was preoccupied with city-management issues. John Stein told the *New York Times* that when he was mayor, some residents were censoring books they found offensive. "People would bring books back censored," he said. "Pages would get marked up or torn out."

Chase did recall the matter and was present when Sarah brought it up at the end of the public comments portion of a council meeting. "She said she was at the library and noticed this book, and she didn't think it had any business in the library," she said. Department heads attend all council meetings, and Emmons, the library director, was present. "Mary is fiery when provoked," said Chase, who requested the book so she could review it herself. "I found it to be a sensitive book about showing love for additional family members. I took the book to show the other council members and said I felt it was inoffensive and suggested for everyone to read it, but there were no takers. I said, 'Sarah, why don't you take it home and read it?' I could tell by her body language she cringed at the idea. I was shocked. It blew my mind that she wouldn't look at it. I remember [Emmons] telling Sarah that the book stays put, and Sarah said stuff like, 'That's okay, if it stays behind the reference desk, but it shouldn't be in a place where kids can get it without their parents knowing.' She said she wouldn't object to someone taking it out. I argued, 'It's not pornographic.' "

The censorship matter came up again after Sarah was elected mayor. Curiously, in 2008, Chase made a special trip to the Wasilla library to see if the book was in the collection. "It's not there anymore," she said. "There is one copy, but it's all the way out in a library in Talkeetna, a fringe community where hardly any people live," she said.

Fringe might be a word used to describe the Alaskan Independence Party, a group that has pressed for a vote on whether Alaska should remain a state. It was around this time that Todd became involved in the organization. In 1994, he attended the party's convention in Wasilla, said Doyle Holmes, a store owner who co-chaired the group at that time. But he could not remember if Todd participated in the discussion. Todd signed on as a member in 1995 and again in 2000. His ties to the group ended in 2002, the year Sarah first ran for state office.

Two prevailing thoughts dominated the debate in 1994: total secession or a position toning "it down a bit," Holmes told the *Washington Post*. Among other issues, the group has advocated less government interference and turning all federal lands back to the state. In addition, one of the stated goals of the party is to allow Alaskans to vote on remaining a state; becoming a territory; becoming a commonwealth; or becoming a fully independent nation—the choices residents had in 1958 when they elected statehood. For the record, Sarah was never a member of the party.

Wasilla's 1996 mayoral race represented a break

from tradition. For one, Sarah entered the race and challenged Stein, a three-time incumbent, and a popular one at that. Mayor since 1987, Stein was vying for a fourth term; most council members figured it would be his last and were willing to wait him out. "People were satisfied with the job John was doing, and he was an extremely popular mayor," said Chase. "He got the sales tax passed, but we didn't want to see the money blown."

The sales tax was both a blessing and a curse. While it supported the police department and pumped up city reserves, it also created tension, because there was no consensus about what to do with the surplus. Police Chief Irl Stambaugh led an effort by the city department heads to have their jobs reclassified in order to raise salaries. This didn't sit well with fiscal conservatives on the council, led by Sarah.

A survey was conducted and compared the city positions to similar jobs in the oil industry in Anchorage, which in Chase's mind skewed the results in favor of the employees. That opened the door for criticism that spending was unchecked. "It alerted me that the tail was wagging the dog, and perhaps John was getting tired," said Chase, who had left the council in 1995 to take a position working for State Senator Lyda Green, whose district included Wasilla. "I think some of us were waiting for him to retire, but Sarah wanted to jump in at that point. It surprised me when she did, and I was conflicted, because I knew them all."

In August 1996, Sarah announced her intention to run, promising voters "fiscal responsibility without raising taxes." Sarah would call her opponent a "good old boy" out of touch with his constituency. Stein vowed to increase public services, and his campaign slogan was "Protect the Progress." The lines were drawn. Political opponents would borrow a nickname from Sarah's ferocious basketball play to describe her campaign tactics and ability to turn on old mentors like Stein: Sarah Barracuda.

Her opponents weren't exactly wallflowers, either. Todd told *People* magazine that when Sarah announced her candidacy, one of the council members said, "You can't run because you've got three negatives: Track, Bristol, and Willow." "When you tell her that kind of stuff," Todd said, laughing, "she just gets all fired up."

Chase went to work for Sarah as her campaign manager, with the understanding, she believed, that she would become the deputy administrator if Sarah won. In the past, said then *Frontiersman* editor Victoria Naegele, it seemed the mayor got elected based on whether you enjoyed hunting with him or not. This campaign turned into a scrum. City department heads lined up behind Stein and collectively wrote a letter of endorsement that was published in the *Frontiersman*. National politics were also trickling down to Wasilla. In 1996, conservatism was sweeping the country, and the Alaskan interior saw a population increase, with new residents pouring in from places like Oklahoma and Texas to work the Prudhoe Bay oil fields. They didn't know it at the time, but moderate Republicans like Stein were in trouble. Confident in Sarah's candidacy, the state's Republican Party decided to throw its considerable weight behind her, injecting partisan politics into what was traditionally a nonpartisan campaign.

Backing Sarah were two state senators and two members of the Alaska House of Representatives, who promised constituents that her election would "enhance our efforts to serve Wasilla." This kind of prominent GOP backing demonstrated that there was a larger agenda at stake than simply managing one of the fastest-growing cities in the state. Even then, Sarah was clearly being groomed for bigger things. This push came at the behest of the national Republican Party, which urged the local GOP to develop younger candidates, regardless of their experience. Regionally speaking, Sarah was regarded as a shining star.

Stein also made some missteps, coming down on the wrong side of Republican state senator Lyda Green, who supported legislation that would loosen restrictions on carrying concealed weapons in places such as drinking establishments. Stein backed Alaska's Democratic governor, Tony Knowles, who vetoed the bill, one that Sarah had endorsed. The NRA also got involved, labeling Stein "anti-gun" and literally giving Sarah its stamp of approval, which she promptly featured in ads and mailers

"The thing was, John was a hunter, and he wasn't against guns," Chase said. Sarah also backed a proposal that would allow bars to stay open until 5 a.m. For Chase, it wasn't so much Sarah's stance on the issues but how she fought the fight. Chase was caught off guard when an anti-abortion group leafleted the community, emphasizing Sarah's conservative family values, and she was surprised again when a pro-Palin flyer contained not only Sarah's "new ideas" and "fresh perspective" but the NRA logo. Sarah, according to Stein, also questioned why Stein's wife used her maiden name. "There were a few things Sarah did on the side that I didn't know about," Chase said. Still, others felt Sarah wasn't acting out of line. Chas St. George, a friend of the Palins who worked on Stein's campaign, told *Time* magazine that the primary issue was that the city coffers were growing, and "John was for expanding services and Sarah wasn't. That's what the race was about."

"Wasilla had never seen a campaign like that before," Carney said. "She ran on partisan politics and got the Republican Party to back her, even though John was a Republican himself. She ran on issues that had nothing to do with the city. We were all about preserving the lakes and improving highways and maybe joining Palmer to share services—the library was overloaded and inadequate— and those issues should have captured the campaign."

Local voters liked her personal touch, and many knew her father and mother, who were enormously popular. The former Miss Wasilla and co-captain of the state championship basketball team had broad appeal and a conservative message that appealed to this growing community. Fueled by the seventies oil boom, the area attracted many Christians from Texas, Louisiana, and Oklahoma to work the fields on the North Slope and worship in the community's growing number of evangelical churches.

Sarah also ran as a fiscal conservative. "Vote for conservative, more efficient government," her campaign literature stated, emphasizing that she supported budget cuts and tax decreases while Stein did not. She pushed for term limits and considered no issue too small. Taking Stein to task for the computerized phone voice-mail system the city had installed, she said it created a "communication gap" between the people and city hall.

Sarah, as always, campaigned hard, knocking on the door of every registered voter in the city and sending handwritten letters to dedicated voters. "Sarah has the ability to talk to a person and make them feel like you are the only person on the planet," Chase said. "And she was in television and well versed in media presentation." Her campaign promises included cutting property and business inventory taxes and controlling government spending.

"Streamline administrative costs and increase service to the public," Sarah promised in her literature. "As mayor I'll start the ball rolling by taking a pay cut." Which she did, reducing her salary from $68,000 to $64,200 after she got into office. Then she took direct aim at her old aerobics pal. "Wasilla is ready for new ideas and the fresh perspective you can't get from a four-term mayor."

Ouch. Stein felt some of the tactics by Sarah were underhanded. "Sarah comes in with all this ideological stuff, and I was like, *whoa*," Stein told the *New York Times*. "But that got her elected: abortion, gun rights, term limits, and the religious born-again thing. I'm not a churchgoing guy, and that was another issue: 'We will have our first Christian mayor,' " said Stein, recalling one TV station's mention of Sarah. Stein was raised Lutheran. He said he also felt compelled to produce a marriage certificate after Palin commented that Stein and his wife had different last names.

Judy Patrick, a friend of Sarah's who was elected to

city council that same year, said the mud was slung in both directions. "The main conversation when we got elected was that we were accused of improprieties. We had unseated a popular mayor and derailed his direction and angered a group of citizens. He had a plan for Wasilla that involved all these grandiose buildings, and they just became angry."

On election night, October 1, 1996, a pro-Sarah crowd gathered at the Mat-Su Borough government offices, and officials tallied the numbers on a display board. Sarah won convincingly, defeating Stein 651–440. "The second I knew we had what we needed, I walked over and congratulated her, 'Hey, we just did it.' I got a hug, and then she walked away to meet the press," Chase recalled. Sarah rattled off some names on her thank-you list and left Chase off. She thought it was an oversight until Sarah did it again.

A couple of days later, Sarah called with bad news: she wasn't going to hire Chase as the city administrator, because it smacked of cronyism, possibly a wise choice given all the heat during the election. Could she make a recommendation for the $50,000-a-year job? A subdued Chase suggested an old co-worker, John Cramer, who worked for Lyda Green. Sarah remembered the name and would later take a hit when critics said hiring Cramer smelled of party patronage. The next day at the campaign office, Chase said she refused a consolation check for $1,000 from Sarah and sniped, "You're lucky you have Todd to put up with all of this since he's the one taking care of the kids." Angry at the remark, Sarah wrote her the next day and said she had no right to comment on her relationship with Todd. But there were no hard feelings. Sarah gave Chase a job recommendation later and provided a glowing letter. "She wrote she would not have won without me," Chase said, beaming. "We spent almost every night working together during the campaign, and she is an amazing politician, and I'm really proud of everything she's accomplished, but I don't think she's any different than the good old boys she replaced."

Stein wasn't done with Sarah by a long shot, but the people had spoken for now. "Stein's a good person," said R'Nita Rogers, who had lost a city council race to Palin two years earlier. "I think he's just been in too long."

Sarah's political trajectory, meanwhile, seemed poised to clear Mount McKinley. During a late-night meeting before the election, Chase and Sarah were discussing the candidate's future, and Chase suggested she could run for governor in ten years. It's doubtful that even the GOP leaders lining up in support could have anticipated the reply from the ambitious thirty-two-year-old mayor-to-be. "I want to be president," she said.

SIX

SHAKING UP THE OLD GUARD

he headline in the September 3, 2008, *New York Times* spelled out Sarah Palin's rocky start as mayor of Wasilla:

"Palin's Start in Alaska: Not Politics As Usual."

Between 1994 and 1996, conservatives across the Mat-Su Borough had scored election coups over liberal and moderate incumbents. Sarah was riding that conservative momentum into office, a mere two years after Representative Newt Gingrich issued his new playbook for the GOP, the Contract with America. Hours after Sarah's victory, she announced she was going to shake up the administration, proposing cuts in the city's museum budget while increasing funds for such basic necessities as roads and sewer lines. She also was prepared to offer property-tax relief for homeowners in a city that was benefiting from rapid business growth and a two percent sales tax that left the budget $4 million in the black. Though the city wasn't short of money, its employees had to be accountable to taxpayers, herself included, Sarah said.

While Sarah's opponents questioned whether her experience was sufficient, Wasilla's top executive has limited responsibility compared to other cities. Schools and firefighting are managed by the regional government, the Mat-Su Borough. The state is in charge of running social services and overseeing environmental matters, such as drainage and water systems for construction projects. Not only does this division of power limit the scope of the mayor's control, it also enables communities like Wasilla to keep property taxes low or nonexistent. Much of Wasilla's revenue is directly attributed to the city's two percent sales tax, most of which is generated by shoppers outside the city. The city's shopping plazas and big-box stores are ubiquitous in their presence along George Parks Highway. Most residents live in two distinct areas. Many are outside of town in rural pockets, nestled in clearings surrounded by birch woods, and connected to paved streets by gravel roads. Others live in newer subdivisions, complete with all the amenities.

When Sarah surveyed city hall, she took the approach of a basketball coach taking over a losing team of malcontents: it was time to shake up the roster. Sarah had received support from the Republican legislative delegation in the Mat-Su Borough, and state GOP leaders were enthusiastic about her future. Now Sarah wanted the full support of her staff, but most had publicly endorsed Stein, including Police Chief Stambaugh. Sarah found this unacceptable. She decided it was time for new blood, but she didn't make her move right away.

The next confrontation came when the new council tried to fill two vacant seats on the six-member council. A unanimous vote was needed by the then four-person council, and Carney blocked candidates he perceived to be Sarah backers. When the process came to a standstill, Sarah threatened to pick them herself if they didn't reach a resolution, and then applied some muscle by bringing in two Anchorage attorneys. But her opponents felt she would be in violation of the city code, drawing more criticism from Carney and the *Frontiersman*.

"I said we should go back to the election results and take the two highest vote getters who lost, but 'nooo,' " Carney recalled. He blocked the nominations of two candidates that he felt Sarah would control. Instead, the city advertised for the positions, and two new names emerged—Darlene Langill, whom Carney supported, and Dianne Keller, a future Palin protégé who would eventually succeed her as Wasilla's mayor. These selections were approved unanimously.

Frontiersman cartoonist Chuck Legge couldn't resist editorializing about Palin's maneuvering and her aborted attempt to make unlawful appointments to the council aided by two Anchorage lawyers. He drew a cartoon inspired by Hans Christian Andersen's fairy tale "The Emperor's New Clothes," a story about a king who gets swindled by two con men who promise him new clothes made with the finest fabric, which are invisible only to those who are stupid or unfit for office. The emperor pretends to see the invisible clothes, fearful of looking dumb, and his ministers do the same. As he marches through town to show off his "new" clothes, a child shouts, "He has nothing on!" In Legge's cartoon, the obsequious Anchorage lawyers play the role of the con men ("These clothes we made you are divine," they said) while the public cried out, "Quick! Appoint the council seats and maybe she'll change back!"

Todd Palin was not amused by the cartoon. He was especially upset that caricatures were ogling his "nude" wife. The cartoon showed a group of people, eyes bugging out, looking at Sarah standing on a stage. The cartoon just showed bare legs. Vicki Naegele, then the editor of the *Frontiersman*, recalled Todd storming into the newspaper offices demanding to speak to the editor. "He was furious," Naegele recalled. "We tried explaining it to him—that the idea behind the editorial cartoon was based on a fable—and he didn't seem to get it, or it didn't matter, he was still angry." It wouldn't be the last time in Sarah's political career that Todd would attempt to fight one of his wife's battles.

At the same time, Sarah went ahead and hired a deputy administrator, a $50,000-a-year position that had been vacant for a few years. Critics lashed out at her, saying that this demonstrated that she was unfit for the job. Stein, with a degree in public administration from the University of Oregon, managed the city himself. But Sarah argued that the city's growth justified filling the job. Judy Patrick, a recently elected council member who was recruited by Stein to run for council the same year Sarah ran for mayor, agreed that the job was too big for one person and Sarah needed help. "I said it was crazy to do it by yourself," said Patrick.

A week before Halloween, Sarah made her boldest move yet. Calling it a loyalty test, she asked all the top managers to resign and reapply for their jobs with updated résumés. "Wasilla is moving forward in a positive direction. This is the time for the department heads to let me know if they plan to move forward or if it's time for a change," she said.

Laura Chase got an early inkling of what was in store a couple of days after the election, when Sarah told her she was going to shake up the bureaucracy. "I think I'm going to get rid of them," she told her. She had spoken about it with Todd's father, Jim Palin, a general manager of a local utility company.

"You could see the good old boys had been running things for some time and it was time for some new faces and younger attitudes," Jim said. "We needed some new blood in there. I agreed she needed to make changes. Those guys were adamant and vocal supporters of Stein. I said, 'It takes a team to run the city, and if you don't have a team approach, you have to find new team members.' "

In her first meeting with department heads, Sarah had been blunt. "I told them I had understood they had supported Mayor Stein. But I told them they couldn't continue to support him now that he was out of office."

The group included Stambaugh, public works director Jack Felton, finance director Duane Dvorak, and librarian Mary Ellen Emmons. The city museum director, John Cooper, was also asked to resign; he subsequently quit, and Sarah eliminated the position. Cooper knew the writing on the wall. He consulted an attorney after receiving notice from Sarah and found he had no legal recourse; he was serving at the pleasure of the mayor and was essentially at her mercy. Cooper gave up without a fight.

While the department heads remained silent, former mayor Stein told a reporter that there was confusion because the managers thought they had squared things away with Sarah, and it would be business as usual. In office less than two weeks, Sarah seemed exasperated when she met with reporters to explain her decision. "My goodness, I've been here eleven days," she said. "Give me a chance, please."

When a reporter tried to reach Emmons for reaction, he was informed she could not comment without permission from the new mayor. Sarah said it was a temporary order until the department heads were clear on her policies, but the *Frontiersman* editorialized that Palin had overstepped her bounds, calling Sarah's directive "a gag order." The paper and Palin already had a strained relationship over the contentious election. When Palin called and asked two city hall beat reporters to lunch at the Windbreak Café, bringing a bouquet of flowers as a gesture of conciliation, the move came as a surprise. "We thought things would be amiable," recalled Naegele, then the editor-in-chief. "But we felt asking all the department heads to resign was unjust and inappropriate," he said. "She felt she could do things her way, and we didn't agree."

Despite asking for the resignations, Sarah didn't take any immediate action. Nick Carney was disturbed by the treatment of the department heads and the hiring of deputy administrator John Cramer for $50,000 a year. "The day-to-day was beyond her," Carney told the *Anchorage Daily News* in 2006. "It was the barracuda in her that came out, that 'Those guys were on the side of John Stein, and I'm going to get rid of them.'"

Unperturbed, Sarah told a reporter that Carney was consumed with their rivalry, and it distorted his perception. "I couldn't do anything without Nick Carney griping about it. That was the nature of our relationship. I could have walked across Lake Lucille on the water, and he would have griped about me splashing."

Judy Patrick discounted the critics who complained that Sarah ran a partisan race. Wasilla's demographics had changed, and candidates, especially women, stood to gain by clarifying their values for voters. "I'm an artist and a woman, and people are going to have presumptions," Patrick explained. "I thought it was important to emphasize I was a Republican, specifically because of my gender and profession."

Sarah faced a loyal bureaucracy that had been led by a popular incumbent mayor, who had served since 1987. "Sarah didn't like the way things were going," Patrick said. "During the campaign, I remember her coming to my house and asking, 'Judy, I need to know where you stand. The council is talking about building a new city hall with taxpayer money. Do you agree with that?' "

Nick Carney and John Stein were indeed part of a core group of Republicans who recruited Sarah to run for council in 1992, Patrick said. They "liked to think they could control you, and if you didn't agree with them, they'd turn on you."

Central to Sarah's candidacy was her concern over taxes. Though the sales tax had generated substantial revenue, it seemed imprudent to both Sarah and Patrick simply to spend the money because it was available. Once it was clear Sarah wasn't going to be supportive, "she became the enemy," Patrick said. "Nick Carney came into her office after she was elected mayor and said he was going to oppose everything she did; he was very cantankerous and went against everything we were in favor of."

"My problem with her was her method of attack," said Carney. "She fired all these people before she could hire people to come in and take the job. If you cross her, she's vindictive. I got her elected [in 1992], but once I had crossed her, I got nowhere with her."

Carney was concerned that if Sarah let all the managerial talent in the city go, she would have to go outside the city to replace it. "We didn't have a big workforce," he said. "I could have been comfortable if she had gone out and recruited the new management first."

Sarah and her supporters rejected that argument, and regardless, she had the backing of the city code. "I thought it was fair, and she ran up against this entitlement mentality," Patrick said. "But the truth was the department heads served at the pleasure of the mayor, and the form of government we had called for had a strong executive, which the newspaper never bothered to explain. It seemed like everyone was in denial, but this wasn't any different than a president coming into office and changing out his cabinet. Our mayor has a lot of power."

A week before Christmas, when the days in Alaska were shrinking rapidly and the snow was accumulating on the peaks of the Chugach and Talkeetna mountain ranges, the *Frontiersman* broke an intriguing story headlined "Palin: Library Censorship Inquiries 'Rhetorical.' "

The article quoted library director Mary Ellen Emmons, saying that on two separate occasions after Sarah was elected on October 1, the new mayor broached the subject of censorship and wanted to know how Emmons would react. Emmons recalled that in the first conversation, Sarah just touched on the subject. Then on October 28, Sarah explicitly asked her if she could live with the censorship of library books. This was during the same month that Sarah was requesting resignations from all of the city's department heads as a way of expressing loyalty, the *Frontiersman* reported. "This is different than a normal book-selection procedure or a book-challenge policy," said Emmons, who also served as president of the Alaska Library Association. "She asked me if I would object to censorship, and I replied, 'Yup.' And I told her it would not be just me. This was a constitutional question, and the American Civil Liberties Union would get involved too."

Sarah told the paper that no individual books had been mentioned when she posed questions to Emmons. She raised the issue, she said, in a "rhetorical" context. When the book-censorship matter came up in the 2008 presidential campaign, she reiterated that she opposed censorship. In 1996, she said she was just doing her job—trying to get acquainted with staff by discussing a wide range of topics. "Many issues were discussed, both rhetorical and realistic in nature," she said in a written statement. "All questions posed to Wasilla's library director were asked in the context of professionalism regarding the library policy that is in place in our city. Obviously the issue of censorship is a library question . . . you ask the library director that type of question," Sarah said. In a third meeting with Emmons in December, the mayor brought up the censorship matter again. "I just hope it was a trial balloon," said Emmons, who at the time was fine-tuning Wasilla's book-challenge policy. "Because the free exchange of information is my job, and I will fight anyone who tries to interfere with that."

After the holidays, Sarah decided it was time to part ways with two directors—police chief Stambaugh, a staunch supporter of John Stein, and library director Emmons. For the time being, Felton and Dvorak stayed on, but they resigned later in the summer. In her termination letter, Sarah wrote that she didn't feel either Emmons or Stambaugh supported her efforts to govern, according to the *Anchorage Daily News*. Both directors said they received letters of termination at their office on a Thursday afternoon. The letter stated the positions were eliminated as of February 13, but it was no longer necessary to show up for work.

Emmons was a seven-year veteran of the library, and Stambaugh had twenty-six years in law enforcement. He had been the city's chief since the department was formed in 1993. Prior to that, he served the Anchorage police department for twenty-two years and had attained the rank of captain. Both administrators took the news as a surprise, feeling they had worked out their differences with Sarah, despite persistent rumors that

Sarah was dissatisfied with their performance. In fact, both administrators had met with the new mayor the day before receiving their termination letters, and neither had any warning of what was about to happen.

"After the initial roller coaster, we were ready to work for Mayor Palin," Emmons said in an interview at the time. "Unfortunately I think we were both fired for politics." Stambaugh said he was disappointed. Citing his experience in the field, he said, "I take pride in what I've gained. I would never do anything to undermine the city or the police department." Sarah emphasized politics wasn't influencing her decisions, but she declined to elaborate, because these were personnel matters. She actually backed off on whether they had been officially let go, telling a reporter that she had not yet spoken directly with the department heads and that there had been "no actual terminations."

Stambaugh begged to differ and was prepared to seek a legal remedy; his contract stated that he could only be fired with cause. He repeated the letter's contents to *Anchorage Daily News* reporter Stephanie Komarnitsky. "Although I appreciate your service as police chief, I've decided it's time for a change. I do not feel I have your full support in my efforts to govern the city of Wasilla. Therefore I intend to terminate your employment."

On that Thursday, friends and supporters paid Stambaugh a visit at his home. Stein joined the gathering. "It's just a huge loss for the community," he told a reporter.

The move led to another harsh editorial from the *Frontiersman*. "I wrote a scathing editorial," said Naegele. "I can't say these were the world's best employees, but we felt it was unjust and inappropriate."

But Sarah changed her mind. Emmons, with community support, fought for her job and persuaded Sarah that she would stand by her. Twenty-four hours after firing her, Sarah said Emmons would stay on. Still, in the wake of Stambaugh's ouster, a group of residents, who called themselves the Concerned Citizens of Wasilla, met to consider mounting a recall drive against Sarah. About sixty attended the first meeting, including councilman Nick Carney and former museum director John Cooper. The group created a list of questions to pose to the mayor: Why fire the police chief without a replacement? Is there an ethics code? Would she leave office to avoid a recall? The chairwoman of the recall group, Kathryn Rounds, said Sarah deserved a chance to be heard before they made any decisions. Sarah seemed unimpressed. She said the critics were the same group of naysayers who had been after her since she came into office. "I don't remember any past mayors . . . having to face a firing squad," she told a reporter.

Sarah had a point, and legally she was in the right. She explained that the city code specified that department heads served at the pleasure of the mayor. It was just that in small-town Wasilla, nobody had bothered to assert the opportunity. Chief Stambaugh, who went on to hire an attorney and sue the city, did not get a second chance from Sarah, who argued that the chief's contract was invalid since it was negotiated under the previous mayor.

According to Patrick, Sarah wanted to maintain command over the police chief, and Stambaugh had been lobbying the previous council and Stein to make his position exempt from mayoral control. If that happened, the mayor would lose the authority to hire and fire the chief.

Stambaugh eventually lost his suit; a judge ruled Sarah was within her rights to fire him.

As for the recall, the effort fizzled. The *Anchorage Daily News* reported that residents debated for two hours over how to proceed, but the consensus was that no one wanted a fight, as they figured it would be more productive to work with the new mayor. The meeting itself was message enough, said seventeen-year Wasilla resident Laura Miller. "At least it will get her to pay a little more attention," she told a reporter. "I don't want to start a fight if it was just miscommunication."

Sarah forged on and had a new police chief in place by March, Duwayne "Charlie" Fannon, the former chief of police in Haines, Alaska, the city near Sarah's old home of Skagway. He accepted the job to direct Wasilla's eleven-man force and manage a budget of $1.3 million. Wasilla's department was double that of Haines, but Fannon had ten years of experience. In his lawsuit, Stambaugh claimed Sarah was pressured by Wasilla bar owners and the NRA to fire him because he wanted to cut back on bar hours to reduce alcohol-related car accidents, and he supported efforts to limit carrying concealed weapons.

Fannon had his own opinion. "I have a philosophy that every time there's a new ordinance, we lose a little more of our freedom," he told the council on the night they affirmed his hiring. "I don't think the answer to crime is restricting people's freedom more and more." Rather than restrict operation hours, Fannon said he preferred a personal approach—communicating directly with bar owners and visiting schools to discuss the perils of drinking.

On April 2, Sarah decided after a stressful winter of running the city, it was time to do a little shopping. She told Todd she was driving into Anchorage to pick up some things at Costco, but she had other ideas. Before noshing on the Costco snacks the store serves up between aisles, Sarah wanted a taste of celebrity and made a beeline to the J.C. Penney's cosmetics department. There, with five hundred other Alaskans, she got an up-close look at Ivana Trump, who was in town plugging her new line of perfume. Perched at a table next to a photo of herself, signing autographs and posing for pictures, Trump, her blond hair "coiffed in a bouffant French twist," and outfitted in a light-colored pantsuit and pink fingernail polish, looked every bit the purveyor of fame and style. "We want to see Ivana," Sarah told the *Anchorage Daily News*, "because we are so desperate in Alaska for any semblance of glamour and culture."

The day was a nice, light departure from the tumult of Wasilla politics, which never seemed to let up. Just when the situation was starting to simmer down, the three-woman staff at the city's historical museum resigned en masse. The "three gray-haired matrons," as the *Anchorage Daily News* described them, had worked at the museum since the early 1980s and were fixtures in the valley. The museum, now called the Dorothy Page Museum, was housed in a building constructed in 1932 and displayed a collection of mining equipment and homestead artifacts that chronicled Wasilla's early years. There was an ore stamp mill built in 1900 that was used by Chinese laborers to pulverize ore and an early version of a foosball game that miners crafted of plastic. The women themselves were veritable encyclopedias of knowledge. Opal Toomey, then seventy-seven, homesteaded in the community and used to travel to Anchorage by train, the only way into the city. A Mat-Su Borough anthropologist, Fran Seager-Ross, said she frequently relied on the women for details about the region's past.

Sarah and the new council had their eye on the museum and its hefty $200,000 budget. Sarah wanted $32,000 cut and left it up to the staff to decide how. But who would go? Opal Toomey, Esther West, or Ann Meyers? Rather than lay off a worker, Patrick said the group could have cut back their hours collectively to meet the goal. But instead they chose to make a political statement. "Sarah liked them, we all did, and we didn't want to get rid of them," said Patrick. "We asked them to decide how to do it. We didn't care how they did it—one could leave, or they could go to working part-time. But we were portrayed as being mean, and once again it became a personal attack."

In August, the ladies retired en masse, which made headlines and cast the Palin administration in a dubious light again. "We hate to leave," Meyers told a reporter. "We've been together a long time, but this is enough."

The trio was frustrated, they said, because the city was far from broke, and they reasoned that there was no purpose for cutting the budget. Mayor Palin and some members of the council argued that they were brought into office to make infrastructure improvements, and that was the priority. Yes, there was $4 million in reserves, but that didn't even cover an entire year's budget, Sarah noted. "I think everyone was in agreement there were ways to make the museum more efficient, to spend taxpayers' dollars wiser over there," Sarah said to the *Anchorage Daily News*, noting the cost of the museum based on foot traffic was around twenty-five dollars per visitor. "If you talk to someone in Wasilla about where they want their tax dollars to go, nine out of ten say, 'Fix my road. I still don't have water in my area. And protect our lakes with a sewer system.' "

Sarah brought in a new curator and a part-time employee, and cut back the museum's hours. She also would go on to create an annual community Christmas celebration that included a tree-lighting ceremony, music, and artistic contributions from children attending Wasilla schools. The museum also produced a gold rush exhibit at the Alaska State Fair, and the new curator cleaned up displays and artifacts. "Sarah truly cared about those ladies," Geri McCann, the curator who replaced John Cooper, wrote in a blog. "She wanted the history of Wasilla preserved, but with fiscal responsibility."

Cooper weighed in from Hawaii, saying he felt his support of Stein and his proposed expansion of the museum led to his dismissal. He packed up his family and moved out of state. "Our lives were really coming together in Wasilla, and Sarah Palin tore it apart," Cooper said recently from his home in Hilo, Hawaii. He told a reporter in September 2008 that he was a "casualty of Sarah Palin's rise to political prominence." Then, speaking of his former colleagues, he said despite their skills as department heads, Sarah was more committed to her political friends. "We all knew what we were doing, and we were good at it. But we represented a change that the reactionary forces didn't want. They won, and we lost."

Patrick said John Cooper was a good example of Sarah's attempt to keep costs under control. "He was making $70,000 a year, and they would get something like one or two visitors a month in the winter. He wanted a big fancy museum, but we're talking about Wasilla, Alaska, here. We wanted to turn it into a seasonal museum. She wanted to streamline government and consolidate departments. We were looking for ways to be more efficient."

Later in her first term, Sarah captured some sorely

needed victories, though not all without controversy. Voters approved a $5.5-million bond to finance road-paving projects in the city. She also fulfilled her campaign promise to lower taxes as the council voted to drop the town's personal-property tax and the business-inventory and aircraft taxes. Critics would claim later there might have been a conflict of interest on some of these votes. Though her father-in-law owned a plane, she cast the tie-breaking vote on the aircraft tax, according to an Associated Press report. She also supported Wasilla's repeal of taxes on other property, such as snowmobiles. Todd owned a snowmobile shop at the time. However, Alaska being where it is, many residents owned small bush planes and snowmobiles, so the vote certainly benefited more than a few. Sarah did recuse herself from a discussion when the council convened over a grant for the Iron Dog race. The lost revenues from Sarah's tax cuts were made up by the town's share of a borough vehicle tax. She also would cut the property tax rate from 2.0 to 1.2 mills. "We're not sticking it to the property owner anymore," she said. Her new hire, deputy administrator Cramer, was helping smooth things over with the city departments that were undergoing transitions. Sarah also reduced her salary from $68,000 to $64,200.

"She said, 'I'm embarrassed to be highest-paid

mayor in the country [per capita],' " recalled Patrick. "I remember when she tried to cut her salary and Carney opposed it. It turned out the mayor can't adjust her own salary, and we had to wait for the next budget cycle, so it took a little bit longer. Then, since it was tied into a salary matrix for all employees, it went up automatically a couple of years later. So it went down for her second year in office, and then it went back to $68,000 in her third year, and then she froze it."

In September 1996, Carney wrote a scathing opinion piece for the *Frontiersman* that was critical of Sarah on several fronts. She didn't provide support for the overtaxed library system and had lost several key employees, including public works director Felton. "Mayor Palin has failed to weld the council into a cooperating group and has been unable and unwilling to communicate fully with the council," he wrote. He also questioned her replacements, including a public works director who lacked an engineering degree that would enable her to sign off on projects. She was the wife of a key aide to a previous Republican governor and would last only a year on the job.

"Sarah always did and still does surround herself with people she gets along well with," former councilwoman Darlene Langill told the *Washington Post*.

One of the last city officials to go was the city attorney Dick Deuser, a University of Minnesota law school grad well versed in legal precedent and constitutional law. In a 2008 interview with the *New Republic* for an article titled "Barracuda: The Resentments of Sarah Palin," Deuser told a reporter how the council had asked him about the legality of banning group homes in Wasilla and how he explained that such a ban would be unconstitutional. Sarah, who supported the ban, appeared "impatient" with the explanation and its potential repercussions. "I would describe it this way: Sarah was not an in-depth person. Never has, never will be," Deuser said. "Her instincts are political as opposed to evaluative."

He was eventually voted out of a job by the council, an exit that Carney claimed was engineered by Sarah because his decisions "conflicted with what she wanted to hear." He was replaced by Ken Jacobus, a counsel for the Republican Party. Jacobus, however, met the approval of the full council before he came on board.

Anne Kilkenny, the city hall gadfly who attended most of the council meetings in Sarah's first year as mayor, and who also authored the anti-Palin e-mail that circulated after Sarah joined the McCain ticket, believed Sarah had a bias against intellectuals like Stein, Deuser, and her biggest nemesis of all, Carney. In fact, she seemed intimidated by them, according to former campaign manager Chase. It was an opinion advanced by

Norm Scheiber of the *New Republic*. "A trip through Palin's past reveals that almost every step of her career can be understood as a reaction to elitist condescension—much of it in her own mind," he wrote.

Patrick disagreed. "I think she appreciates smart people—but in her heart she is for the common man. I remember we would pack in the crowds at city council for an important issue and argue contentiously. Sarah reminded us, 'I want to remind you that we keep hearing from a vocal minority, and we represent a silent majority who had elected us.'"

Sarah may have been on to something there. She survived the difficult first year and fought off the groundswell of a recall effort. She made some unpopular decisions and in later campaigns admitted those first months on the job were "rocky" but that she was better for it.

One of her replacement managers, Don Shiesel, who was hired in 1998 to direct public works, said she was excellent at delegating tasks and providing the autonomy so department heads could do their jobs. "She's a quick study," he told a reporter in 2008 during the presidential campaign. "She's a heck of a public speaker and works her magic on people. Give her four years with some training, and she'll be up to snuff. She's not dumb; she'll be able to catch on to stuff real quick."

When she ran for governor in 2006, one of the negative *Frontiersman* editorials was doctored into resembling a front-page news story and resurfaced during the eleventh hour of the Republican primary, prompting *Frontiersman* publisher Kari Sleight and former editor Naegele to condemn the mailer sent out by one of Palin's opponents. "As a community newspaper, we held her feet to the fire," Naegele said of those turbulent months in 1996–97. "I remember the need for such harsh words diminished as the months wore on. At times during my tenure as editor, there was praise for Palin."

Sarah had these reflections on her first year as mayor. "If nothing else, the old *Frontiersman* editorial points out the importance of administrative experience at the chief executive level," she said. "I grew tremendously in my early months as mayor, managing the fastest growing city in the state, and I turned my critics around."

SEVEN
BUILDING A CITY

T he winter of 1998 was snowless, again. Wasilla had already lost the start of the annual Iron Dog snowmobile race in February. Now the Iditarod sled-dog race was moving out of town, making it the third time in five years that the race was moved thirty miles up George Parks Highway to the community of Willow. Snow wasn't the only problem— gale-force winds were also spoiling the starts. For a mayor who supported small businesses, this was a tough blow. In later years, Sarah disputed the notion that man was completely responsible for the global-warming crisis, but she certainly couldn't deny the weather changes in her hometown. "We used to have good, normal Alaskan winters here with tons of snow," Sarah told a reporter. "But the last few years, nothing." When she looked out over the field where the race traditionally started, just off Main Street, all she could see was dry brownish grass and trails of frozen dirt. "It's empty, lonely, and bare," Sarah lamented.

Typically, the start of the Iditarod race, scheduled on the first Saturday in March, draws thousands of spectators and family members of the teams, which number from fifty to one hundred. It has been a bonanza for local merchants since the race commenced in 1973. The race lasts seventeen grueling, frigid days and covers 1,150 miles over Alaska's most rugged terrain. The mushers and their dog teams race in pursuit of a share of an $875,000 purse. Today, the race is more visible than ever. Last year's winner, back-to-back titlist Lance Mackey, a throat-cancer survivor from Fairbanks, appeared on the *Conan O'Brien Show* in September to promote Discovery Channel's airing of a TV series on the race, calling it *The Toughest Race on Earth—Iditarod*. Sarah's rise to prominence will no doubt add to the popularity of the event, but in the late 1990s, she was just another frustrated politician praying for snow.

"It's a bummer," said Wasilla Chamber of Commerce executive director Ed Brittingham, reacting to fans and mushers driving past Wasilla en route to Willow. One consolation, with or without snow, was that Wasilla kept the special events dedicated to the race. The Iditarod Days Festival, which featured arts and crafts shows, an ice-golf tournament on Wasilla Lake, and a microbrew festival, remained in town.

In 1998, Sarah made strides as a manager, overcoming the growing pains from her first year on the job. In an interview with the *Frontiersman,* she took credit for engineering the city's growth. "What's amazing is to be able to see it and know we're helping to grow a city and not just saying we're the fastest growing city in the state but living it every day and knowing that 'Oh my gosh, this is new, and this is new, and every day it seems like some new development wants to come in, or some new residential area is going to be developed.' It's pretty exciting."

The city was developing its airport and extending access roads. Water and sewer-line expansion was drawing new businesses, including Wal-Mart and retailer Fred Meyer, which, of course, added to the city coffers. The state Department of Environmental Conservation was concerned that the stores' storm-runoff systems might pollute Wasilla Lake, where Sarah lived in a three-bedroom shoreline home with her family, but the systems passed muster, and the mayor was satisfied. "I live on that lake. I would not support a development that wasn't environmentally friendly," she said.

Sarah's liberal detractors found an unusual ally—local skateboarders, who felt Sarah's wrath in October

1998 when she supported a ban prohibiting them from riding their skateboards on public and private property in the city. The ordinance, which included provisions for confiscation and a hundred-dollar fine, coincided with the opening of Wasilla's new $233,000 state park.

In 1999, John Stein decided to make another run for mayor. The *Anchorage Daily News* called it a race "that promises to be a test not only of the candidates' personal appeal, but also of a broader struggle for political dominance in the Valley." Stein raised $5,000 for his campaign, while Sarah's war chest reached $15,000.

There were two prevailing visions. Stein represented the opinion that rigorous planning and land-use regulation would make a better life for residents. Hot-button social issues like gun control and abortion were irrelevant in local elections. The second view was championed by Sarah: minimal government with a conservative stance on social issues. Stein even switched parties to emphasize the contrast, while Palin remained Republican. She would rest on a pro-development campaign, pointing to the retail growth of Wasilla and maintaining that the city should "stay the course." She also had implemented a property-tax rate decrease from 2.0 mills to 1.2 mills, which translated into an eighty-dollar decrease annually for owners of $100,000 homes, and she persuaded voters to accept the $5.5-million sewer bond.

Pundits pointed out that there was a role reversal in this watershed election. In Wasilla, the mayor is in charge of the police department, a library, a planning office, a parks and recreation department, and a modest history museum. Now it was Stein being critical of proliferated spending by Sarah, whom he accused of spending too much on administration. The budget for general government salaries—the mayor's office, city council, and planning and finance employees—went from $1.3 million in 1998 to $1.9 million in 1999. The so-called fiscally conservative mayor, he said, was guilty of expanding government. Sarah countered that much of the budget increase could be attributed to $400,000 in interest due on the voter-approved infrastructure bonds and new jobs that were added to the payroll after she arrived in office. Stein wasn't a big fan of the sewer bond because the debt service was so high, leaving the city in a difficult spot if the economy soured. The city also could have slowed down the construction and postponed a paving project that would have saved $2 million. But Sarah said the communities along that road were in desperate straits, and there was no time to wait.

He also criticized Sarah for driving away the staff he had originally brought in, noting that only five of the six department heads remained from Sarah's first day on the job. Stambaugh was fired and replaced; librarian

Mary Emmons had recently resigned, amicably; and three other department heads had moved on months ago. Sarah felt she needed to shake up the staff to put her plans into effect and that since then, there had been little turnover. Stein and Carney also accused her of bringing in "good old boys" from the state Republican Party, including Cramer, who worked for state senator Lyda Green, and Jacobus, the new city attorney who previously served as counsel to the state Republican Party, though Sarah argued that the council approved the hiring of Jacobus, not her. Gone, too, was Wasilla's deputy mayor, Dave Chappel, who served two years under Palin but clashed with the mayor over some city appointments and a policy ban prohibiting the reimbursement of employees for educational and professional travel outside Alaska.

However, Chappel said he saw growth in Sarah as a leader. "When I first met Sarah, I would say Sarah was a Republican, with the big R, and that's it," said Chappel. "As she developed politically, she began to see beyond the R and look at the whole picture. She matured."

In 1999, Wasilla moved the start of the Iditarod race out to the airport, and Wasilla citizens finally got the race back to town. Sarah officiated at an August wedding in the Wal-Mart store. Standing in the aisle next to the menswear section, the couple, Wal-Mart employees Jake McGowan and Rosalyn Ryan, exchanged vows and said, "I do." "It was so sweet," said a teary-eyed Sarah, who shopped in the store. "It was so Wasilla."

Wasilla liked her. On election day in October, Sarah defeated Stein, running away, 826–255. "The community has made their choice, and that's fine," said Stein, who later moved to Sitka, Alaska, to work for the city administration. "I think folks are just too happy with the present situation." Sarah said she was the beneficiary of a strong economy. "Wasilla has been on a roll," she said.

Sarah's supporters gave her high marks for responding to their concerns and making herself available to voters. "She truly listened to what we wanted in our town, and she's got it done," Richard Clayton, a local bike shop owner, told a reporter.

Finishing number one was an old habit for the Palin clan. A month after Sarah's victory, Todd plunked down his share of a $1,730 Iron Dog racing fee and began training in earnest for another shot at winning the two-thousand-mile race. Though Todd was out of the business of selling snowmobiles after giving up his Valley Polaris shop in Big Lake in 1997, which he operated for three years, he still enjoyed competing and snowmobiling professionally. In February 2000, he won his second Iron

Dog in forty-one hours and ten minutes, besting a field of thirty-four racing teams. He and teammate Dusty Van Meter charged out of the blocks in Wasilla, completed the first 362-mile leg of the trail in nine hours and twenty-seven minutes and never looked back. Though conditions change from race to race, it's interesting to note that when Todd won in 1995, his time was seventeen hours slower, at fifty-eight hours and twenty-four minutes.

In March 2000, Sarah Palin breathed a big sigh of relief when a federal judge dismissed Irl Stambaugh's $500,000 wrongful-termination claim against the city. U.S. District Court Judge James K. Singleton ruled that the 1997 firing was legal and the mayor had the right to terminate him for almost any cause, even political reasons. Sarah, he said, was justified in her decision if she felt she couldn't trust Stambaugh to abide by her policies. As for Stambaugh's claim that he was protected by his contract, the judge ruled that the provisions were never in force because the city council hadn't voted on them. "It's really good news for Wasilla," Sarah told the *Anchorage Daily News*. In explaining her actions four years earlier, she said she just felt she didn't have Stambaugh's support. "It was no secret to anybody in Wasilla that he wasn't happy to see a change in the mayor's seat," she said.

The *Seattle Times* reviewed a federal archive in

Seattle and found another black mark against Stambaugh: his failure to take seriously Sarah's request for weekly progress reports that required "at least two positive examples of work that was started, how we helped the public, how we saved the city money, how we helped the state, and how we helped Uncle Sam." Stambaugh and his ally on the council, Nick Carney, felt the reports were a nuisance.

When the ruling came down, Stambaugh had already left town for Juneau to work as the executive director of the Alaska Police Standards Council. Carney also had pulled up stakes. After finishing his term on the council in 1998, he sold his garbage-collecting business and moved to Utah. He still remains in touch with his Wasilla friends, including Todd Palin's parents, Jim and Faye, who golf with Carney and his wife when they visit.

When Sarah's second term began, the city had pressing needs. The library needed more space, and city hall was getting by in cramped quarters. Meetings were held in the basement of the main building, a converted school. Sarah had expanded her budget to attract business—her formula was increase police and public works, but limit library services and city planning. She also found $38,000 to recruit a Washington, D.C., lobbyist, a former aide to U.S. Sen. Ted Stevens, to attract federal money to the city through earmarks. Stevens at the time was chairman of the Senate Appropriations Committee. "Sarah was hungry for earmarks just like everybody else," said Larry Persily, who later worked under Governor Palin for the Alaska state office in Washington, D.C. "Everyone was feeding at the trough."

That strategy brought $27 million to the city for a $1.9 million bus station, $900,000 in utility repairs, $15 million for a railroad project, and $1 million for a communications center, which was actually $1.6 million until the government shaved $600,000 from the project. The city also led an expansion of Parks Highway from two to four lanes along a congested 2.5-mile stretch that was being used daily by thirty thousand motorists, most of them commuting to Anchorage. While an argument can certainly be made that Sarah's quest for federal dollars was done on behalf of the city and its residents, it would create awkward moments during John McCain's presidential campaign.

In 2001, John McCain, who opposes earmarks, actually criticized two Wasilla projects, asking why a city of 5,500 needed $2.5 million for road upgrades. But some local Republicans familiar with the projects sided with Sarah. "Her obligation was to provide basic services," said one Mat-Su Valley official. "Federal and state projects were accepted, and they were fair game."

Not all the legislation being enacted reflected positively on Sarah. In May 2000, Governor Tony Knowles, Sarah's future opponent in the 2006 governor's race, signed a piece of legislation designed to prevent cities from billing rape victims for the costs of investigating the crime. When a woman is raped, hospitals conduct physical exams and test swabs to collect evidence to determine if a crime has taken place. The rape-kit exam costs $300 to $1,200, and some municipalities, including Wasilla, were billing the victims. This legislation made that practice illegal.

The day it went into effect, chief of police Charlie Fannon spoke to the *Frontiersman* and said he disagreed with the new law because it would require cities to come up with funds to pay for the evidence-gathering exams. "In the past we've charged the cost of exams to the victims' insurance company when possible," he said at the time. "I just don't want to see any more burden put on the taxpayer." He said it would cost the city $5,000 to $14,000 annually to cover the cost of gathering evidence for the sexual assault crimes. Ideally, he said, the burden should fall on the criminal as part of restitution to the victim, and he intended to bring that up in court when the opportunity arose.

The *New York Times* and other national media wrote about Wasilla's old policy during the presidential campaign in September. Then-Governor Knowles explained the reasoning behind House Bill 270, which had been sponsored by former Anchorage representative Eric Croft. "We would never bill the victim of a burglary for fingerprinting and photographing a crime scene, or for the cost of gathering other evidence, nor should we bill rape victims just because the crime scene happens to be their bodies," Knowles said.

The *Times* also reported there was no record of Sarah's opinion about the issue or whether she knew it was in the budget, but Fannon's comments came after the bill had passed. Croft, a former Democratic lawmaker, told the *Times* that the policy was reflected in budget documents that then-Mayor Palin had signed. During a September interview with the *Frontiersman*, Sarah didn't answer whether Wasilla had billed rape victims for tests under her watch, but she said she rejects the practice in principle. "The entire notion of making a victim of a crime pay for anything is crazy," she said in an October 10 interview. "I do not believe, nor have I ever believed, that rape victims should have to pay for an evidence-gathering test. As governor, I worked in a variety of ways to tackle the problem of sexual assault and rape, including making domestic violence a priority of my administration."

That year, the Palins also broke ground on a new

home on the shores of Lake Lucille. Todd, according to old friend Tom Whitstine Jr., had a couple of great years in commercial fishing to help finance the move, and Todd kept costs under control by doing much of the work himself, with the help of contractor pals. Spenard Builders Supply provided Todd with the materials and some labor to build the home, according to the *Village Voice*. They also were a sponsor of Todd's snowmobile team. Later in 2004, they would hire Sarah to do a state-wide TV commercial. They also were listed as one of the subcontractors to one of the biggest building projects in Wasilla history, the multimillion-dollar sports complex and hockey rink that Sarah promoted in her second term as mayor. According to the *Village Voice*, it's unclear who the other contractors were who helped the Palins build their new home, since Sarah, "as mayor, blocked an effort to require the filing of building permits in the wide-open city."

But by all accounts, Todd helped pour the concrete foundation, installed the electrical wiring, and put in the heating and ventilation system for the two-story wood-frame residence. With its majestic picture windows overlooking the lake and the Chugach Mountains beyond, the four-bedroom, four-bath house is considered prime real estate in Wasilla. The 3,500-square-foot home, part of the Snider subdivision along Lake Lucille, is assessed at $552,000 and sits at the end of a two-acre lot, protected from view by a ten-foot-high wooden privacy fence that spans one side of the property. Nearby is a halfway house for people recovering from drug and alcohol abuse.

In Wasilla, lakefront homes can be had, but it's hard to find one near a paved road. The Palins live near a main highway and shopping center, and the lake is float-plane accessible, an important asset since Todd owns a two-seat 1958 Piper float plane that has been in his family for two decades. The red-and-white plane is parked on the property's waterfront and is used as a backdrop by many photographers who visit their home. "Todd did a little bit of everything on that house," said Whitstine, who works for British Petroleum on the North Slope with Todd and checked out their heating and ventilation system. Whitstine estimated that they probably spent a couple of hundred thousand on materials and another $40,000 for the land, so it wasn't a massive financial undertaking.

Their new home is different from the Wasilla Lake house in other ways. Besides having an additional bedroom, it's more child-friendly and more private. The Wasilla Lake house was built too close to neighbors and right by the water's edge, requiring a steep stairway to reach a boat ramp. Small children were a serious safety concern to the Palins after Sarah became pregnant with her fourth child in July 2000. Little Piper Indie Grace Palin was born the following March 19 at 11:37 a.m., arriving right on her due date at seven pounds, thirteen ounces at Mat-Su Borough's old Valley Hospital. It was Sarah's second birth while holding public office and her first as mayor. The birth earned a write-up in the *Frontiersman,* which noted that Sarah did not take leave on the day after Piper's birth, showing up to work briefly to forward e-mail and phone messages to her home. "Not only is she perfect and amazing but also so convenient," Sarah said. "She's right on time, and she's everything we ever dreamed of." Dad was equally ecstatic, describing the new addition as "just perfect." They chose Piper for her name because, like the other children's names, it was related to Alaska and sports. "I've always loved the name Piper," Sarah said. Indie, she explained, wasn't merely a brand of snow machine but also a shortened form of the word *independence*. Grace stood for "grace of God." Palin took some accrued sick leave and asked deputy mayor Judy Patrick and city administrator John Cramer to handle any city-related affairs. The family wanted to "savor" those first several days with Piper, because after having three children, Todd and she knew how quickly time passed with an infant, she told the newspaper. Sarah's aunt Katie Johnson made a trip to

Sally holding her baby daughter Sarah in Skagway, Alaska, in 1964. The Heaths lived in Skagway for five years before settling in Wasilla. *(Photo courtesy of Heather Bruce)*

Sarah posing for her second-grade school picture in Wasilla in 1971. *(Photo courtesy of Heather Bruce)*

Chuck Jr., Heather, Molly, and Sarah outside their Wasilla home in October 1971. They are standing by their father's Rambler with a dead caribou their father had shot tied down on the trunk of the car. "We were close enough to bring the caribou right home," said Sarah's sister, Heather Bruce. *(Photo courtesy of Heather Bruce)*

Sarah reading a newspaper during her senior year at Wasilla High. She would later intern at her local newspaper and work in broadcasting for Anchorage TV stations. *(Wasilla High School via Mat-Su Valley Frontiersman)*

Wasilla point guard Sarah Heath (Palin), #22, during the 1982 state basketball championships. *(Anchorage Daily News archive)*

When she was competing in beauty pageants in 1983–84, Sarah Palin played the flute for the talent portion of the event. *(Mat-Su Valley Frontiersman)*

Sarah won the Miss Wasilla pageant and followed that up with a second-runner-up finish in the Miss Alaska contest in 1984. *(Mat-Su Valley Frontiersman)*

Palin appears at a press conference for the NRA. Palin, an avid hunter, has been a lifelong supporter of the NRA. *(Mat-Su Valley Frontiersman)*

Gov. Sarah Palin fields orders while serving sloppy joe mix at the annual Governor's Picnic, held Saturday, July 19, 2008, on the Delaney Park Strip. *(Erik Hill/ Anchorage Daily News)*

Sarah Palin and her husband, Todd,
at home in Wasilla. *(Marc Lester/
Anchorage Daily News)*

In December 2006, the Heath family gathered in the governor's mansion in
Juneau to celebrate the holidays. Left to right: Heather, Sarah, Sally, Chuck
Sr., Chuck Jr., and Molly. *(Photo courtesy of Heather Bruce)*

Alaska governor Sarah Palin visits soldiers of 3rd Battalion 297th Infantry Regiment Alaska National Guard at the Life Support Area, Kuwait Dining Facility, on July 24, 2008, to learn more about their mission. *(Photo by Pvt. Christopher T. Grammer)*

Lt. Col. David Cogdell helps Alaska governor Sarah Palin test out the Engagement Skills Trainer at Camp Buehring, Kuwait. *(Photo by Pvt. Christopher T. Grammer)*

Governor Sarah Palin gives her husband—the "First Dude" Todd Palin, four-time Tesoro Iron Dog winner—a hug at the start on Big Lake on Sunday, February 10, 2008. The snowmobile race covers 2,000 miles of Alaska wilderness, going to Nome, before finishing in Fairbanks. *(Bill Roth/Anchorage Daily News)*

Sally and Chuck Heath at home in Wasilla the day they learned Sarah had been nominated to run for vice president. *(Mat-Su Valley Frontiersman)*

Todd, Trig, and Sarah just days after Trig's April 2008 birth. Palin kept her pregnancy a secret from her children and the public until just weeks before Trig's birth. *(Mat-Su Valley Frontiersman)*

Republican vice-presidential candidate Alaska governor Sarah Palin, right, holds her son Trig, as she is joined by her family on stage after her speech at the Republican National Convention in St. Paul, Minnesota, on September 3, 2008. From the left are son Track; daughter Bristol and her fiancé, Levi Johnston; daughters Willow and Piper; and husband, Todd. *(AP Photo/Ron Edmonds, file)*

Republican vice-presidential candidate Alaska governor Sarah Palin addresses supporters during a campaign rally in Green Bay, Wisconsin, September 18, 2008. *(AP Photo/Stephan Savoia)*

Wasilla that year to visit Sally and check in on Sarah and the new baby. "I remember seeing Piper after she was born—there was not a care in the world with that child, and she was so cute," Johnson said.

"That birth was normal, just fine," said Patrick, who remembered that Sarah brought Piper to work a few days later. "She kept Piper in a baby rocker under her desk. She would nurse her and then put her to sleep," said Patrick, adding that Sarah said she breast-fed all her kids. Later in the month, Patrick and a dozen friends and family gave Sarah an airplane-themed baby shower at the Grouse Ridge shooting range, which has a nice clubhouse for events. "Everyone brought airplane-themed gifts, authentic instruments, pilot logs, Piper aircraft signs. We had a great time," Patrick said.

EIGHT
ASPIRATIONS

*F*ive months after Piper's birth, tragedy struck in Wasilla when it lost one of its favorite sons, Sarah's old boyfriend, Curtis Menard Jr. A married father of four, he died in a solo plane crash near Beluga Lake, close to Tyonek, Alaska, about 70 miles west of Anchorage. The thirty-six-year-old orthodontist was a loss to the Heath family as well. Curtis Sr. and wife, Linda, had known the Heaths since the early 1970s. Curtis Sr. was the town dentist and treated all the Heaths. He also was a prominent Republican, serving in both the Alaska House and Senate between 1986 and 1994 and mentoring Sarah as she ascended the Wasilla political ladder. Linda, a longtime member of the Mat-Su Borough School Board, also stayed close to Sarah after guiding her through the beauty-pageant circuit in 1984. Like Sarah, Curtis Jr. loved the outdoors and enjoyed flying, hunting, fishing, running, basketball, and cross-country skiing. In high school, Sarah and Curtis ran track and played basketball. During the trips, Sarah used to kid Menard about his choice of music. "We'd have our rock 'n' roll, and Curtis would be listening to Barry Manilow on his boom box," Sarah told friend Judy Patrick. His wife, Carole, concurred. "He wasn't a big rock person," she said. In Menard's 1982 Wasilla High yearbook, Sarah wrote, "Don't go off to college and get married . . ." But Curtis did, meeting a fellow dentist in 1990 while studying orthodontics at the University of Iowa. He and Carole Brodeur married in May 1992, and they had four children. "But Curtis and Sarah remained friends, and the families were very close," Carole said.

When Sarah formed a task force to look into the development of a regional sports complex, she tapped Curtis and his father to work on the project, a $14.6 million, 104,000-square-foot indoor recreation facility that would house both an indoor NHL-sized hockey rink, basketball courts, and a soccer field outfitted with a rubberized surface. Just before his death, Curtis went to visit Sarah in the mayor's office and confronted her about something personal. He felt her career might be getting in the way of raising her children. "Curtis was an old-fashioned kind of guy, and he was concerned that Sarah was juggling being a mom of young children while in office," Carole said. "It's not that the kids were in danger, but he was more conservative and appreciated a mom that stayed home. But they were friends enough that he felt he could go and talk to her about it."

On August 9, 2001, Curtis was piloting his Cessna 185 floatplane alone when it went down about one and a half miles from Lake Beluga. Three relatives were waiting there for Menard to pick them up for a return flight to Wasilla. Rescue crews discovered the flight was missing when an emergency beacon started transmitting a distress signal. Investigators couldn't reach the crash scene to recover the body until the next day. A memorial service was held the following week at Wasilla's Assembly of God church, the only building in town that could accommodate a standing-room crowd that numbered more than one thousand. "As difficult as it was to be there, it was a nice day because so many people spoke of Curtis and his wonderful character, including Sarah," Carole recalled. Sarah, she said, spoke of Curtis's involvement in the community and even divulged details of their conversation about Sarah's career and children. "I know he came back from the meeting feeling better, and their friendship remained," Carole said. "Sarah has a strong family network, and they support her aspirations."

Those aspirations changed forever one afternoon in

November 2001 when Sarah was contacted by Senator Frank Murkowski, who was vacating his junior seat in the U.S. Senate to run for Alaska governor. His name and reputation were so respected that several other Republican candidates thinking about the governor's job virtually ceded the nomination to Murkowski and decided to run for lieutenant governor. Now the senator wanted to know if Sarah would throw her name in that hat, too.

At the time, Judy Patrick was still serving on the council and also acting as Sarah's deputy mayor. "It was widely recognized that Sarah had a bigger career outside of being the mayor of Wasilla," Patrick said. Running for a House seat, reasoned Judy, was not a logical choice for Sarah because she came from an executive position. "In Alaska, you can only make big jumps because there are no incremental political platforms to go to," Patrick said. "She is wired to go for things, and she has known inside of herself that she was destined to do certain things, and that's what moves her."

Sarah was certainly a younger candidate, but she had plenty of backing from powerful friends in the Republican Party. She would have to prevail in a primary to get on the GOP ticket. Her competition had more years of combined experience in Juneau than Sarah's age, which was thirty-eight. She was up against Senate majority leader and fourteen-year legislator Sen. Loren

Leman of Anchorage; Gail Phillips, a moderate Republican from Homer with experience as both House speaker and majority leader; and Robin Taylor, a former judge from Wrangell who had eighteen years of legislative experience. Phillips said GOP state party chairman, Randy Ruedrich, was talking Sarah up privately as a "bright and shining star," she said. "There was a lot of preference for her within the leadership, but the three of us would discuss it among ourselves. We were saying, hey, how about experience?" Sarah conceded she couldn't match her opponents in that regard, but the state was in need of something she had to offer: "new energy and fresh ideas."

"I think the biggest difference between me and my Republican opponents in this race is that I'm not running for governor, I'm running for lieutenant governor," Sarah said.

Tuckerman Babcock, a Republican Party official, said Sarah believed working with Murkowski would be a terrific opportunity to be mentored. "She had a lot of confidence she was going to win that race," he told a reporter.

On lunch hours, evenings, and weekends, Patrick and Sarah pulled together a grassroots campaign. "She became the fresh face," Patrick said. They held a couple of local fund-raisers, and Patrick, a professional photographer, helped put together some mailers and advertisements. "Sarah's a chocolate fiend, so we had a fund-raiser at her house, and people showed up with her favorite chocolate dishes to win a prize, and they would drop their checks in a basket," she recalled. Patrick, who had commercial-photography clients in the oil industry, introduced Sarah around the Anchorage Petroleum Club, soliciting $500 donations. That night, Patrick recalled being approached by an executive from VECO Corp., the oil-field service company that had contributed to the cleanup of the *Exxon Valdez* oil spill and later was embroiled in several bribery scandals. This company was investigated by the FBI for its role in the remodeling of U.S. Sen. Ted Stevens's Girdwood, Alaska, home that eventually led to the senator's 2008 conviction for failing to report tens of thousands of dollars in gifts on financial-disclosure forms. Patrick recalled the VECO representative saying, "Your girlfriend is not going to get elected unless we decide to support her."

Unbeknownst to Patrick, Sarah, like many politicians at the time, did accept contributions from individuals tied to VECO Corp., a major player in the Alaska political scene before a corruption scandal unraveled the company. Sarah's campaign finance-disclosure forms showed $4,500 in VECO-related donations in late 2001. However, most of her campaign support would come from individual donations and from small businesses set in the Mat-Su Valley.

Early in 2002, Todd won his third Iron Dog race, beating out sixty-two snowmobilers with partner Dusty Van Meter. They split a purse of $25,000. At the starting line in Big Lake, Sarah gave her husband a hug and then, in her official capacity as mayor, waved the traditional green flag to begin the weeklong marathon. Back in Wasilla, Sarah returned to watching the progress of the proposed sports complex, which was expected to be a close vote. Some residents were hoping for a new library, said Anne Kilkenny, reasoning that a second ice rink wasn't going to add anything to the community and the library was in dire need of expansion. Initially, the city looked into building a second indoor ice surface to relieve the crowding at Mat-Su Valley's only indoor facility, the Brett Memorial Ice Arena, which was booked around the clock during hockey season. Four high schools shared the surface with many club teams. Once the committee realized they couldn't get support for that project, they attracted more voters by expanding the scope, Patrick said. When they added an indoor soccer field and basketball courts to the plan, more voters took interest, even though it drove the projected cost from $5 million to more than $14 million. A larger facility also had the added value of hosting trade fairs, conventions, and graduations.

There's little question that the valley needed a new ice rink, but the issue was how to pay for it. To finance the project, Sarah supported floating a $14.7-million general-obligation bond to be financed by a half-cent sales-tax increase, which needed a majority approval from voters.

Political and community leaders were concerned about other matters they hoped a new community and sports center could address: the growing crime problem in Mat-Su Borough and finding productive activities for youth. The methamphetamine problem was still in its early stages, but it was significant enough that state troopers reported uncovering nine meth labs in 2003. The problem would only get worse in the years to come.

In a regional Mat-Su crime report that surveyed crime in the borough (begun in 2003, the report was published in 2005), Wasilla's new chief of police, Don Savage, said, "We are seeing more extremes in violent crime with a total disregard for human rights or even the perpetrator's own self-protection. There is a population that is extremely dangerous. There are increasing numbers of 'homeless and aimless' juveniles in the Mat-Su area, starting at the age of twelve and thirteen, who are living in the woods or 'couch surfing' and not going to school. Sex abuse, child abuse, and neglect issues are keeping kids out of school. Statistically the Mat-Su area has the highest incidence of sex abuse per capita in the state. The vast majority of offenders are not in the cities, and some people choose to live across an invisible dividing line, which allows them to receive government services but have very little interference. Mandatory reporting by schools and medical staff often identifies the problem. Kids who are sexually abused are showing up as homeless and aimless juveniles or substance abusers."

George Boatwright, the Palmer chief of police, pointed to a program in Anchorage that was effective in limiting the recidivism rate with intervention and follow-up programs for youth criminals: "A wide variety of activities are needed; the Boys and Girls Club is one of the biggest single things that [Anchorage] has going for young people."

In that respect, the sports complex for the region was sorely needed. Two boosters were Dave Tuttle, an insurance agent, and former state senator Curtis Menard Sr. At a February chamber of commerce meeting, they arrived with buttons proclaiming "Something for Everyone" and "Build It Now." "We're asking you to be ambassadors for us," Menard told the crowd of forty. "I'm saying, let's look at the big picture and build it now. We feel the pluses outweigh the minuses dramatically."

Critics thought the committee was downplaying the

actual costs. They wondered how a facility of this size could be run with just a staff of eight. At what cost would Wasilla extend utilities to the arena? How much would they have to pay for the land? Also, could they really fill the arena in the summer season with convention customers? The other concern was that given the timetable and site selection, the city would have to start building the complex on land it didn't own. All voters really had to go on to make a decision was the $87,500 design concept and assurances from the committee that the project was feasible. Tuttle said at the meeting that they were asking residents to "take a leap of faith," since without voter approval of the sales tax, they couldn't even proceed with the architectural plans. Tuttle and Menard argued that the existence of the facility could make a difference for someone deciding where to live in Alaska, and it would draw users from the entire region. There was also the assurance that the sales tax would pay the interest on the bond until a sunset clause took effect in 2012. "Everyone knew it would have to be subsidized to some degree," said Patrick. "But Wasilla had no large gathering place, and it was sorely needed for sports and recreation."

In March 2002, the city voted, and the measure barely passed, 306–286. Palin noted that the close election showed that folks were fiscally conservative and placed the burden on government to make sure the complex was built efficiently and "operated in the best possible manner for the community."

The city council likely dropped the ball on the last directive. When the city broke ground on the sports complex later that summer (the hockey rink was named the Curtis C. Menard II Memorial Ice Arena), it was built on disputed land. The city eventually obtained a seventy-acre parcel from the original owner, Gary Lundgren, by claiming eminent domain in late 2002 under Mayor Dianne Keller's new administration. But in a subsequent legal battle, not only did the city have to pay Lundgren $1 million for the property, but it got stuck with more than $830,000 in legal fees and court costs, which required the city to dip into the general fund. Critics argued the city should have bought the land first and then proceeded with construction, but Sarah may have pushed through the ballot initiative for the half-cent sales-tax hike so she could take credit for the project before her term expired. In the end, the city wasted taxpayers' dollars by overpaying, critics said. But Wasilla's public works director, Archie Giddings, told the *Frontiersman* that the costs were worth it because the land "serves a valuable and vital public use" and that in the end, the city has ownership.

"We spend so much time inside because of the

weather, so this place is used constantly," said one Wasilla hockey mom. "It's an asset having another indoor rink, and with all the other activities we can do here—running, a playground, soccer field, basketball, graduations and fairs—it's wonderful."

That summer, Sarah focused on the lieutenant governor's race. She needed a full-time campaign manager, and the Murkowski campaign suggested that she meet with Willis Lyford, a political strategist from Anchorage. "We both knew he was brilliant," said Patrick. "He will tell you the first day they met, Sarah was wearing this skirt that stopped above the knee. And she got up and came around her desk, and Willis thought to himself, 'She's young and attractive; this is not a look you see on a Republican.' "

Since their budget was tight—Sarah's campaign would raise $58,000 to Leman's $230,000—they primarily stuck to direct mail and advertising to reach voters across the state. Lyford urged Sarah to go out and meet the people to take advantage of her personality and communications skills. Sarah attended community parades and events, anyplace that would get her in front of voters and give her an opportunity to speak. Todd also offered to volunteer. "Todd was our sign man," Patrick explained. "We made these four-by-eight-foot yard signs, and Todd would put them in his truck and leave

Wasilla early in the morning, drive three hundred miles to Fairbanks, another seventy-five miles to Delta Junction, and then back to Glennallen, and then he'd be back in Wasilla by three a.m. He'd cover seven hundred miles in a day." Otherwise, "He was off doing his own thing or at home managing the kids."

To reciprocate, Sarah would leave town with the kids when he was getting ready for the Iron Dog. "I remember she took the kids to Hawaii for a week so he would have time to work on his machine and practice until three a.m. It was each of them supporting the other when they did their thing," Patrick said.

Sarah set up a campaign office in her house, served as her own treasurer, and wrote her own thank-you notes to donors. Sarah did hire a housekeeper, who also doubled as a babysitter for her young children, who ranged in age from one-year-old Piper to twelve-year-old Track. Her mother, Sally, helped out, along with Sarah's younger sister, Molly, who has a daughter the same age as Piper. Molly was married to Michael Wooten, who graduated from the Alaska State Trooper Academy and had joined the force in 2001. "Chuck and Sally gave Molly and Mike a barbecue to celebrate his graduation. Everyone was there, and they were all so proud of him. They had a lot of hopes as a couple, and things looked good in the beginning," Patrick said.

Meanwhile, Sarah continued in her duties as mayor during her campaign for lieutenant governor. "Wasilla is a small town, and there's no commuting time," Patrick said, explaining how Sarah was able to manage both jobs. "She could go home for lunch or leave early at three p.m. and be home in a few minutes. Being mayor was a twenty-four/seven position, and you worked nights and weekends so there was flexible time. You make it work."

The campaign heated up in the summer after school got out. Sarah took her kids with her on trips. "Any situation where she was allowed to bring her kids, she would," said Patrick, who has three kids of her own. "It was a way to spend time with them, and it was a win-win because they got a special experience and she got to see them."

The kids joined Sarah at town parades in Kenai and the Alaska State Fair Parade in Palmer. In the five-mile Golden Days Parade in July, Sarah took the children to Fairbanks and carried Piper in her arms along the route. A woman in the crowd felt so sorry for her that she gave Sarah a stroller, telling her she could keep it. Patrick had volunteers handing out campaign flyers. "Everyone wanted her picture, and it was a big asset, so we put her image on everything," Patrick said. "My friends in real estate always said, 'People remember a face.' Suddenly, we had all these volunteers when we started with nobody."

Sarah loved getting out and pressing the flesh, but it took a while for her to warm to the idea of using her looks in the campaign. While she first rejected the idea of having her face on every piece of campaign literature ("I don't want to be known for that," Sarah said), Patrick explained it was an economic necessity. "I'm sorry, girlfriend, this is all we have. We have no money, so we have to use this."

Still, it took some cajoling. "I remember taking her to my hair stylist for a change of pace, and Sarah said, 'Whatever you do, don't cut it.' So much for a new haircut," Patrick said.

In July, Sarah participated in a candidates' forum at the Palmer Moose Lodge. Robin Taylor wore a red, white, and blue American flag jacket and talked about opening up state lands for development. Gail Phillips, the other woman candidate in the race, cited her administrative experience in Juneau where she served as Republican House speaker, and Sen. Loren Leman cast himself as a conciliator, urging closer communication between the governor's office and the legislature. When Sarah's turn arrived, she described herself as a "hard-core fiscal conservative," who supported spending cuts and natural-resource development. She cited her tax-cut measures as mayor and said her lack of experience in Juneau was a plus. "Less divisiveness and new voices are needed," she said.

Two days later, Sarah lost a key endorsement. The Alaska Outdoor Council came out in favor of Robin Taylor. The council announced to the media that it made its decision based in part on responses to a questionnaire. Sarah was curious—she figured she was a natural for an endorsement, since the organization lobbies for hunters and trappers, access to state parks, and habitat protection. She never received a questionnaire, and neither had the other two candidates she checked with, Phillips and Leman. Patrick confirmed that Sarah sent off a pointed e-mail to the AOC from her city hall office asking about the phantom survey, but the move proved to be a careless mistake. The law states that any campaign has to be kept separate from the mayor's duties. When she ran for governor in three years, Sarah apologized for using city hall staff, phones, and computers to aid her campaign for lieutenant governor. There was even a campaign-related plane flight inadvertently expensed to the city that Sarah reimbursed when she found out about it a couple of weeks later, the Associated Press reported.

Patrick takes some of the responsibility for the transgressions. "That was caused by people like me," she said. "Sarah was insistent on not doing anything from city hall—and we did the lieutenant governor's stuff during lunch from her home or after work. But if I needed an answer quick, I'd send it to her at the office, and she would get really mad about it. My way of think-ing was the mayor's job is twenty-four/seven—you're on call nights and weekends, and what is the big deal if you answer a couple of e-mails in the middle of the af-ternoon. I was a culprit. Maybe there were a dozen in-stances where she did something from the office."

As July turned into August, Sarah began to make a move in the polls. She won an endorsement from former Anchorage mayor Tom Fink, who appeared in her lone TV ad touting her conservative politics and job as Wasilla mayor. He also felt she'd enhance the Republi-can ticket because the leading Democratic candidate, Lieutenant Governor Fran Ulmer, was a woman. "They're both personable, relatively young women," he told the *Anchorage Daily News*. Sarah's female oppo-nent, Gail Phillips, begged to differ: "If something were to happen to Frank Murkowski, I'm prepared to step in and run the state government. I don't think she is."

What Sarah's campaign lacked in finances (each of the other three candidates raised more than $100,000 in August, while Sarah had raised $39,000), Sarah made up for in performance. "It was clear to people she was the real deal," Patrick said. "What's funny to me is seeing similarities I saw on the state level on display on the na-tional level. She has talent, a fashion sense, and the abil-ity; that's what people saw in her in Alaska."

The money problem limited the scope of Sarah's campaign, preventing her from reaching the Republican enclaves in southeast Alaska. "We couldn't mine that area at all," Patrick said. Less than a week before the election, Sarah felt the pain of being on the receiving end of negative campaigning. The media was anonymously informed of the 1993 fishing violation, but it had been entered into the books as a felony. The court fixed the error and sent a letter of apology to Sarah, who issued a statement. "I think it's pretty cowardly," Sarah said at the time. "Somebody is peddling this five days before the election, obviously trying to smear my reputation."

It's hard to say whether more funds or the news of the fishing violation made a difference, but the race was closer than expected. On August 28, Leman won the primary, with Sarah coming in a close second, just two percentage points and 1,424 votes behind the leader after ninety-nine percent of the votes were tallied. Critics suggested Sarah and other conservatives benefited from a closed primary system in which only registered Republicans could vote for a person in their own party. But Sarah attributed her strong showing to Alaskans interested in new approaches. "Collectively, my three competitors have served in the legislature longer than I have been alive," she said.

Summing up the campaign, Patrick felt Sarah's impressive showing was enough, especially for a job that is primarily responsible for certifying elections. "We didn't view it as a loss," Judy explained. "It put Sarah on the map."

Back in Wasilla, Sarah had just two months left on her final term as mayor. She dismissed deputy city administrator John Cramer, surprising many residents. Ground had been broken on the new sports complex. Sarah and Todd also had a personal matter to attend to, and they needed help from the Wasilla planning commission. The Palins were getting ready to move into their new home on Lake Lucille, and it was time to sell the old house. Sarah had a buyer ready to purchase the $327,000 home, but in order to close the deal, the city had to waive the zoning violations with a variance. The original owner apparently built the home too close to the shore, and too close to neighboring properties, and included a carport that almost touched a neighboring property. The request for a variance was being disputed by neighbors and a planning official. Clyde Boyer, a neighbor, wrote the city and said that being a public figure should not give anyone special benefits. He asked that the Wasilla planning commission apply the same rules to the Palins' situation that it would apply to other families making similar requests.

The Palins didn't create the violations, but they should have been aware of them when they purchased the residence, wrote Susan Lee, a zoning official with the Mat-Su Borough, who recommended against the variance. But the final decision lay with the city. According to the Associated Press, which investigated the case, Wasilla planner Tim Krug approved a variance for the shoreline setback and for the side of the house to be close to the other property, as long as the carport was removed. On September 10, the Wasilla planning commission approved the variances, and a few days later, the Palins signed a deed to sell the house. But the carport was never removed.

While Sarah Palin was waging a campaign for lieutenant governor, there was another Palin entering the field of politics. Faye Palin, Todd's stepmother and the wife of Todd's father, Jim, entered the Wasilla mayor's race in August, against Sarah's good friend, city councilwoman Dianne Keller, and two other candidates. The town waited with bated breath to see whom Sarah would endorse for the $68,000 job in this typically nonpartisan race. There was silence.

In September, the *Anchorage Daily News* ran a headline, "Wasilla Elections Low-Key; Apathy: Few Residents Seem Overly Interested in Local Politics." The city was in good financial health, thanks to the sales tax

John Stein implemented ten years earlier. Borough residents flocked to the city to visit big-box stores such as Wal-Mart and Fred Meyer, and revenues were in excess of $6 million annually. Politicians never had to face unpopular decisions like raising property taxes and cutting vital services. But traffic for the city of 5,500 was getting worse, and many roads still remained to be paved. Still, "I couldn't have asked for a better time to be mayor of this city," Sarah told the *Anchorage Daily News*.

Faye Palin, said to be a pro-choice Democrat, raised more money than anyone in the race, $11,000, and cited her experience as vice president at the Matanuska Telephone Association. She had retired from the utility company a few years earlier but had been in charge of maintenance, construction, and customer service.

"What she didn't get, however, is an endorsement from her stepdaughter-in-law," the *Daily News* reported. Sarah told the *Daily News* she was friends with Keller and didn't want to publicly endorse one candidate over the other.

Faye played it down. "I would hope the voters, however they vote, would do that because I'm capable of doing the job, not necessarily because of some affiliation that has nothing to do with my skills," she said for the story.

The final days of the campaign were contentious.

Time magazine reported that Faye's campaign signs were defaced with "Baby-killer." Mat-Su political insiders also said Sarah's view on abortion—she opposed it even in the case of rape and incest—was the reason Faye didn't get Sarah's endorsement. In Wasilla, a long-time politician explained, Faye was perceived as pro-choice and Sarah's anti-abortion views were well known to voters. The issue might never come up at city hall, not in a million years, but to Sarah it didn't matter. "It was deeply rooted in Sarah and she wasn't going to budge," he said.

Keller defeated Faye, 402–256.

"Neither of them got an endorsement," said Patrick. "We did recruit Dianne to run, and we wanted someone in office who thought like we did. But Sarah did not endorse Faye, and she did not endorse Dianne. No one got the endorsement. I don't know why she didn't endorse Faye, and I was encouraging her to endorse Dianne; we wanted Dianne to have it, and she earned it; we were all in the trenches together. Dianne was conservative, and we thought Faye was more of a moderate, and we wanted a fiscal-conservative course."

NINE
WAITING YOUR TURN

After Sarah left office, she had coffee with Patrick, and they discussed Sarah's next move. One of the reasons Sarah wasn't so broken-hearted over losing the lieutenant governor's race was that there was a "bigger carrot" dangling from newly elected Governor Frank Murkowski's stick: his vacated U.S. Senate seat. The buzz for Sarah started shortly after her strong showing in the lieutenant governor's race. Political pundits were speculating that Sarah would get the appointment outright, or even land the lieutenant governor's chair after all if Murkowski chose running mate Loren Leman to serve. Sarah had been a dutiful campaigner for the Murkowski-Leman ticket, appearing at events, in print ads, and on television. Murkowski had even gone on television recently and indicated there was a place in his administration for Sarah, though he didn't mention specifics. "At times it seemed Sarah was more visible than Murkowski's running mate, Loren Leman," the *Frontiersman* reported. Sarah also visited Murkowski's campaign headquarters and had been quizzed by his aides on what she was interested in doing next. "Everything is up in the air still. I know that I don't necessarily want to retire, and with Todd's flexible schedule it allows me to serve in a couple of different capacities if they want me to," she told the *Frontiersman*. "That's the best thing I have going for me—Todd's support—anyplace that I can serve that's good for Alaska, he'll support me in that." Todd's job as a production operator for British Petroleum on the North Slope oil fields allowed him to work one week on and one week off.

By December, Murkowski had pored over more than two dozen candidates in his search for the state's next junior senator, and Sarah had made the short list. Liz Ruskin of the *Anchorage Daily News* said word of the appointment was so quiet, "suspense has given rise to baseless speculation."

"The number of rumors, obviously, is very significant," said state Republican Party chairman Randy Reudrich. "If you listen long enough, you can find one that contradicts the one you heard earlier." The unofficial conservative Web site GOPUSA.com had already done a survey of sorts and had its choice picked out: Sarah Palin.

Sarah's supporters noted her youth and solid showing in the lieutenant governor's race. Other candidates included former state lawmaker John Binkley and Murkowski's own daughter, Lisa Murkowski, a respected moderate Republican in the state House and counterbalance to Democratic governor Tony Knowles if he decided to run for the Senate seat when it opened up in 2004. The move would make Murkowski the first father to appoint his daughter as a U.S. senator. By mid-December, she was looking stronger as the odds-on choice to replace her father. Murkowski's late cuts included Sarah, who predicted Lisa Murkowski would get the nod.

On December 18, the headline in the *Anchorage Daily News* tipped Murkowski's hand: "Daughter Could Serve Dad's Senate Term"; two days later, he appointed his daughter, a two-term Republican state representative who had recently been chosen House majority leader, to his old Senate seat. Her selection drew complaints of nepotism among Republicans, but the new governor said, "Above all, I felt the person I appoint to the remaining two years of my term should be someone who shares my basic philosophy, my values . . . someone whose judgment I trust in representing the state and all of its people."

Lisa Murkowski was a former attorney for the Anchorage District Court, but her moderate voting record annoyed many conservatives. Still, most Republicans praised the pick. Sarah was not happy.

"It was a big blow to Sarah," said Patrick. "She made the short list and worked hard for him during the gubernatorial campaign, and then he appointed Lisa. She felt betrayed. It's not that Lisa was a bad choice—she was a state representative, and she was well liked. She did get reelected on her own merit." The chief complaint was why go through the process of interviewing twenty-five candidates when, in the end, Murkowski was probably going to select his daughter all along?

But Governor Murkowski didn't forget about Sarah. "I remember we were having coffee, and I was telling her, 'Something is going to come up,' but we just didn't know what. It was a big waiting game. Sarah was offered commissioner of administration, which primarily handles union negotiations, but she thought about it and turned it down. He was tossing her a bone, but Sarah was interested in directing commerce and economic development, but she was passed over for that one."

Murkowski came back with a second offer—an appointment to the independent Alaska Oil and Gas Conservation Commission (AOGCC). The three-member team was responsible for the oversight of the state's oil and gas industry with the priority of maximizing the recovery of Alaska's most-valued natural resources. With a staff of more than two dozen engineers, geologists, and petroleum inspectors, the commission safeguarded groundwater and surface water during drilling and investigated oil-well accidents and illegal waste-storage sites. It also ensured that oil and gas wells were up to code and didn't threaten aquifers during drilling. Sarah was appointed to the public seat on the commission; she said her tenure as mayor and councilwoman provided her with some background to fulfill her responsibility. She was joined by state Republican Party chairman Randy Ruedrich, who was given the engineering seat on the commission. He had a doctorate in chemical engineering and thirty years of experience in the oil and gas industry. But critics said both appointments smacked of political patronage, especially Ruedrich's selection. Why would Murkowski name a prominent GOP fund-raiser to a sensitive commission spot without Ruedrich resigning his Republican Party post? Regardless, the legislature confirmed the appointments.

The third member of the commission was a holdover from the previous administration, geology expert Dan Seamount.

Sarah's new salary was a substantial bump from her job as mayor, from $68,000 to $110,000. When Murkowski named her chairwoman of the commission and ethics supervisor, she got another $15,000 increase. Todd's blue-collar job on the North Slope was not considered a conflict of interest, since it was doubtful that any ruling Sarah made would affect her husband's job. However, she looked forward to finally understanding the more technical aspects of what her husband did for a living. "Maybe by the time this is all through, I can have an intelligent conversation with my husband about work," Sarah said, chuckling.

After the job was announced in February, Sarah went out and bought a minivan for the daily commute to Anchorage. "She hated the van," Patrick said. "We're not mommies with Odyssey minivans; we like our trucks and SUVs. But Sarah couldn't justify that. The minivan gets better mileage."

That minivan would be sold in a year.

Energy issues were at the forefront of Alaska politics, and Sarah was excited by the prospect of having a key role. At first, she was overwhelmed by the amount of technical knowledge required for the position. At the recommendation of staff, she read several books on energy matters. "The need, obviously, is for objectivity and fairness and for being able to absorb a lot of information and be able to maneuver yourself through that information," she said, describing her job to a reporter. "It's all very technical," she told the *Frontiersman*. "And all these things make for a pretty sharp learning curve."

A quick study, Sarah did her best. Seamount told the *New Republic* that Sarah felt insecure about her performance on the commission. "She would say she wasn't qualified for the job," he said. "I differed with her. She brought a lot."

Sarah was unexpectedly thrust into the role of playing commission cop. She was ethics supervisor, so staff and public complaints regarding commission activities came to her. She was on the job just several months when she began getting tips that Ruedrich was conducting state party business from his commission office. Some of those private contacts included oil companies he had previously worked for and which were presently having violations adjudicated before the commission, creating a conflict of interest for himself. Ruedrich, who was simultaneously serving as the chair of the state Republican Party, also was expensing travel to party events, which he would later deny.

In September, staffers were complaining that Ruedrich was doing party work from the office, sometimes spending hours each day taking calls on a private cell phone. Then Sarah heard from residents of Sutton, a Mat-Su Borough town on Sarah's home turf. They called to complain that Ruedrich participated in an August meeting to promote a private company's plan to drill for coal-based methane gas under their homes. Residents were furious that the state had leased the mineral rights literally out from under them, but it was the Department of Natural Resources' problem. Homeowners were upset over the late notice and feared that their water supplies could be threatened by the drilling. Then Ruedrich took over the floor and started explaining how safe the development would be, using a series of slides to explain the process. Chris Whittington-Evans, president of the nonprofit Friends of Mat-Su, recognized Ruedrich and wondered to himself, "Oh my God, why is he here?"

The slide show was familiar to Evans because he had seen it a couple of weeks before, when an Evergreen executive had displayed it to them at a breakfast meeting in Palmer. Adding to the confusion was Ruedrich's role. Whom was he representing, the state, the public, or the company Evergreen Resources Inc., a coal-based methane-gas developer that his independent commission should have been regulating?

As chairwoman, Sarah was required to submit a quarterly report that said there were no ethics violations on her watch. That fall, she refused to sign it without disclosing the breach. "I was having lunch with Sarah, and she was telling me her dilemma," Patrick said. "She was getting advice to just sign the report and that it wasn't a big deal. But to her, it was lying; she has a huge sense of right and wrong. It really ate at her. She was trying to report the ethics violation, but there was no response, and it was pushed up the ladder to attorney general Gregg Renkes and it ended up with Jim Clark."

On September 3, Sarah alerted Murkowski's chief of staff, Jim Clark, of the problem, and she got a callback three weeks later, assuring her that he would handle the matter. When Sarah gave Ruedrich a heads-up that Clark would be calling, he said he had already heard from Clark. In fact, he heard from Clark every Sunday. "He asked me if I was doing anything wrong. I told him no," Ruedrich told Sarah.

Sarah tried to persuade Ruedrich to end his activities, but he resisted her advice. In fact, Ruedrich and oil-company executives had hosted a September 16 fund-raiser for a Fairbanks Republican borough mayor. And in October, he sent out an e-mail notice of a fund-raiser for the state House Republican Majority Fund at the Petroleum Club in Anchorage. The *Daily News* reported that the October 13 e-mail, titled "Mark your calendars," invited recipients to a House GOP fund-raiser for Anchorage legislator Ramona Barnes, the Republican House speaker. The message also noted the new contribution limits for the Alaska GOP: $10,000. Ruedrich disputed that he sent the e-mail, saying he had accidentally forwarded it after receiving it from a GOP official without inspecting its contents.

Again, Sarah said she was "concerned" to hear about the e-mail, explaining to a reporter that she had spoken to Ruedrich and other state officials about his fund-raising activies. "I have been assured, Randy has told me, that he is not soliciting funds or raising funds on a state level." But Democrats were already circling the possible scandal. "It raises some serious ethical questions," Anchorage Democratic representative Ethan Berkowitz said.

Ruedrich was creating other problems for the commission. He wanted to investigate the political affiliations of staff members and root out the Democrats who had supported former governor Tony Knowles. He targeted commission attorney Bob Mintz, whom he labeled a "liberal Democrat" though other staff and commissioners found his recommendations and briefs to be nonpartisan. Commissioner Seamount, the *Daily News* said, fumed one afternoon when Sarah asked him to serve as an expert on a radio call-in show, only to discover Ruedrich had beaten him to the phone after overhearing Sarah asking Seamount to make the call. "No, no, no, this isn't right. He should not be doing this," Seamount told her.

"I thought you called in," Sarah told Seamount. "So I turned it on and went, 'Oh, no.' "

Meanwhile, Ruedrich continued to show up at Evergreen's meetings and advocate the coal-bed methane development project. The link went deeper when it was discovered that Ruedrich had e-mailed a confidential AOGCC memo, written by the assistant attorney general assigned to the agency, to an Evergreen lobbyist. The lobbyist, Kyle Parker, was tied to a law firm that was developing legislation designed to diminish local control of coal-bed methane projects, the *Daily News* reported. Sarah, too, was an early supporter of the project and had attended some of the same meetings, staying mostly neutral. But later she changed her mind and decided not to support the drilling effort. "Her decision may have been expedient, but I believe she realized this was making people unhappy, and she bowed out," Evans said.

Evans found no such transformation in Ruedrich. He fired off an e-mail to Sarah on November 6 and demanded that Ruedrich be removed from the commission. Sarah replied, "This will not be swept under the rug." She sent along Evans's e-mail to Clark, Renkes, and commissioner of administration Mike Miller. Ruedrich met with the governor and two days later resigned his post. He said he left in the best interest of the Republican Party and felt the ethics violations were "way overblown."

In response, Sarah said the conflict-of-interest issue damaged the commission's credibility and that she was prepared to leave if nothing was done about it. "The right thing has been done here," she told a reporter.

"It broke open after that," Patrick said.

The attorney general's office ordered Sarah to break into Ruedrich's computer and round up his e-mails. Sarah complied and then asked if an investigation would be launched. Renkes's answers were ambivalent. In December, she sent the attorney general documents from Ruedrich's computer but didn't hear back for a month. On January 2, 2004, she mailed Murkowski a letter asking for an investigation, so that she couldn't be blamed for a cover-up. Though assistant attorney general Paul Lyle did begin an investigation, there was no acknowledgment that it was under way. On January 16, Sarah resigned from the commission. That same day, Gregg Renkes announced he was recusing himself from the investigation because of his political ties to Ruedrich, putting the investigation into the hands of an assistant, Barbara Ritchie. State lawyers told Sarah to remain quiet. "I'm forced to withhold information from Alaskans, and that goes against what I believe in as a public servant," Sarah said.

But Sarah didn't remain silent. Some of her Republican mentors felt she should have just passed on the information to the state and let the investigation take its course without making a big scene. "The impression I got was she didn't want to do it," said Roy Burkhart, a district Republican head from Mat-Su, from whom Sarah sought advice. "But the evidence was there, and it was going to get worse if she didn't do it." While he didn't have a quarrel with her decision to turn in Ruedrich, he felt she should have allowed authorities to investigate and stayed quietly in the background. But that old Sarah was gone.

TEN

HOCKEY MOM BENCHED

Sarah hadn't soured on politics, but she was getting signals that it was a time to step back. Conservative supporters were pushing her to challenge moderate Republican Lisa Murkowski, whose U.S. Senate seat was up that year. However, when Sarah gathered her family to discuss the possibility and the move to Washington, D.C., if she won, Todd and the girls gave yes votes, but Track, fourteen, resisted. In an interview with writer Kaylene Johnson, Sarah explained that she wouldn't pursue the office without a unanimous vote from her family. "It had to be a family decision," she said. "Track did not want me to run. And he was adamant about it. He had to bless me."

Instead, she chose to endorse Mike Miller, who had recently resigned his administrative post in Governor Murkowski's office to run against the governor's daughter. "Sarah is a very energetic person, and I look forward to having her support," Miller said.

It wasn't until June that the state took action against Ruedrich, but the outcome wasn't what everyone had hoped. While he admitted that he had committed three violations as a former regulator of the oil and gas industry, including conducting partisan political business from his office, he was able to negotiate a settlement that included paying a $12,000 fine, the largest of its type in Alaska history. Much to the chagrin of Democrats, he kept his job as Republican Party boss after a party committee gave him a vote of confidence. Governor Murkowski signed off on the settlement and said the ethics law had been "justly applied." But Governor Murkowski's political stock was in a free fall. In September the *Anchorage Daily News* was calling the Ruedrich affair "a scandal" and lambasted Murkowski for calling Ruedrich "a survivor." "Do you suppose that sent a good signal to the party, to Ms. Palin, to other potential whistle blowers?" the newspaper asked.

Before the year was out, Sarah was embroiled in another conflict with Governor Murkowski's handling of a conflict-of-interest dispute with a staff member. The *Anchorage Daily News* had broken the story about a multimillion-dollar trade deal that attorney general Gregg Renkes had negotiated, which would enable Taiwan to import coal from Alaska's Cook Inlet. Renkes lined up KFx Inc. and its patented coal-drying process for use on the exported coal. KFx stood to benefit financially, good news to its stockholders, which included Renkes. He owned more than $100,000 in KFx stock and was buying more as he negotiated the September 2004 deal without the governor's knowledge, although Renkes had disclosed it in filings with the Alaska Public Offices Commission. While Murkowski insisted it was an insignificant amount and within state guidelines, Sarah teamed with Democrat Eric Croft, demanding that both Renkes and Murkowski be investigated for ethics violations. "People are asking, 'What's the governor's role in this?' " Sarah told the *Anchorage Daily News*. "Not only do Alaskans deserve to know the truth, but both gentlemen deserve a fair hearing." The governor was less than sanguine in his response, calling Sarah and Croft's letter the "action of a few politicians who have run in the last few years and have future political ambitions."

Sarah would reply in a sharply pointed letter published in the December 17 issue of the *Anchorage Daily News*. In the letter, Sarah asked, "What political motivation? What political ambition? I am, as one morning talk show audience was reminded this week, 'just an unemployed housewife from Wasilla.' Well, doggone it, besides being 'just a housewife,' I'm also a hockey mom.

It's said the only difference between a hockey mom and a pit bull is lipstick. So with lipstick on, the gloves come off in answering administration accusations."

A pit bull in lipstick? The label would be used again.

Sarah went on to stress that she voted for Murkowski and campaigned diligently for him and then discreetly laid the groundwork for the nonpartisan rallying cry of her future gubernatorial campaign. No matter how a voter identifies himself on a ballot, Sarah wrote that all Alaskans, regardless of affiliation, "were united seeking better governance," citing herself and Croft as examples.

A closer look at the editorial reveals that the former Wasilla mayor and president of the Alaska Conference of Mayors also updated voters on what she had been doing with her time in the past year. She identified herself as manager and scorekeeper for Track's hockey teams, exhorting her son "through the glass to stay out of the penalty box."

For the past year, Sarah had been in a penalty box of her own. She did stay in the public eye by doing statewide television ads for Spenard Builders Supply and a state fire marshal public-service announcement on cooking safety. She also contrived a funny response to a private e-mail leak in which Ben Stevens, the son of U.S. Sen. Ted Stevens, called Mat-Su Valley residents "Valley trash." Sarah donned a T-shirt with the derogatory label and appeared on a local Web site. She also did an ad with several prominent Republicans supporting an all-Alaska natural-gas line, a position she would later reverse after more inspection on the issue.

Though the unemployed former mayor craved to get back into the action, she was able to spend more time with her children. Part of the political intermission was spent watching Track play hockey in Wasilla and her daughters compete in basketball and soccer. Her father had instilled in her that sports was a training ground for learning life's lessons, something Sarah passed on to her children and the community at large. During a speech she gave at the 2005 Colony High commencement, she encouraged the students to savor the life lessons from athletic competition—the self-discipline, the grace in defeat and victory, the drive, the work ethic, and "translate that into family life, community life, and business," she said.

Track had been playing hockey for as long as he could walk, his relatives said. In the winter, he played for two teams, the Wasilla High Warriors hockey team and a local club or "comp B" team, the Mat-Su Eagles, which would suspend play for the older kids when high school hockey season was in progress. Home games and practices were played in the Brett Memorial Arena and the new Curtis Menard ice rink at the recently completed sports complex. Sarah was a regular, often arriving at games in a down coat accompanied by Bristol, Willow, Piper, and Todd, if he was in town.

In 2004, Bristol turned fourteen, Willow turned ten, and Piper was just three. "She really fit in with the rest of us and didn't look out of place at all," said one Wasilla mother whose son played with Track. She asked to remain anonymous. "I usually sat next to Sarah. We talked about the kids, the game, activities, but not politics. She cheered, but she was not hard on the refs, the coaches, or her son. I remember her daughters would get a little bored, and she would let Piper comb and brush her hair when she wasn't working in what we call the box."

The "box" was an enclosed area by the ice where Sarah could sit and keep score or run the game clock behind a sheet of fiberglass. "She was very familiar with the rules of the game," the hockey mom said. "One year she served as a manager, and that meant keeping in touch with the other parents on practice times and the team party. It's a commitment, because Track played on two teams, and that keeps you busy from September to April, at least one game a week. And we did travel, usually to Fairbanks, Anchorage, and Kenai areas."

When Track scored a goal, Sarah would leap to her feet with a shout-out to her son. But otherwise she contained her emotions. "She was not a screamer or yeller. I heard she was a real competitor in high school, but she took it all in stride, even the bad calls or if her son got tripped," the mom said. "I can't remember one instance where she acted inappropriately. We always have a few parents who got worked up, but Sarah wasn't one of those. Sarah would get excited for everyone on the team, not just Track. She used to help carpool to games and practices, and if she had extra space in her car for an away game in Fairbanks, she'd make room for one more. She was always willing to lend a hand, and so was Todd when he wasn't working on the slope."

Willow and Piper used to volunteer for the chuck-a-puck contest during the Warriors games. "They would walk through the stands—Piper would carry the bucket of numbered pucks, and Willow held a clipboard to write down who bought which puck and collect the money (a dollar a puck)."

At intermission, the fans would heave their pucks toward center ice, and the puck stopping closest to the face-off circle was declared the winner. The winning chucker was awarded half the money collected in the bucket. On a good night, that might be forty dollars, with the balance donated to the booster club.

That winter, Todd debated whether to compete in the Iron Dog as Sarah helped him nurse a bad back. He had finished second the previous year with partner Scott Davis. Thousands of miles of training and competing had taken its toll, Todd said, adding, "The Alaskan lifestyle is wear and tear on backs."

Davis was a six-time winner of the race when he joined forces with Todd after the 2002 event. He is five years Todd's senior and knows something about the pain Todd was going through. "As each year goes by, you have to do more and more training. As you get older, your back and shoulders ache, there's dehydration and exhaustion. You have to watch your eyes, because terrain racers really rely on vision, and it's one of the first things to go."

In the weeks approaching the race, their training regimen includes snow-machining fifty to one hundred miles in a night and two hundred to three hundred sit-ups per day to strengthen the core muscles and abdominals, which play a huge role in supporting the vulnerable lower back. Maximum speeds can exceed a hundred miles per hour, and Todd and the other top racers have acquired Indy-car-racer reflexes to avoid dangerous and hidden obstacles, such as stumps, fallen trees, ice formations, and hardened snow drifts. Sometimes, the obstacles move. Racers have been known to collide with moose.

Training does take Todd away from his family, especially in the month leading up to the race. "It's a little bit of travel since we live two hundred miles apart and since we build our machines together in my shop, so there's a little more driving on Todd's part," Davis said. "We try to coordinate training with working on our snowmobiles, and we also train individually, and as we get closer to the race, we train together. You have to get used to driving with the snow dust in your eyes. It's all about the hours you put in and the miles you put on your machine, so you find time when it allows."

Todd and Scott have different skills, and they find that one's weakness is the other's strength. Out on the course, Todd rides in back while Davis takes the lead. It seems like a small tactic, but it's tough on the rear man. "When we race, the river runs are hard, because the snow dust kicks up, temperatures are super-cold, and it's hard for the guy riding in back. You need to stay far enough apart so the snow dust can clear for the guy in back," Davis said.

While Davis is considered a whiz with the wrench, Todd gets high marks for his navigation skills. "Todd is a pilot, and his flying experience helps with his navigation ability. He is familiar with GPS and navigation devices, and he's a good field mechanic as well, and when you're out there, two heads are better than one. Navigation, mechanics, teamwork—it takes a combination of those abilities to be successful."

A sympathetic family helps, too. "You either got the support to do it, or it's not possible," Davis said. "Every year before we do this, we talk with our families before we make the commitment. Sarah is very competitive herself, and she cares about Todd's racing. It's expensive, dangerous, and places demands on the family. Todd and Sarah have a great network that helps care for the kids, and Todd makes it seamless. He comes here early and then leaves at a certain time, and the next thing I know, I'm talking to him while he's at an event for the kids or doing something with Sarah. He makes good use of his time, and if we have to, we reschedule. We're versatile."

In the heat of competition, Davis said, you want a teammate you can trust. "When it's fifty below, stuff's breaking down, it wears on you as the years go by, and he doesn't get discouraged. I think the mental toughness he possesses helps him everywhere in life. You can't pay attention to what everyone else is doing; if someone is faster, you still have to run your race."

Run your own race; pay attention to what you're doing; shore up your weaknesses with training and help; solicit family support. That February, Todd and Scott finished second in the Iron Dog again, not bad for a guy with a bad back. Just as the race was about to get under way, a headline blasted from the *Daily News:* "Embattled Renkes Resigns; State Attorney General Blames News Media, Political Attacks."

Unable to fend off questions about his role in a coal-trade deal that could profit a Denver company in which he had $110,000 in stock, Renkes said he stepped down to save his family from "the vicious politics of personal destruction." An investigation by an independent counsel had concluded there was no wrongdoing on Renkes' part because the stock he owned was deemed legally "insignificant" to be a conflict of interest. Eric Croft and Sarah immediately withdrew their complaint with the state personnel board. But a few months later, Sarah said the Murkowski administration remained in "denial that there was any wrongdoing."

The parallels between running a two-thousand-mile snowmobile race and a political campaign seemed uncanny.

ELEVEN

BACK IN THE HUNT

As the summer approached, Sarah was getting the itch to compete in another race of her own.

A poll was released on June 6, 2005, showing Governor Murkowski's popularity plummeting. His disapproval rating hit sixty-six percent, which ranked him the second-least-liked governor in the United States. The door was now wide open for fresh candidates.

Patrick recalled having a conversation with Sarah, and they discussed the significance of losing the 2002 lieutenant governor's race and how beneficial it could be for Sarah not to be affiliated with Murkowski. Ironic? Lucky? Not at all, Patrick explained. "I'm a Christian, and so is Sarah, and we don't believe in luck," Patrick said. "We talked about this. When we look back on it, Sarah was earnest about becoming Murkowski's lieutenant governor, but it turned out bad for him. She believes in God, and I believe in God and faith, and we feel it plays a role, that a Christian God gives you a role and a plan and a purpose for your life."

The next day, Sarah hinted at her intentions to run for governor when she slipped up during an interview with the *Anchorage Daily News*. Explaining her desire for an executive office, she said, "It was like when I was on the city council . . . making decisions . . . but I realized that in order to really set a tone . . . I needed to run for governor, I mean run for mayor."

Clearly, she was a little rusty dealing with the press, which happens when a politician drops from the public eye for seventeen months. In the story, Sarah caught folks up on her activities. She had been a hockey mom for Track, car-pooled for school and her daughters' basketball and soccer games, and gave a commencement speech for Palmer's Colony High School, reminding students to take what they've learned in high school and transfer it to their family and community. She also obtained a business license to open a marketing and consulting firm, called Rouge Cou, "a classy way of saying red neck in French," she explained.

At the time, Palin realized she might have been a lone voice in the wilderness, since there were "deep divisions" between herself and the party leaders. There's another word for people who run up against established hierarchies.

Maverick.

"Randy Ruedrich," she said, "used to think I could do anything . . . but now I am the enemy, because I asked questions and did my job as [AOGCC] supervisor." Admittedly, Sarah was frustrated with Alaskan politics, but she hadn't given up hope. "My interest is serving Alaskans in whatever capacity Alaskans see fit in the future."

But Sarah already had that figured out. If she took the next big step, she would run a nonpartisan campaign and appeal to Alaskans. While she may not have had the support of the central players in the state GOP, she did have one other party in the fold. "I certainly have the blessing of my husband and my kids, my family, to get out there and run for whatever I want to run for," she said. "I've been home enough, seventeen months, and I think my kids are really ready for me to go do something. I'm in their business all the time."

On October 18, Bristol's birthday, Sarah invited forty-five of her closest friends and family to her home on Lake Lucille. Sure, there was a little birthday celebration and some cake for her oldest daughter, who turned fifteen. But Sarah had another announcement: she was seeking the Republican nomination for governor. "Keeping it simple is my philosophy," she said. "My desire to see small, efficient government that's going to provide the basic services for Alaska, that's shared by the majority of Alaskans. And in keeping it simple we know that Alaskans, we crave, we deserve leaders who are not going to approach all of our issues with just merely a partisan approach. . . . Alaskans who are independent in their thinking and are not obsessed with partisanship, they're going to be voting their conscience, voting for that individual that will bring them that positive change."

Right around the time Sarah was contemplating making a run at Governor Murkowski, she was supporting her sister Molly McCann through a personal crisis: her four-year marriage to Alaska state trooper Mike Wooten was falling apart. Problems had been brewing for a while, both at home and on the job. His employer had reprimanded him for negligent damage to a state car and such traffic miscues as speeding, unsafe lane changes, and not using turn signals. He had also been criticized for using his cell phone to make personal calls and had been tardy on the job.

Bigger problems for Wooten surfaced when his employer investigated several allegations brought to their attention by Molly and her family. "All I got to say is, check [Wooten's] record and see what he's like as a cop," said Chuck Heath.

One of those issues occurred in 2003 when Wooten

shot a cow moose without a permit. He was hunting with Molly and a friend in the Jim Creek area, and she had a permit to take a cow. Such permits are coveted by hunters because so few are given out. Drifting in a boat, they spotted a female moose onshore. Molly balked at firing the weapon—no surprise there. Her father said she wasn't into hunting. "Molly would go hunting with us, but she never shot anything," Chuck said. Wooten took the rifle and killed the moose himself, a criminal misdemeanor in Alaska, though he was never charged.

Later, after troopers learned of the illegal kill, Wooten was removed from his duty as wildlife investigator for the department. The moose was reportedly butchered by Chuck Heath and shared with family members, including Todd and Sarah.

Another disconcerting moment during their union came when Wooten demonstrated a Taser on his eleven-year-old stepson. Wooten had just completed an instruction course on how to use the demobilizing weapon when Molly's son from a previous marriage begged him to try it on him. The boy wanted to show off to his cousin Bristol Palin, who was also in the house. The boy said his mother, Molly, was in another room warning them not to do it, but they went ahead anyway. Wooten told the boy to kneel down so he wouldn't fall, and he secured a probe to his arm with tape. Pillows were placed around the child, and Wooten said he "turned the Taser on for like a second, turned it off." The boy jerked. "He thought that was the greatest thing in the world, wanted to do it again," Wooten said to the investigator. In the report, Bristol testified that her cousin got scared and the force of the Taser knocked him back. The jolt hurt for a split second, her cousin said, and left a mark on his arm.

An expert on Tasers spoke to the *Anchorage Daily News* for its July 27, 2008, story, "Is Wooten a Good Trooper?" Explaining how the device is used in the field, he said a law enforcement officer would fire the probes into the body surface of a suspect and turn on the device for five seconds. The suspect is briefly incapacitated. In demonstrations, if the Taser is safely attached and turned on for a second, "it would feel like your funny bone was hit, but the quick jolt wouldn't knock you over," the expert said.

A third incident in the Wooten investigation involved Sarah and Track. In February 2005, around the same time attorney general Renkes submitted his resignation and Todd was preparing for the Iron Dog, Molly called her sister in a panic and said Wooten was on his way home, and he was furious. She put the phone on speaker so Sarah could listen in. Track, fifteen, was also in the room. McCann recalled in her interview with troopers that her husband said if her father, Chuck, hired an attorney for her, he would "eat a f'ing lead bullet. I will shoot him."

Sarah recalled that her brother-in-law kept yelling, "I'm gonna f'ing kill your dad if he gets an attorney to help you." However, she couldn't say what specifically Wooten was referring to. Molly clarified that later in a protective order, saying she and Mike were separated, and he was upset that she was hiring an attorney to resolve their custody dispute. Track confirmed he heard the same thing as his mother. Sarah said she was concerned enough to drive over to her sister's house and observe through a window. Wooten appeared angry, she said. A neighbor watching with Sarah said Wooten was upset, but it didn't appear that Molly was in any danger. Wooten later denied that he said he would harm Chuck, but trooper officials found him culpable of a policy violation. No crime had been committed because the threat wasn't made directly to his father-in-law.

Finally, there was testimony submitted for the investigation regarding Wooten's drinking. Two neighbors living near Mike and Molly, Adrian and Marilyn Lane, longtime friends of the Heaths, said they were alarmed one day in 2004 when Wooten dropped by their house in his white patrol car and drank a beer he had retrieved from a refrigerator in the Lanes' garage. On his way out, he grabbed a second can, opened it, and hopped into his patrol car to drive away. The Lanes told him he needed to be careful. Wooten denied he did this, but investigators concluded he had. "I do not drive drunk," he said in court papers.

In another instance, about a month before Molly filed divorce papers, Wooten had a confrontation with a bartender at a local Wasilla haunt, the Mug-Shot Saloon. Wooten had gotten into an altercation, and Wooten's pal and the bartender intervened to keep the two from exchanging blows. When the other man didn't get ejected from the bar, Wooten got into it with the bartender and flashed his badge. " 'Lemmie introduce myself, I'm State Trooper Wooten,' " the bartender told authorities he said. Wooten left in a car with his buddy and was pulled over by state trooper Dave Herrell a couple of blocks away. The bartender, it turned out, had alerted police that Wooten was leaving the bar and appeared drunk. Wooten identified himself as a trooper to Herrell, who concluded Wooten wasn't under the influence. Still, he asked him to park his car and then drove the pair back to the friend's house. Wooten called Molly to come pick him up. By Molly's account, her husband bragged, "Oh, I can play a good sober when I need to." In an affidavit, Wooten said the bartender got angry with him because he told him not to serve the belligerent person anymore.

The relationship came to an official end on April 11,

but it didn't end amicably. That day, Molly requested a domestic-violence restraining order from the court and filed for divorce. For Wooten, then a thirty-two-year-old Air Force veteran who had joined the troopers four years earlier, it wasn't the first time a marriage had gone south. Chuck also contacted the troopers and told them of the protective order Molly had filed against his son-in-law. The contents accused Wooten of "extreme verbal abuse and violent threats and physical intimidation," Molly wrote in her petition. She said that her husband had made threats to hurt her father and told her to "put a leash on your sister and family or I'm going to bring them down," she said in the document. In addition, a neighbor called the troopers and said Wooten had a drinking problem and that of late he appeared "disconnected."

Wooten said in his divorce affidavit that he had "never hit her or threatened to hit her," adding that they had been having marital difficulties for quite some time. They had separated in March.

The next day, Wooten's supervisor reiterated the court order and ordered Wooten to turn in his badge, gun, trooper ID card, and vehicle for the twenty-day period the order remained in force.

Later in the month, an internal investigation was launched, and relevant witnesses were questioned, including Sarah, Chuck, Todd, Track, Bristol, Molly,

Wooten, and other troopers. Sarah's participation didn't end there. In August, two months before her announcement that she would run for governor, she wrote a letter to Colonel Julia Grimes, head of the Alaska state troopers. In it, she complained that the troopers were dragging their feet over taking measures against a law enforcement officer many classified as a "loose cannon" and a "ticking time bomb." The Palins were concerned enough that they hired a private investigator.

Troopers wrapped up the investigation shortly after Sarah announced her intention to run for governor. In January, Molly's divorce from Wooten was finalized, though disagreements over custody and visitation remained unresolved. Two months later, Grimes acted on the charges and found Wooten guilty of three violations, and a fourth would surface later. She suspended Wooten for ten days. But the penalty was later reduced by fifty percent after his union, the Public Safety Employees Association, complained the initial penalty was too harsh. "The record clearly indicates a serious and concentrated pattern of unacceptable and at times, illegal activity over a lengthy period, which establishes a course of conduct totally at odds with the ethics of our profession," wrote Colonel Grimes in her letter of suspension.

Another lapse by Wooten would cost him his job,

she warned the trooper. He is currently still employed by the state. He has also publicly apologized.

Union chief John Cyr told the *Anchorage Daily News* that Wooten was disciplined appropriately. "Basically, end of story," he said. But it wasn't end of story. Far from it. Sarah and Todd believed his transgressions merited stronger action and should have cost him his job. Wooten, they believed, was a danger to her family and the community.

Recalling the divorce, Patrick said it was causing a great deal of strife for Sarah and the rest of the Heath family. "They're a tight family," she said. "The kids were little; Molly was nursing Heath. He was getting custody of the kids, and often he wasn't there, and his girlfriend's teenagers were watching their kids. Sarah was concerned about safety issues and the well-being of her own daughter since Molly watched Piper a lot [Molly's daughter, McKinley, is the same age]. Sarah is hardwired like that. If there's a wrong there, it strikes a chord in her."

Molly has treated all of Sarah's kids like her own. With Chuck Jr. and Heather living in Anchorage, Molly is the only other Heath sibling remaining in Wasilla besides Sarah. Growing up, one of the hardest obstacles the Heaths faced was getting by in a hardscrabble town without any family in the area, as Sally's family remained in

Washington and Chuck's parents lived in Idaho. So the Heath kids made an unofficial pact—they would stay close to one another in Alaska and raise their families together. It seems to have worked out and has been especially beneficial to Sarah, who could rely on family instead of hired help to take care of her kids when Todd was away and she was busy with her political career. "I could not do my job without my family," Sarah told *People*. Of her siblings, Molly was the baby in the family, the one everyone always looked out for and protected.

Later, as Sarah forged a political career and Todd, between juggling a full-time job on the North Slope and spending part of the summer in Bristol Bay fishing and a good part of the winter preparing for the Iron Dog, it was Molly who took on the lion's share of watching Sarah's kids and attending their sporting events if Sarah or Todd was away. In return, Sarah and Todd always had Molly's back, her problems with ex-husband Mike Wooten no exception. In fact, Sarah has been a bastion of support throughout her ongoing custody struggle with Wooten, telling her to stay strong and that she's fighting the good fight.

But the matter would have to wait. Sarah was busy on the campaign trail; the election for governor was just several months away.

When Sarah announced her candidacy in October

2005, Murkowski was still undecided about running for a second term. Sarah and Todd decided to make a bet whether the governor would enter the race, with the loser having to sit for a tattoo. If Murkowski was in, Sarah had to get the Big Dipper etched on her ankle. If the governor declined to run, Todd would get a wedding band tattooed on his ring finger, Sarah told the Associated Press.

Life in the governor's office was not going smoothly for Murkowski. He was embroiled in talks with major oil companies about building a natural-gas pipeline that would provide the resources to the Lower Forty-eight. He also was dealing with low approval ratings that consistently ranked him forty-ninth out of fifty in the United States, just ahead of Ohio governor Bob Taft. Since coming into office in 2002, he had to make some unpopular choices when the price of oil started to dip. He cut the longevity bonus for the elderly, which provided $250 a month for seniors who turned sixty-five by 1996. He dropped direct payments to local governments and raised oil taxes.

In one of his more controversial moves, Murkowski purchased a state jet for travel. He explained to baffled voters that his goal was to improve the Department of Public Safety's turboprop fleet with a newer plane that could be used for emergencies and to whisk inmates to a prison the state had a contract with in Arizona. Murkowski would also use the jet for his own travel, noting that much of Alaska is accessible only by air and that he traveled outside the state to negotiate trade deals and attend conferences. Defying legislature disapproval, Murkowski went ahead and bought the Westwind II anyway for $2.6 million, along with $200,000 more for pilot training and upgrades. He managed that by selling one of the turboprops and paying for the rest with a controversial lease-to-purchase finance deal, which didn't need legislature approval. Regardless, the incumbent was confident. "If I decide to, I will run, and I will win," he said.

The drop in oil prices beleaguered Murkowski's administration since it cut into the state's share of oil revenue, which covers eighty percent of the state budget. When gasoline prices go up, it's bad for consumers but good for Alaska. When oil prices drop, that's bad for Alaska. In October, Murkowski had also fired his commissioner of natural resources, Tom Irwin, who had been critical of Murkowski's closed-door meetings with North Slope oil firms about building the natural-gas pipeline. Irwin felt Murkowski was providing too many concessions, and negotiations needed to be open to the public.

Sarah had strong early poll numbers but faced an uphill battle in a primary, because it would be closed— open to registered Republican voters only—with independents and nonpartisans on the outside looking in. If she was nervous about it, she wasn't letting on. "Seventy percent of Alaskans will be able to pick up that Republican ballot and cast their votes for me," she said. The field did expand just before Christmas when John Binkley entered the race. A fifty-two-year-old businessman from Fairbanks and a former state legislator, Binkley was one of Murkowski's finalists along with Sarah for the U.S. Senate seat he'd awarded to his daughter, Lisa. Binkley was running his family's tourism business, and he had strong ties to the state's rural communities thanks to his years as a state senator from Bethel, 340 miles west of Anchorage on Alaska's west coast. The Democrat entrants included Eric Croft, Sarah's partner in the Renkes coal controversy. But they had their eye on former Democratic governor Tony Knowles, who had yet to declare. With eight months until the August primary, nobody was counting out Murkowski.

One afternoon, Sarah got a call from her Wasilla hairstylist, Jessica Steele. Steele owned a local shop called the Beehive and had recently seen Sarah on TV. She had a couple of new ideas. Would she like to come in and brainstorm about hair color and style for the campaign?

Steele had been coloring and cutting Sarah's hair on and off since 2002, when her term as mayor was ending and she was running for lieutenant governor. "We have experimented with different tones over the years," Steele said. "But we have always kept the classic silhouette of an updo." Sarah wanted her hairstyle to be quick and easy and something she could duplicate herself."

For the 2006 governor's race, Steele wanted to tweak the color. There would be several televised debates and many TV appearances. And make no mistake about it, after four wins in five elections, Sarah was cognizant of her strengths, two of them being youth and energy.

The updo had been a standard style for Sarah since her days as Wasilla mayor. By keeping her hair in a bun and away from her face, Sarah always believed she could keep someone's attention during a meeting or a conversation. In politics, a candidate may only have a minute, even less, to make an impression. The trick was to make it a lasting one. Sarah walked into Steele's shop wearing a parka over a tracksuit, little Piper in tow. Walking into the Beehive salon always brought a smile to the face of Wasilla's political maverick. The 1,400-square-foot shop is painted Barbie pink and draws an eclectic clientele; the chatter ranges from shopping trips to Anchorage to stalking a grizzly bear during hunting season. A haircut is thirty dollars, and color treatments run ninety-five dollars. The scene is like "*Steel Magnolias* on permafrost," Steele told the *New York Times*.

Steele set up a head mannequin for Piper, complete with wig, bobby pins, and comb. With Piper preoccupied, Steele got down to business with her favorite politician. She wanted to try a lighter color on Sarah's hair to give her a softer look. What Sarah likes best about the updo is its practicality; it's easy to pull back with barrettes or bobby pins, something Sarah could do in just a minute between meetings or appointments, "so she can focus on getting the job done," Steele said. "The updo can have fancier curls or bangs, depending on the event."

Sarah is a naturally rich, dark brunette, so Steele tested out blond highlights, but they looked gray on camera, and the darker highlights couldn't be seen at all. The solution: caramel and darker beige-blond and red and coppery highlights. "She wants to look professional," Steele explained. "She's very beautiful, but she's not confident about her own beauty; she wants to downplay it. She thinks if you have hair in your face and you're trying to say something, the hair can be distracting. She doesn't want her looks to distract from her message, and she wants to make sure you are paying attention to what she's saying and not be distracted by her hair, so it's off the face. It's not like she thinks, 'Oh, I'm pretty.' In politics, which men dominate, she wants to be taken seriously. But the color has to be applied just right, because if she's gone for three months, I can't have something that will grow out."

Sarah is very aware of how she wants to be perceived. She applies her own makeup and settles on a natural look. No stranger to a tanning bed, she never has to overdo it. "Sarah has a natural glow and much different skin coloring than her sisters. The makeup enhances her natural beauty, so she keeps it light," Steele said.

That day, Sarah sat in her chair and relaxed, scrolling through her BlackBerry as Steele applied the foil to her hair. "We talk about our kids mostly," said Steele, who had three at the time. "Sarah always asks me about my kids and talks about her own. I'm always asking her advice about something; she's so knowledgeable."

Back in 2003, when Steele was going through a custody battle with an ex-husband, Sarah and she, who both attend Wasilla Bible Church, would say a prayer together. "Sarah said there's a reason for everything, and God was in control, so have faith," Steele recalled.

The friendship grew, and in June 2006, when Steele got engaged, she invited Sarah to her bridal shower. Sarah gave her a red coffeepot. At times, Steele has been torn by conflicting demands—being a full-time mother at home or running her salon with the kids in a nursery downstairs from the shop. In these instances, Sarah often would give one of her pep talks. "Sarah believes you can have it all," said Steele. "She said if I stayed at home, I'd miss doing something that I love. So don't apologize for that. Be true to yourself, and you'll be happy."

As for her fashion sense in those days, Sarah shopped at any number of stores, a consignment shop in Anchorage specializing in designer clothes, and Nordstrom at a downtown Anchorage mall, to get her brightly colored blazers and skirts. Even now, "Sometimes I'll just pick something up for her," said Patrick, who works near Sarah's favorite consignment shop. "If I see something that's right for her, I'll get it, because I know she doesn't have time to shop."

Sarah usually completes her look with heels because they make her appear taller; aided by the updo, and she can add a couple of inches to her height. "Better for the TV cameras," Steele has told her. "And always glasses for her. In 2006, she had rims and different styles and colors. So the final look is stylish, pulled together, and elegant."

In May 2006, Murkowski finally declared he would run for a second term. Sarah, meanwhile, had been pounding home her nonpartisan message for seven months, reaching out to voters in every corner of the state. At a luncheon with the Bartlett Democrats at the Royal Fork restaurant in Anchorage, she delivered a speech that was upbeat as she proposed a new era in Alaska politics where practical ideas and transparent government supersede party politics. As if to drive home her conciliatory tone, she embraced local Democrats Eric Croft and Ethan Berkowitz, who were running in the Democratic primary for governor, and Andrew Halcro, a one-time Republican lawmaker running as an independent, as fresh faces in Alaska politics. Halcro is a Sarah critic, but he knows a formidable candidate when he sees one. Her innate ability to sense when the political tide is shifting, even in the heat of battle, is one of her strengths. During a televised debate in the 2006 governor's race, Halcro faced off against Sarah and watched her absorb repeated questions about her strong opposition to abortion, which she personally believes should occur only when the mother's life is threatened. She gently asked the host if those same questions would be posed to her opponents, who came off resoundingly pro-choice. She also made her point, Halcro explained to *Time* magazine, that this line of questioning devalued her larger mission: fixing the leadership in Juneau.

She targeted Murkowski's handling of the closed-door gas-pipeline negotiations. "Alaskans are wondering whose interests are being served," she said, urging open negotiations and a goal of an all-Alaskan line that would provide fuel for homes instate and out. She promised to reinstitute the longevity bonus and took aim at Murkowski's Westwind II jet. "The jet . . . strange priority," Sarah told the crowd. "It exemplifies everything that's wrong right now with state government."

In August, Palin also visited Ketchikan, where there was much discussion about building a bridge that would provide access to Ketchikan's airport on Gravina Island, which had a population of about fifty. The price tag was $233 million in federal money, and it was a pork-barrel project engineered by Alaska's U.S. senator, Ted Stevens. Alaska's lone congressman, Don Young, also supported what would later be labeled "The Bridge to Nowhere."

So did Sarah at the time. "We need to come to the defense of southeast Alaska when proposals are on the table like the bridge, and not allow the spinmeisters to turn this project or any other into something that's so negative," Sarah said in August 2006, according to the *Ketchikan Daily News*.

Old friend Steve MacDonald, who supervised Sarah when she worked at KTVA CBS in the early 1990s, was now KTUU NBC news director. "Whatever you want to say about Sarah Palin, never underestimate her. I remember her as a young mom who didn't seem politically astute and said she was going to run for city council, and then she won two terms. Then she ran for mayor against John Stein, and I said, 'That's brutal, Stein is enmeshed in Wasilla. She will get creamed.' And she beat him! And then Stein went after her in 1999, and she creamed him. That's when I said to myself, 'OK, I will never underestimate her again.' So when she ran for lieutenant governor in 2002 and barely lost to Sen. Loren Leman, a guy who was politically connected and had the backing of the Republican Party, that's when they knew what they had in Sarah. After that, they asked her to help Governor Murkowski get elected." Yet even after Sarah had her much-publicized falling out with the state GOP over the Ruedrich and Renkes scandals, MacDonald said it would be foolish to write her off. "Don't underestimate her," he said.

Sarah's message got through, and she surged to a double-digit lead in the polls a month before the August primary vote. As she moved ahead, both Murkowski and Binkley launched negative campaigns, with Binkley extracting an old editorial from the *Frontiersman*, the one that blasted Sarah's credibility as mayor and hinted that a recall might be in order. In a response to Binkley's ad, Sarah characterized those difficult days as a learning experience that prepared her for future executive service, and then she ripped Binkley for putting together "the worst of several ads" that he and Murkowski distributed to distort her record. The *Frontiersman* also issued a statement saying Binkley's mailer was misleading, and there was "praise" for Sarah later in her administration.

Murkowski drummed up the old charge that Sarah had used the Wasilla mayor's office to aid her campaign for lieutenant governor. This was done to detract from her effort to have Republican Party chairman Randy Ruedrich kicked off the AOGCC. Sarah came out and apologized for any mistakes she committed as mayor but characterized the attack as a "smear campaign." She was not formally accused of any ethics violations.

Murkowski was a victim of bad luck, bad policies, and the youthful energy that characterized Sarah Palin. He lost badly to Sarah in the August Republican primary in what was regarded as one of the biggest upsets in state political history. Sarah garnered fifty-one percent of the vote to Murkowski's nineteen percent, with Binkley coming in second with thirty percent. Crucial to the campaign was the state's goal of constructing a natural-gas pipeline from the North Slope into Canada, a project critical to the state's economy. "It has to be pushed hard," Sarah said after her victory. "It is the future of the Alaska economy."

Just after the primary, the state political scene was shaken when the FBI searched the offices of six Alaska legislators. Authorities were looking for financial links between lawmakers and the now-defunct oil-field services company VECO Corp. In May 2007, VECO executives Bill Allen, CEO, and Richard Smith, vice president, pleaded guilty to charges of paying out $400,000 in bribes to Alaska public officials to gain support of a crude-oil-profits tax favoring the oil industry. Four lawmakers were later arrested, and VECO-related investigations were begun on Congressman Don Young and Sen. Ted Stevens, who was later convicted on seven felony counts after Allen admitted he had company workers remodel Stevens' Girdwood, Alaska, home. The wrongdoing would cost Stevens his Senate job in 2008, when he was defeated by Democratic challenger Mark Begich, the mayor of Anchorage. None of the candidates for governor was involved, but it raised the whole question of ethics reform and voter trust, issues Sarah had been harping on for months. KTUU TV journalist Bill McAllister, who later went to work for Sarah, had a name for this phenomenon—this innate ability Sarah had for knowing just which issues to present to voters: "Sarah-dipity."

On primary election night, her grassroots volunteers gathered at the Captain Cook Hotel in Anchorage to watch the results come in. A victorious Sarah led 400-plus volunteers and campaign workers on a downtown march to the election center in the Egan Building four blocks away. They waved "Palin for Governor" signs and chanted Sarah's name. On the night of her victory, she boldly asked rival Randy Ruedrich to resign as Republican Party chair—he refused. She subsequently learned the Republican cupboard for the governor's race was bare, though Ruedrich said they did manage to come up with about $70,000. By October, Sarah and her lieutenant governor running mate, Sean Parnell, had raised $788,319, about $70,000 less than Democratic nominee Tony Knowles. However, the Palin ticket was helped by the Republican Governors Association, which sprang for a series of TV ads. Sarah also rallied 1,200 volunteers around the state to spread her message.

In the last weeks of the campaign, Sarah was absent from a few scheduled events and didn't appear sharp in a couple of forums. As the front-runner, which she was for virtually the entire race, she had the prerogative to pick and choose what she would do. But in one education forum, Knowles, sixty-three, delivered a four-year plan to improve education, while Sarah talked generally about making education a high priority and then shared her personal story about growing up as the daughter of a schoolteacher. Her opponents scoffed, and newsman Bill McAllister, who was working on Sarah's campaign, said Knowles couldn't comprehend why the media didn't jump all over her for not providing specifics.

Her opponents couldn't make anything stick. She said she would favor Mat-Su Valley if she were elected governor, which caused her rivals to suggest that other Alaskans should be worried. Just as when she was mayor, abortion became an issue in a candidates' debates, and later, when Knowles, trailing in the polls, sent out 8,000 letters to pro-choice voters stating that Sarah wouldn't say if she'd block or support an abortion ban if elected. Sarah said everyone knew her personal position, and it was a nonissue, but she added she would not sign into law anything that would supersede the Supreme Court's ruling. Creation science also entered the debate when Palin said she would support teaching it alongside evolution in public schools. "Teach both," she said in a debate on KAKM Channel 7, though she backed off the statement later, saying she would not urge the state board of education to add creation-based coursework to required curriculums.

She also got involved in the Mat-Su Borough mayor's race, supporting old friend Curtis Menard Sr. over her former Wasilla police chief, Charlie Fannon, whom she had backed and worked for in his unsuccessful bid for Mat-Su mayor three years earlier. Radio talk-show host Rick Rydell asked, "Can she keep focused on the bigger mission?"

She did. In the stretch run, the race tightened and

would be decided by the ten percent of the voters who were undecided. Sarah got a key endorsement from popular U.S. Sen. Ted Stevens, who had yet to be tainted by scandal. Knowles, a former two-term governor, did well, picking up endorsements from major corporations such as Conoco Phillips, Providence Health Systems, and Northrim Bank. The major daily papers in Juneau and Anchorage also rallied behind Knowles. Knowles spent $1.3 million to Sarah's $900,000. But on November 7, Sarah Palin, all of forty-two, became Alaska's youngest ever and first female governor. She bested runner-up Tony Knowles forty-eight percent to forty-one percent, with Halcro earning nine percent. When she became the statistical winner, she shouted, "All right, are you ready for a new Alaska?" The Egan Convention Center rocked as several hundred supporters waved their red-and-white Palin signs and cheered mightily for the governor-elect. "I think this is unlike anything Alaska has seen before."

The fresh perspective, her staunch support of ethics reform, her mandate for change, and her profile as an outsider formed an immovable foundation to her campaign. Knowles and Halcro were more politically savvy and had a better handle on the issues. They insisted she lacked experience. Even Sarah admitted as much in a debate, complimenting Halcro for his grasp of facts and figures but coyly adding she wasn't certain any of it mattered. "The voters aren't looking for perfection," she said. "If they are looking for perfection, they should vote for God," she told a reporter. "They aren't looking for professional politicians who are going to pretend to have every answer. They are looking for honesty. For people who are ready to work with others to build a state."

The small-town mayor's message resonated in many of Alaska's small towns, from Palmer to Kenai. They liked her lifestyle—basketball jock, hockey mom, hunter, snow-machiner, and political outsider who grew up on moose burgers and caribou steaks. Her catch-phrases "new energy" and "fresh faces" caught on. They liked her plain talk even though she didn't have all the solutions. This fight was the precursor to the Joe Sixpack campaign she would run in two years with John McCain. "It's about timing," she said.

Even primary opponent John Binkley was sold. He said she was carried by "everyday Alaskans who have been empowered by Sarah Palin. I think she's going to restore faith and trust of the Alaskan people in the government."

TWELVE
NEW SENSATION

O n the day of her gubernatorial inauguration, December 4, Sarah turned to an old friend and mentor, Paul Riley, her former minister from Wasilla Assembly of God church, to give the convocation prayer before four thousand people. "It was the most exciting thing I had ever gone to," said Helen Riley. "Paul was very humbled."

While Sarah clearly holds affection for Riley, she had left the Wasilla Assembly of God church, having switched to Wasilla Bible Church in 2002. A close family friend, Adele Morgan, told the *New York Times* that the Palins moved over to Wasilla Bible because it was less extreme and more tolerant than the Assemblies of God, where some parishioners speak in tongues and practice miraculous healings. Todd also may have had something to do with the change. "Sarah is the more religious of the two," said Jim Palin, Todd's father. "I think he is spiritual. But he doesn't go to church as much as Sarah does." So perhaps a place of worship that was a little less intense was preferable.

At Wasilla Bible, Sarah and Todd can arrive late and leave early, sitting in the back and worshiping quietly without a barrage of political sermons. Assemblies minister Ed Kalnins once suggested that supporters of John Kerry in the 2004 presidential election would never get to heaven, according to the *Anchorage Daily News*. Kalnins later said the remark was meant as a joke. Wasilla Bible Church has also come under scrutiny, participating in a program that counsels gays to overcome their homosexuality through prayer. Sarah would join another Christian church in Juneau to attend when she wasn't in Wasilla.

After the inauguration, she sought out Riley for some spiritual advice. Sarah was in search of a biblical example of a great leader, and she wanted to know the secret of his leadership. Riley cited the Old Testament story of Esther, a beautiful queen and the hero of the Jewish holiday of Purim. Esther was married to a powerful Persian king who was unaware of his wife's Jewish heritage. One day, when the king's prime minister convinced him that all the Jews must die, Esther intervened and not only saved the Jews but had their enemies in the plot put down. Riley's point was that when Esther was called to action, God granted her a power she never knew she had. "God has given [Sarah] the strength to serve," he told the *New York Times*. "And God has given her the strength to carry out her goals."

In the first months of her administration, Sarah's critics watched her closely to see if her faith would influence her governing style. Sarah, though, had learned long ago not to let her religious beliefs guide her policy. While she had said that she wouldn't mind seeing creationism taught alongside Darwinism, she kept her pledge and did nothing to promote the idea. She also vetoed legislation that would have rejected health benefits to workers in same-sex relationships, heeding advice that it was unconstitutional. And later, she refused to grant a special session of the House and Senate on two abortion proposals because they would have impeded the special session she was holding for her most important issue: the bill promoting a new natural-gas pipeline.

Days after winning the race for governor, Sarah made a to-do list and began the process of shaping her administration. It was still to be determined how she and Todd, the man she introduced to the state as "First Dude," would split the family between Juneau and Wasilla. It was expected that Todd would take some time off from his job on the North Slope.

The early campaign promises included:

- Restoring the longevity bonus, a $250-a-month payout to Alaska's elderly. Low oil prices had caused Murkowski to jettison the program because the state was short on revenue.

- Unloading the state jet purchased by Murkowski. After the election, Sarah met with her rival, Murkowski, who warned her she would regret selling the jet once she started traveling for the job. Sarah wasn't about to change her mind, saying she'd use one of the King Air propeller planes, which are cheaper to run, or fly commercial. "I will figure out the best way to get rid of it," she told a reporter.

- Mending fences with the legislature, which had a strained relationship with Murkowski.

- Submitting a budget for the legislature by mid-December.

- Beginning negotiations with companies that would like to build the gas pipeline.

Sarah also had to make a multitude of appointments to various state board, cabinet, and agency posts and review thirty-five appointments Murkowski made in his last hour on the job. "We'll keep the good ones," she said.

While she kept most of the appointments, she did reject the selection of Jim Clark, Murkowski's chief of staff, to the sensitive Alaska Natural Gas Development Authority Board, which was charged with negotiating with oil companies to build the Alaskan natural-gas pipeline.

A week later, she made five other appointments, none more curious than Talis Colberg of Palmer, a small-town worker's compensation lawyer Sarah chose as her attorney general. Sarah cited his honesty and work ethic and his prior experience serving on the Mat-Su Borough Assembly, similar to a county government.

Colberg himself seemed somewhat surprised at the appointment, having expressed no opinions on the prevailing issues of the day, such as benefits for partners of gay state employees. Nor did he have any criminal trial experience or management background to supervise a department of five hundred employees. "Certainly it's an improbable event that I would be here today," he told a reporter. "There's no doubt about it." Sarah said she wanted someone without a personal agenda on issues, and she wanted objectivity. She liked that he was coming in with a clean slate. But legislative leaders didn't have a clue about his background.

"He's something of a blank slate," said Democratic Anchorage Sen. Hollis French. "I'm looking to get to know him better."

In the weeks that followed, Sarah made several other appointments—old pals from Wasilla High and members from her church, according to the *New York Times*. While critics raised questions about the qualifications of some of her choices, Sarah prized loyalty above all else. Moreover, it's not surprising that several of her appointments also worked on her campaign, which is fairly standard party patronage for an incoming executive.

For the $95,000 directorship of the State Division of Agriculture, she chose Franci Havemeister, a former real estate agent who "cited her childhood love of cows as a qualification," the *Times* reported. For the $82,908 head of the economic development office, she named old high school friend Joe Austerman, who ran a Mail Boxes Etc. franchise. For the position of legislative director, she picked junior-high band mate John Bitney, but the *New York Times* reported that he later lost his job because he fell in love with the wife of a close Palin friend. He was later hired by Alaska's speaker of the House, Republican John Harris, who told the *Times* he subsequently received a call from Todd Palin saying he was unhappy that Bitney was working for him. Todd reportedly said he never mentioned Bitney by name in the conversation. Bitney married the woman, Deborah Richter, who was Sarah's gubernatorial campaign treasurer and was later hired by Sarah's administration to serve as director of the state division that disburses dividends to Alaskans from the state's oil-wealth savings account.

Arranging the family move to Juneau was another priority for Sarah. She had visited the governor's mansion once before, as a teenager playing for her high school basketball team. "It was locked, and we couldn't go in," she told a reporter. This time, she got a set of keys when she moved in with Todd and her three daughters in December. Bristol, Willow, and Piper picked out their new bedrooms and enrolled in the local Juneau schools. They also helped their mother and father host an open house at the mansion, which drew thousands of Juneau residents who had never been inside the residence before. Dubbed "The People's House" by Sarah herself, it was decorated in a holiday theme with wreaths, ornaments, and red ribbons. Sarah and Todd stood in the receiving line for almost four hours. "Everything was beautiful," said Sandy Parnell, wife of Lieutenant Governor Sean Parnell.

Back in Wasilla, Track stayed behind, spending part of the year playing junior hockey in Michigan before returning home to wrap up his senior year at Wasilla High. Todd went back and forth between Juneau and Wasilla—he was training for the 2007 Iron Dog with partner Scott Davis. A year before, they were part of the

Iron Dog's closest finish ever. Todd and Scott had the lead going into the last leg of the race and lost by one second—that's right, one second after two thousand miles of riding.

When the race got under way in February 2007, Sarah was the official starter. She traveled from Juneau to Anchorage with the three girls, charging the state $519.30 for each round-trip ticket for each daughter, according to the Associated Press. Little noticed at the time was that she noted on her expense report that her girls joined her for the trip to "open the start of the Iron Dog race." Later, that expense form was corrected to explain the girls' business as "First family official starter for the start of the Iron Dog race."

Several days later, she waved Todd and Scott across the finish line in Fairbanks—in first place. That was the second time Todd and Sarah had scored back-to-back firsts, the last time being Sarah's victory in the 1999 Wasilla Mayor's race and Todd's win in the 2000 Iron Dog. Todd now had four Iron Dog titles under his belt.

As the legislative session got under way in Juneau, Sarah was still trying to figure out how to sell Murkowski's jet. In December, she put the plane up for sale on eBay, a fact she alluded to a year later when she spoke to the Republican Convention crowd in

Minnesota. But she never sold the plane through the auction site, despite trying to sell it there three more times. Sarah was gunning for $2.5 million, but the state could only muster a $2-million offer in January, when the plane was posted on the site for the second time. In the end, Sarah hired a private broker to unload it, at a loss of more than $400,000.

Meanwhile, the state was stuck with $62,000 in quarterly payments for the loan on the twenty-three-year-old jet, which was finally sold to an Alaskan businessman for $2.1 million later in the year. "The eBay thing didn't work out very well," a state official said. But the company sure got great publicity thanks to Sarah's speech.

Back in Palmer, Curtis Menard Sr. was sitting at home one day when his wife arrived with a new puppy, a bloodhound. She decided the Palin girls needed a dog to keep them company in Juneau. Sarah named the cuddly pup AGIA, after the Alaska Gasoline Inducement Act, a bill working its way through the legislature that would allow the state to license an oil company to build the 1,715-mile natural-gas pipeline from Prudhoe Bay to the Alberta hub in Canada. Lawmakers approved AGIA, and the license was eventually awarded to a Canadian company, TransCanada Alaska.

As for AGIA the dog, he was a hit with the Palin

girls but made a mess of the governor's mansion. Everyone was too busy to train him. When the family returned to Wasilla that summer, AGIA went with them, and Sarah asked if the Menards wouldn't mind taking him back. She figured AGIA deserved a better fate and would have more fun running around the Menard homestead than being cooped up in a mansion.

Still, the governor's honeymoon was in full swing. Sarah's approval ratings were chart-topping. In May 2007, the numbers came in making her the most popular governor in the nation. Ivan Moore Research recorded an approval rating of eighty-nine percent, with a second poll by Dittman Research showing a ninety-three percent approval rating. Not bad for someone on the job six months. Even Randy Ruedrich was a believer, telling the *Anchorage Daily News*, "She's managed to communicate well with Alaskans, and that's what popularity is all about."

The VECO Corp. scandal also may have kept her ratings up, as executives Bill Allen and Richard Smith pleaded guilty to bribing lawmakers. The negative news only seemed to amplify Sarah's "anti-establishment and anti-corruption" credentials, said Larry Sabato, a political scientist at the Center for Politics at the University of Virginia. The momentum enabled her to put through a bipartisan ethics-reform bill that she signed into law later in the year. It required lobbyists to report food and drinks they bought politicians in excess of fifteen dollars, and it prevented donations to lawmakers above $250 from the same person in a year. In addition, all contributions to campaigns above $1,000 must be reported publicly.

In late May, Sarah returned to Wasilla to speak at Wasilla High's commencement ceremony. Track was a member of that class of 2007. Sarah took the stage to cheers from her hometown crowd and spoke to the largest graduating class in Mat-Su Valley history, 270 seniors. "Warriors, what a shining season we've had," she said, referring to state titles won by the boys and girls basketball teams. "This is a class of champions."

Palin watched as two senior-class officers and three valedictorians addressed the students and their families. Her sympathies ran with the underdogs in the class. "For those of you feeling like you're middle of the road, lost in the crowd," she said to the graduating class, "that's most of us." Every graduate "has a specific destiny," even the most "undistinguished student has an important role in the final cosmic calculus. Seek what it is you are created to do," she said. "Nothing is an accident."

Back in Juneau, Sarah also looked around the mansion itself to make cost-cutting measures. In June, she let go the governor's chef, Stefani Marnon, who had been cooking for governors since the mid-1990s. "Bottom line is the governor does not need a gourmet chef at the mansion," said Sarah's spokeswoman, Meghan Stapleton. "From the start, she has been very uncomfortable with a gourmet chef. It's a luxury item she doesn't think Alaskans should be paying for." Sarah viewed Marnon's departure as a sacrifice she had to make because other departments were cutting back. "She wants to do her part," said Stapleton. Sarah also felt it was superfluous to have a full-time chef if she was not living at the mansion year-round. She told voters that she would get by just fine; she could cook a meal, and the kids could make sandwiches in a pinch. As for events at the mansion, Sarah felt it was more economical to hire someone as needed, such as during the winter legislative session when the governor did more entertaining.

Marnon wasn't actually laid off. The *Anchorage Daily News* reported that she was reassigned as a "constituent relations assistant" in the governor's office before finding a position as a chef for the Alaska legislative lounge.

But her departure from the mansion sent a signal to Juneau lawmakers. It meant in all likelihood that Sarah and the Palins were not going to make Juneau their full-time home in the future, which would be a first for a sitting governor. Sarah wasn't saying yet what her plans were, but after the Palin girls finished up the school year in Juneau, they returned to Wasilla with their mother, who would work out of the governor's Anchorage office.

Later in the summer, Sarah made her first overseas trip as governor, traveling to Kuwait to visit the 575 Alaska National Guard troops based in the Middle East country. She watched training exercises and participated in firearms drills, though not with live rounds. During the trip, she met with soldiers, got a tour of the base from commanding officers, and posed for a famous picture showing Alaska's governor looking very comfortable aiming a rifle at a camera taking her picture. Meeting with members of the Alaska media via teleconference, she said the temperature was 127 degrees. "It's like taking a steam bath all day long," she said. She was amazed at how native Alaskans survived in such weather when they were used to chilly summers and freezing winters. She also mentioned that her son, Track, had said he was thinking of joining the service, something she wouldn't be opposed to if he decided he wanted to do it, she said.

The office commute was a little longer now—forty miles one way, as opposed to the short walk she enjoyed in Juneau. Sarah commuted in a state-issued Chevy Suburban, and by the end of the summer, her mind was made up. The family would not return to Juneau in the fall. In fact, Sarah announced she would not arrive until the legislative session was under way in January. Later, to accommodate staff, she spent $45,157 in taxpayers' funds to remodel three offices in her Anchorage suite. Critics called the remodeling excessive, while supporters found it reasonable.

In an interview with the *Anchorage Daily News*, Sarah said that while the experience in Juneau was positive, the kids felt more comfortable in Wasilla, where there was extended family, cousins, and grandparents to alleviate the pressures that came with being the children of a governor. "There were a few incidents that would not have happened had I not been elected governor," she said, reflecting on their time in Juneau. In one instance, one of her daughters got a nasty e-mail saying, "Your mom sucks as our governor," Sarah confided to a reporter.

Sarah decided it made more sense for the kids to return to familiar ground; although when the time came to return to Juneau, she would end up taking Piper and Willow out of school in Wasilla and bringing them along to the state capital. If Sarah were needed earlier in Juneau, she could always fly there, she reasoned. "I'll travel where Alaskans need me," she said.

That fall, the girls reenrolled in Wasilla public schools. Todd, meanwhile, had returned to work on the North Slope after spending parts of June and July commercial fishing in Bristol Bay. Sarah joined him for part of the time. Track was attending college and playing junior hockey for the Alaska Avalanche, a program that gets young players ready for college-level hockey. Sarah said even Track wasn't immune to the occasional needling that came with being the son of a governor. "He's getting ready to play juniors there, and some kid is telling him, 'Oh, it's political. [You made the team] just because your mom is governor.' But overall, the experience has been good for the family."

On September 11, Track put his hockey career on hold and made good on his interest in joining the military. He enlisted in the Army, signing up at the recruiting office in Wasilla. "He didn't ask our permission," Sarah told *People* magazine. "He's young, strong, and smart, and this is a good positive step for him. He gave up hockey to do this, and I'm very supportive. I believe in the cause, and hope and pray we have a worthy cause."

Todd was a little less enthusiastic than Sarah regarding Track's decision. While his father, Jim, had served in the Army, Todd told *People,* his only regret was that Track—who has an Alaska tattoo on his shoulder and a Christian fish on his calf—didn't explore other branches of the service more thoroughly before enlisting. But he supported his son's decision. "He's an independent young man," Todd said.

Track received an assignment at Fort Wainwright, Alaska. He was trained to operate an armored eight-wheeled, nineteen-ton vehicle called a Stryker and serve as a bodyguard for brigade leaders. The commander, Army Colonel Burt Thompson, said Track had no preferential treatment during training. In 2008 his unit deployed to Iraq and reportedly was sent to Diyala, the fourth most violent of Iraq's provinces. On the day his unit departed for overseas, Sarah went to Fairbanks and gave a speech to the four hundred members of Track's unit, the Army's First Stryker Brigade, Delta Company. Track stood with his unit as Sarah spoke from her heart: "As you depart us, your parents, your friends and family, allow for a few tears and [allow us] to hold you closer before you're gone."

In October 2007, Sarah held a special session for the legislature to vote on a proposal to hike oil taxes from 22.5 percent to 25.0 percent. The increase would add another $1.5 billion a year for state services. With the support of a bipartisan group of legislators who helped reshape her proposal into even stronger legislation, a strengthened version of Sarah's Alaska's Clear and Equitable Share bill passed both houses by an overwhelming 2–1 margin, despite fierce opposition from the oil industry and influential legislative leaders. It was fortuitous timing, as gasoline prices were climbing. Sarah told a reporter that the bill was designed to extract more for the state when prices were skyrocketing and when the companies could afford it, while including provisions to invest in new fields.

That first year in office also increased Sarah's national profile, as she got high marks as an ethics reformer, for engineering the oil-tax hike and for reinvigorating oil-industry interest in building the gas pipeline, which had roadblocks under the Murkowski administration. The state even hired a media consultant for $31,000 to place Sarah on news shows and in national magazines, positioning her as an oil-and-gas expert who could promote Alaska's interest in building a natural-gas pipeline. As the pipeline project progressed, Sarah's stock rose, and she was invited to appear on Fox News and CNN. *Vogue* magazine did a profile, and just after Christmas 2007, the *Daily News* speculated Sarah might leave the governor's post for higher office before her term expired in 2010. Sarah played it down. "My role as governor is where I can be most helpful right now unless something drastic happens, and I don't anticipate that right now," she told the *Daily News*.

But things were happening. *Newsweek* profiled Sarah in its "Women & Power" issue. Her name already was surfacing as a running mate for a Republican presidential contender.

Ever cognizant of Alaska's image, Sarah reversed herself on her controversial support for the Gravina Island bridge, the cost of which had ballooned to $400 million. She had previously said she would support state funding for the so-called Bridge to Nowhere, but Sarah halted state work on the project in September 2007 when there was a national backlash against pork-barrel projects. The federal dollars for the $400-million bridge were transferred to other state transportation projects. Her office issued a release stating that all state work on the bridge had ceased because the bridge had become "a symbol of what critics said was wrong with federal budget earmarks."

One of those national critics of the bridge was John McCain. "I think that's when [Sarah's] campaign for national office began," Ketchikan mayor Bob Weinstein told the *Anchorage Daily News*.

In Sarah's private life, things were heating up, too. Her sister Molly, who helped her out by driving Piper to and from school and taking her to activities, was still having problems with ex-husband Mike Wooten over their custody arrangement with the two kids they had together, daughter McKinley, six, and son Heath, four. But the public wasn't privy to that aspect of Sarah's personal life.

Sarah had another personal matter to tend to. On

December 4, the anniversary of her gubernatorial inauguration, she was sitting in her Anchorage office when
she got a call from her doctor. She asked if the governor
had some time that afternoon to stop by her office. Sarah
sat up in her chair and politely asked her doctor just to
give it to her straight over the phone. "The baby you're
carrying," she said, "has Down syndrome."

THIRTEEN
A STARTING FIVE

When Sarah and Todd got married, they talked of having a large family. "Let's field a starting five," Sarah suggested. Track and Bristol arrived back-to-back, and then Willow joined the team four years later. When Piper arrived in 2001, they figured that might be it. Sarah was already three years shy of her fortieth birthday, and the couple was convinced they were all done. "We got our final four," they joked to friends. But late in the summer of 2007, that fifth starter emerged in the embryonic form of Trig Palin.

Sarah kept mum about the pregnancy until October. Todd had figured it out but was discreet enough not to say a word. When Sarah finally gave him the great news, she said with a shrug, "Life is full of surprises," she told *People* magazine. Todd was ecstatic. He had always wanted another son, friends said, and his oldest boy had just signed up for a stint in the army, and the country was in the middle of a war. There was no telling what might happen if Track were called to serve in the theater, which he eventually was.

For the next five months, Todd and Sarah kept the pregnancy a secret. Any thoughts of breaking the news early to their kids were scuttled when Sarah learned her baby had Down syndrome after having amniocentesis at thirteen weeks. Todd was away working when her family doctor, Cathy Baldwin-Johnson, called with the news. Sarah drove over to Johnson's office, discussed the implications, and received some reading materials on the disorder. Then she headed home to ponder her fate.

Over the next couple of days, she read everything she could on the disorder. She learned that Down syndrome afflicts 350,000 Americans and affects one in 733 pregnancies, but the odds jump significantly after age forty, when the disease is known to beset one in forty pregnancies. It's caused by the existence of an extra chromosome in the fetal cells and results in physical and intellectual disabilities, which can vary from child to child. Some children cannot speak until age four, and half of the infants are born with a hole in the heart, as was the case with Trig. If the holes don't close, surgery is often required (Trig, fortunately, avoided surgery). Thyroid, intestinal, and vision problems also require treatment. Families are frequently in for a long haul of specialized speech, physical, and occupational therapy.

There was never any question about keeping the baby, and Sarah explained later that the one reason she did amnio was simply to be prepared for any eventuality. It was time, she said, to walk the walk and not just talk the talk.

When Todd returned from his trip, she broke the news to him gently during a quiet moment at home. Tears welling in her eyes, she said, "The good news is we have a boy. But we have a challenge." Unwavering in his support, Todd said, "Awesome! I'm getting another boy."

It may not have been part of their plan, the couple believed, but certainly it was part of a greater plan. "Why not us?" Todd said.

Sarah continued keeping her secret from the public and her children. Not discussing the pregnancy with her daughters, she felt, would shorten the process for them and spare them from unwanted attention. "I didn't want Alaskans to fear I would not be able to fulfill my duties," she told *People*. "Not knowing in my own heart if I was going to be ready to embrace a child with special needs . . . I couldn't talk about it."

Sarah continued her normal activities. She drank her coffee and continued driving to work. Baggier clothes and strategically placed scarves and shawls helped conceal the baby bump. The daily jog fell by the wayside, replaced with the occasional aerobics workout. Sarah made one slipup; one of the girls found a prenatal ultrasound scan of Trig, but Sarah dampened suspicion by explaining it away. When the legislative session got under way after Christmas, Sarah moved to Juneau, this time taking just Piper and Willow. Todd stayed back home working on the slope and training for the Iron Dog. Bristol withdrew from Wasilla High and moved to Anchorage to live with her aunt and uncle, Heather and Kurt Bruce, and their three children. She finished the year up at West High and held down two part-time jobs serving lattes at espresso shops. "I really think she's going to run her own business someday," Heather Bruce said.

"I liked having her around," Heather added. "She stayed in a spare bedroom and did her studies and helped around the house. She was a great girl, and my husband adored her. I loved having her stay here so much I told her if she wanted to come back to Anchorage and go to college, she was welcome. She's very mature for her age. Very athletic and always has a smile on her face."

Heather explained the move was convenient in many ways. Bristol was closer to the airport, so she could get on a plane to Juneau to see her mother or visit her at the governor's Anchorage office when Sarah was in town.

Bristol did have to cope with the physical distance between herself and her Wasilla boyfriend, Levi Johnston, a schoolboy hockey player whom she had been dating on and off for three years. Johnston played club and high school hockey in Wasilla and was known to get into mischief from time to time. In 2007, he was fined $370 for salmon fishing in closed waters, not exactly an uncommon crime in this neck of the woods. On a My-Space Website page, it was said that he liked to "kick ass," but in an interview later on, he claimed a friend posted the page. Local hockey coaches lauded Levi for his hustle and teamwork and his knack for making teammates better. He was prompt for practices and games and was not a behavior problem on the ice. Wasilla contractor Berkley Tilton, whose sons are friends with Levi, said Levi home-schooled during high school and spent part of his junior year at Burchell High School, a small alternative school on the north side of town. He was also studying to be an electrician. Tilton said if Levi had his druthers, he'd rather be hunting moose than sitting in a classroom. "He loves sports and the outdoors," he said.

Though Bristol and Levi were separated by a distance of forty miles, there was certainly no ban on them dating. Levi used to drive to Anchorage to take Bristol out. Heather said, "He used to bring her flowers and take her to dinner and a movie. He would come in and say hello, but he says few words. He's a quiet boy."

In February, Todd and his Iron Dog partner Scott Davis prepared for the 2008 race. Todd and Davis didn't win, but Todd certainly added to his legacy as a tough competitor. "First Dude" was two-thirds of the way through the race and traveling sixty miles per hour in a storm outside Nome when his snow machine collided with a fifty-five-gallon barrel camouflaged by fresh snow. "I didn't see this," he told a reporter. "It just caught me by surprise."

The snow machine came to a halt, but Todd was hurled seventy feet from his overturned Arctic Cat. Davis doubled back and found his partner keeled over in the snow, holding his broken right arm. Davis put him on the back of his machine and rushed him to the closest hospital, but Todd refused to see a doctor, perhaps knowing he could be scratched from the race because of his injury. "He wouldn't let me take him to the doctor," Davis told the *Washington Post*. "It said a lot about his character, not giving up." The next morning, Todd wrapped his arm in duct tape, and they went out to try to repair his machine. They got it up and running, but it conked out fifty miles from the finish line. Davis pulled Todd and his machine the rest of the way in thirty-five-below temperatures.

At the finish line in Fairbanks, Sarah, in a red parka and snow boots, waited nervously in subzero temperatures. It was Sarah's official duty to wave the winners across. Sarah decided to make it a family affair and had brought along the three girls to meet their dad after the race. They stayed at the Princess Lodge in Fairbanks for two nights, and the girls had their own room at a rate of $129 per night, which Sarah later billed to the state. The day before they met Todd at the finish line, Sarah and the girls attended an American Heart Association luncheon. The organizer said Sarah had asked to bring Piper to the event and was caught off guard when Sarah showed up with all three girls. They quickly found two more places at the main table so the family could sit together. "When it's the governor, you just make it happen," organizer Jane Bartels told the Associated Press.

On February 16, Davis pulled Todd and his damaged machine across the finish line. Sarah walked over and gave him a long embrace. "If there's a way he's going to finish the race, he's going to finish it," she said. "The last thing he wanted to do was scratch."

A few minutes before leaving work on March 5, Sarah held a press conference in her Juneau office and finally announced her pregnancy. She said, "Expect a new member of the first family," and then she headed out to a reception at the Baranof Hotel with her family to dine on king crab. Reporters stood there in disbelief. In fact, Sarah had to announce the pregnancy three different ways before anyone knew what she was talking about. "That the pregnancy is so advanced astonished all who heard the news," the *Daily News* reported. "The governor, a runner who's always been trim, simply doesn't look pregnant." Not even her staff was aware until the same day. "I thought it was becoming obvious," Sarah said. "Clothes getting snugger and snugger."

Though the baby was due in mid-May, the pregnancy certainly hadn't slowed her down. She had spent the previous few weeks increasing her national profile; she had traveled to Washington, D.C., for the National Governors' Conference, where she met privately with John McCain and caught the Arizona senator's eye, as a potential running mate for the GOP ticket. "To any critics who say a woman can't think and work and carry a baby at the same time, I'd like to just escort that Neanderthal back to the cave," she said after announcing her pregnancy.

Sarah didn't mention a word about Trig's condition, which was still a secret. Her plan was to announce that about a month before his due date, but Trig decided to come out a little early.

As she approached the last month of her pregnancy, Sarah planned one last trip: attending the Republican Governors Association meeting in Texas. It was going to be her last flight before Trig's arrival. Sarah was scheduled to be a keynote speaker, and she felt it was something she couldn't pass up. On the morning of April 17, the day she was set to address the governors, the Braxton-Hicks contractions that had been plaguing Sarah in recent weeks started picking up their pace. She awoke in her hotel room at 4 a.m., noticed the amniotic fluid was leaking, and called her doctor in Wasilla. Todd got on his phone and arranged another return flight right after the keynote address. If she could, she was going to give that speech, and she did. Then they left the hotel immediately and flew back to Alaska, with a stop-over in Seattle. Perhaps Murkowski was right—maybe Sarah should have kept the jet, because it certainly would have come in handy at this juncture.

Sarah was in touch with her doctor throughout. Her contractions steadied at one to two an hour, which her doctor, Cathy Baldwin-Johnson, who is not an obstetrician but has delivered many children, including Piper, determined was "not active labor," she told a reporter. "I don't think it was unreasonable for her to continue to travel back," she said. However, Dr. Laura Gregg, who works with the American College of Obstetricians and Gynecologists, said there's no difference between water breaking and leaking amniotic fluid. When that happens, she recommends going to the hospital immediately because of the risk for infection to the baby. The organization also discourages flying after thirty-six weeks, putting Sarah right on the cusp. But Sarah showed no signs of distress on the Alaska Airlines flight, an airline spokesman said. Sarah said she wouldn't have risked the baby's health to have him in Alaska. Todd joked, "You can't have a fish picker from Texas."

After her commercial flight touched down in Anchorage, Todd drove her to the regional hospital in Mat-Su Valley, where her family was waiting. On Friday morning—eight hours after touchdown—Sarah gave birth to a six-pound, two-ounce baby boy. Track, an army private, was in Fort Wainwright and couldn't be on hand, but he called in, and they left a line open in Sarah's room so he could hear when the kids met their new brother.

As the girls gathered around the hospital bed, Willow studied Trig as Sarah cradled him in her arms. She noticed the slanted eyes and the lower ears, the characteristics of a baby with Down syndrome.

In her interview with *People* magazine, Sarah recounted the conversation. "He looks like he has Down syndrome," Willow said, looking at her mother. Sarah tried to reassure her daughter. "If he does, you know you will still love him, Willow. It'll be okay." Unsatisfied, Willow asked, "Why didn't you tell us?" Sarah went into an explanation about how she wanted to keep the pregnancy short for their sake, and she also admitted she was busy and hadn't reconciled her own ambivalent feelings. She apologized to her children for the deception but wanted them to understand: "Trig is perfection, and I cannot imagine life without him." Willow was completely forgiving, telling her mother that none of that mattered; Trig, whose name is derived from two Norse meanings—"Brave victory" and "True"—was her brother, and she loved him.

For the rest of the day, Sarah returned to the business of being a governor, sending out BlackBerry messages and even signing a bill. She received a few visitors—old friend Linda Menard from her Miss Wasilla days dropped by—and she issued a press release through her office announcing the birth. She also sent out a two-page e-mail letter to her friends and relatives. Writing eleven days earlier, Sarah used the letter to introduce Trig to his new extended family. The letter talked about Sarah's comfortable pregnancy and how Trig would be a "mischievous" little brother, and, diagnostically speaking, he would always be young at heart. A portion of the letter was published on People.com: "This new person in your life can help everyone put things in perspective and bind us together, and get everyone focused on what really matters . . . those who love him will think less about self and focus less on what the world tells us is 'normal' or 'perfect.' "

Sarah didn't sign her name to the letter. She wrote it

in God's voice and signed it, "Trig's creator, Your Heavenly Father."

When Trig came home, the family chipped in to help with childcare duties. He also started physical therapy to help strengthen his muscle tone. Sarah was back on the job three days after the birth and sometimes took Trig with her to the office. If Todd was free, he drove and watched the baby at the office. The days started early at home. In an interview with *People* magazine, Sarah and Todd shared details of their daily routine and lifestyle. Sarah arose at 4 a.m. to coincide with the start of the day at the Alaska governor's satellite office in Washington, D.C., which lobbies Congress on federal issues affecting Alaska. She surfed the Net for news and caught up on e-mail traffic. Todd usually fixed her a breakfast of toast and apples and helped get the kids ready for school. When Bristol returned to Wasilla in May, she helped out in the morning. Sarah used to put Trig right in bed with Bristol so he would have company as Sarah got ready for work. "I couldn't do my job without my family," Sarah told *People*.

Sarah is on the road by 7 a.m., heading for her Anchorage office, while Todd or Molly takes the younger girls to school. Trig's arrival required a few changes. It forced the Palins to readjust their lifestyle. Todd also tracks the girls' activity schedules and coordinates with

Willow and Piper to make sure they get to their activities in the afternoon. Dinner at home could be simply a pizza Sarah picks up on the way home from work from a local Italian restaurant, or if Sarah is feeling ambitious, she'll whip up a batch of moose-and-salmon stew. "She is a good cook," Steve Becker, Todd's friend, told *People*. At night, Sarah is typically in bed at 10:30 p.m. after catching the nightly news.

One of the secrets to Sarah and Todd's relationship is their unequivocal support for each other's career. Todd is easygoing and fiercely loyal to his wife. He believes Sarah can do anything and overcome any obstacle. Todd is "calm, cool, collected," Sarah said. He also has no problem prioritizing Sarah's career ahead of his. "You just work it out," he told *People*. At the same time, she picks up the slack in the summer when he departs for Bristol Bay for one month of intense commercial salmon fishing, an exploit he loves and the family relies on for income. When they do get away from it all, they snowmobile to a small cabin in the wilderness that they share with friends. Todd says he appreciates that Sarah is low-maintenance. "She doesn't demand or require things," he said.

When Sarah's around her friends, the title disappears from her name, and she's simply Sarah. A good friend from the Elite Six said Sarah showed up unexpectedly to one gathering and brought Trig for all the girls to see. Beehive owner Jessica Steele would stand over Sarah, coloring her hair and asking advice on everything from finances to kids to juggling career and children. "The governor label comes off," Steele said.

Alaska in June turns into the land of the midnight sun. There's snow still on the mountaintops, but the tundra is warming up, and the animals are rummaging through the woods. Last June, a cow moose wandered onto the Palin property overlooking Lake Lucille and eyed little Piper and Willow shooting baskets in the driveway before lumbering into the woods, Chuck Heath recalled. Todd grabbed his youngest daughter by the hand, and they went looking for the moose, inching down the long driveway in his pickup truck as they scanned the forest of birch trees lining the road. Todd brought the truck to a halt when he saw the cow about forty feet from the road getting ready to bed down for the night. Todd and Piper watched until the moose settled down in the thicket, disappearing from sight. A few weeks later, Todd, Sarah, and the kids were relaxing in the house when they looked up and saw the cow moose bound across their backyard with two calves on her heels.

"The cow and her two calves are still living there," Chuck Heath said. "Todd saw them again in the driveway and took a picture."

That's the view sometimes from the Palins' two-story, wood-frame home that overlooks Lake Lucille and the Chugach Mountains. From a nearby wharf, one can see two muskrats patrolling the waterfront near Todd's two-seater Piper Cub float plane, which is moored at a dock. A pair of grebes has nested on a rise in the water, protecting several eggs from a gaggle of marauding ducks and geese lurking nearby.

Inside, it's spacious and clutter-free, said a friend who was there the day Sarah announced her candidacy for governor. Sarah may have her father's drive, but she does not have his penchant for collections and clutter. There are only a couple of animal trophies hanging on the wall—a Kodiak deer and a caribou. A modern black kitchen flows out into a dining room, and the living room, decorated in earth tones, has plenty of space for a big crowd. Trig's Graco rocker, which plays classical music and nature sounds, sits in a corner by the TV, which is often tuned to a hockey game.

Several large windows span from the kitchen to the family room that allow a visitor to enjoy the comforts of the Palin home and a spectacular view of the lake and mountains beyond.

One night, when a visitor from *People* magazine came by, Sarah sat at the kitchen table flipping through her journal. "So I was telling how we can be independent from each other," she said to Todd, "and not be at home for weeks at a time, and I read here, 'It's not so much independence at a time like this, it's a lot of dependence on each other,' " she said. "It's amazing how time passes and it's easier to deal with the circumstances. Don't you think, Todd?"

"Mmm-hmm," he grunted.

Todd and Sarah were put to the test in the summer of 2008. By July, word was spreading around Wasilla that Bristol was pregnant by her boyfriend, Levi. Relatives on Todd's side of the family said they learned of the pregnancy in June after Bristol was a couple of months along. "They were surprised, but these things happen," a Palin relative told *People* magazine. "They are very family people. What's one more Palin running around?"

Protective of her children, Sarah resisted announcing the pregnancy to Alaskans. Rumors flew that Bristol and Levi were under pressure from their parents to get married, but Levi clarified the situation in an interview with the Associated Press. "None of that's true," said Levi, who added that he and Bristol were engaged. Levi, who dropped out of high school and was working as an apprentice electrician, said he and Bristol were ready for the future. "We both love each other. We both want to marry each other. And that's what we're going to do," he said.

The couple began preparing for the baby two weeks after Bristol found out she was pregnant, purchasing a crib and a car seat, *People* magazine reported. Bristol was ready for the challenge. For years, she has been an ace babysitter for her siblings, nieces, and nephews, engaging them with activities and projects, like baking sugar cookies and playing with the girls' hair. Bristol, who is considering a career as a pediatric nurse, also has been a huge help with Trig. "She knows what it's all about," Sarah told *People* magazine.

According to her aunt Heather, Bristol is living at home in Wasilla and taking high school correspondence courses. "She's very mature and very nurturing," Heather said. The family likes Levi, said Chuck Heath. "Levi is a good guy and a hard worker." Asked if anyone was concerned about him dropping out of high school, Chuck said, "People ask me, 'Should I go to college?' I always say, 'Go to college or get a trade,' and he's getting a trade. And he hunts and fishes, too."

Levi is also finishing up his high school work online, but his future plans hit a snag when he left his job on the North Slope after public questions were raised about his eligibility to work for the Arctic Slope Regional Corporation, which apparently requires a high school diploma or equivalent for participation. Levi's father, Keith, an ASRC construction engineer who helped Levi get the job, told the *Anchorage Daily News* that his son will now focus on his education.

Despite the setback, the couple still expects to wed in the summer of 2009. Marriage has been on their minds even before Bristol got pregnant, Levi said, but he admitted he was surprised when he found out Bristol was carrying his baby. "It's going to be a lot of hard work but we can handle it," he said. With a due date in December, he said he was ready for the responsibility of fatherhood and was looking forward to raising a son. "I'm going to take him hunting and fishing. He'll be everywhere with me," said Levi.

That wasn't the only family matter for Sarah to cope with. On July 11, the nasty divorce and child-custody battle between Trooper Michael Wooten and Molly McCann became public when Sarah fired Alaska's public safety commissioner, Walt Monegan. She said the change was prompted because he was insubordinate and protested her fiscal reforms. She had offered the commissioner a job reassignment for about $10,000 less in salary. But Monegan didn't see it that way. He went public, announcing he was let go because he would not accede to the pressure to fire Trooper Wooten.

The effort to remove Wooten had spread throughout the governor's office. Sarah, Todd, and her staff, Monegan said, did just about everything short of actually saying Wooten needed to go, Monegan said in an interview with the *New York Times*. The examples were numerous. Sarah, upon being elected governor, told her security team that Wooten posed a potential danger to her. A month after the election, Todd spoke to Monegan in the governor's office and expressed his and the governor's dissatisfaction over the 2005 trooper investigation and the inadequacy of the five-day suspension that followed. The moose kill particularly concerned Todd.

Monegan reviewed the matter and got back to Todd to tell him the case had been closed. Todd was not happy, and not long after that, Sarah called and said Wooten was "not the kind of person we should want as a trooper." But it didn't end there. The Palins accused Wooten of illegally accepting worker's compensation for a back injury, but personnel officials would check and find no such violation occurred. Monegan thought the family interest in Wooten was over the top. His office was contacted more than two dozen times about Wooten over nineteen months. While Sarah had minimal contact, Todd and several administration officials continued to press. In an interview, Monegan categorized the interest in Wooten as "an obsession."

In August 2007, just days before the Alaska State Fair was to begin, the *New York Times* reported that an aide from the governor's Anchorage office called and said that Sarah had heard Trooper Wooten was going to be working the fair, and if that were the case, something should be done about it since the governor was planning on attending. Trooper Wooten was set to attend, all right—in costume as Safety Bear, the unit's kiddy mascot. Monegan replaced Wooten for that job.

Monegan may have sealed his fate in May 2008, when he visited Sarah in her Anchorage office and asked her to sign an official photo of a state trooper in full dress uniform, standing in front of a local police memorial. The portrait was meant for display commemorating the 2008 Alaska Police Memorial Day event. There was just one problem: the trooper in the photo was Wooten. Sarah signed the photo, but later Monegan got chewed out by one of Sarah's aides for his thoughtlessness. Monegan testified that he had no idea it was Wooten in the photo and had no clue what the trooper looked like.

The moment Monegan was replaced, it was a publicity nightmare for Sarah. Todd was portrayed as a meddling husband, and Sarah appeared vindictive.

A legal adviser counseling Sarah on ethics matters spoke to the *Wall Street Journal* after the Monegan firing and said he had told Sarah that the issue could build into a significant scandal. U.S. Attorney Wevley Shea urged the governor to make an apology for her handling of the case and fire any aides concerned about Wooten. He described the situation as "grave" and said she needed to apologize for any perceived abuse of power in trying to get Wooten fired.

In late July, the legislature got involved and opened an independent investigation of what became known as Troopergate. The Palins and her staff first refused to testify for the investigators, and Sarah argued the matter should go through the personnel board. "We have nothing to hide," she said at a July military appreciation ceremony. The investigation turned into a standoff and was unresolved for the next several weeks.

Meanwhile, Alaskan journalists began snooping around Sarah's travel records and expense reports. At issue was the Palin children's travel expenses that were being charged to the state. Although the news didn't break for two months, an Associated Press investigation found that since the governor took office in 2006, she had charged the state $21,012 for her three daughters' travel expenses, primarily plane tickets for commercial airline flights to join Sarah on official business trips. The first family also used the state plane, a King Air turboprop, two dozen times at a cost of $55,000. Whether one person travels or several, that doesn't increase the cost to run the plane, which is $971 an hour.

The charges included flight and hotel expenses to watch Todd compete in the Iron Dog; a trip to New York to attend a women's leadership conference with

Bristol, which included a $1,385 plane ticket for Bristol; and a four-night stay in a double room at a $700-per-night hotel. The journalists contacted event organizers for several of the trips, and some said they were surprised when Sarah showed up with her daughters "uninvited" and that the governor sometimes asked if the kids could attend with her, the investigation revealed.

After reporters requested the records, the AP story said Sarah ordered changes in the expense reports to explain her daughters' travel. The state doesn't have a policy on expenses for governors' children, just rules detailing expense reimbursements for individuals traveling on state business.

A spokesman for the governor told the Associated Press that Sarah followed policy allowing governors to charge for their children's travel, explaining the governor had invitations requesting the family attend some events. Her aides also said Governor Palin was permitted to charge taxpayers for her children's commercial airline tickets because "they represent the state wherever they go with her."

"There's an expectation that the first family participates in community activities," said Sharon Leighow, the governor's spokeswoman. "They are representing the first family and the state of Alaska."

In late August, some of the members of the Elite

Six, Sarah's group of friends from Wasilla, gathered for a bridal shower. Sarah hadn't seen the gang since May, when she had unexpectedly stopped by a birthday party for a friend to introduce the gang to Trig. The group's sixteen-year friendship was still going strong. The friends were sharing some chicken lasagna and cheesecake when Sarah walked in with her newborn. Sarah was in a hurry. She dropped off a gift and said she planned on taking her girls to the annual Alaska State Fair that Friday. There was no chance she was going to miss a day of feasting on salmon quesadillas and Prince William Sound oysters. Sarah told her friends, " 'I can't stay long,' but can you believe she came by at all?" Amy Hansen of the Elites told *Time* magazine.

Sarah, as on her wedding day, used the fair as a nice cover story, because bigger things were in the works. On Wednesday, she was secretly flown out of Alaska to Flagstaff, Arizona, and driven to John McCain's ranch near Sedona. He was about to put an offer on the table. How would Sarah like to be the first Republican female vice-presidential candidate in history? Sarah jumped at the opportunity.

The speed and sheer audacity of Sarah's acceptance stunned many political observers who felt the inexperienced Alaska governor needed to step back and take a breath, but supporters from her home state weren't surprised by her bravado. Alaskans live in closer proximity to nature than most Americans, and consequently, they live closer to death. As one longtime friend explained: "When there's a chance to seize an opportunity, you take it. Reject it and you may not be around if the opportunity presents itself again."

If Sarah had much notice of what was coming, she kept extended family in the dark. Her parents, Sally and Chuck Heath, found out as they were leaving a gold-mining camp because of a rainstorm. "We're leaving, and it's four a.m., and I get a call from an old student, and he says, 'Turn on the news.'" The phone hasn't stopped since. "We were getting up to a hundred and fifty calls a day at one point," Chuck said.

Jim Palin was in touch with son Todd in the early hours that Friday, but his son was less than forthcoming. "It was Sarah and Todd's twentieth anniversary, and Faye and I were married on August 29, too. The day before, Todd comes over and says, 'Happy early anniversary. I'm going to see Sarah with the girls so we can celebrate ours.' I didn't ask him where he was off to." Jim got his first call at 5:30 a.m. from CBS News in New York. "'Are you related to Governor Palin? We've confirmed she has been named John McCain's running mate.' I'm thinking, 'I should have known.' Ten minutes later, Todd calls and says, 'Don't answer the phone. I'll call you right back.'

He didn't tell me anything. Finally, he calls and says, 'The news release is out.' By then I already knew."

Over at KTUU, old friend Steve MacDonald, the news director, said he was tipped off to Sarah's nomination at 3 a.m. the morning it was announced. "We had spotted the Palin family at the airport earlier that night, and she was on an airplane. We knew she was on the short list, but this was different," he said. "I called the station's political reporter, and we started making calls and getting everyone out of bed. Her staff didn't know anything and told us she was scheduled to do two events that day—a youth academy graduation ceremony, and she was introducing the new Alaskan quarter at the Alaska State Fair. Then we find out that the lieutenant governor had found out he's doing the events. NBC confirmed it, and we went on the air. The staff came in early that morning, and everyone was gathered around the monitors when Sarah appeared and gave her speech. Then it hits you, 'It's Sarah—oh my God!' Your mind knows it, and your eyes can't believe it. This began the most surreal month of my life."

FOURTEEN
HUNTING SEASON

When Sarah Palin was chosen to be John McCain's running mate, it came as no surprise to Christine Garner, the former girlfriend of Todd Palin's brother, J.D. Their daughter lives in Wasilla with her father, and she's close to the Palin kids. "She had been saying for weeks, 'They want Auntie Sarah for vice president.' So I wasn't surprised. I was thrilled, because Sarah had what it took to be a great vice president. She's honest, and she's done so much for Alaska."

On the morning of the announcement, Sarah, Todd, and the kids appeared together at a rally in Dayton, Ohio, with McCain. Sarah publicly accepted the honor of being McCain's vice-presidential pick, and they chose *People* magazine for their first interview. Do you feel ready to be a heartbeat away from the presidency?

"Absolutely, yup, yup," Sarah replied. "Especially with a good team around us."

McCain timed his announcement for the day after the conclusion of the Democratic Convention. There was no surprise with the timing, as the Arizona senator intended to steal the thunder and the weekend headlines from Barack Obama, who was ahead in the polls. Back in Alaska, shocked politicians tried to grapple with McCain's choice, but they said all the right things. Sarah's hometown paper beamed the headline "Alaska GOP thrilled Palin plucked for VP," and state GOP vice chairman Steve Colligan effused, "We think it's the best thing to ever happen to Alaska. There's no better person to identify with Alaskans and everyday Americans." Republican representative Mark Neuman said, "It's going to be great for Alaska, one way or another, win, lose, or draw."

The *Anchorage Daily News* reported the reaction as mixed. Supporters lauded Sarah's energy and message of change, while some veteran Republican politicians were shocked and felt McCain had taken a huge risk drafting a governor who was under investigation for Troopergate and had not been properly vetted by the campaign. John Binkley, who ran and lost to Sarah in the Republican primary for governor in 2006, said Palin was up to the task, and her inexperience wouldn't hurt her: "I'm not certain that will matter."

Rival Andrew Halcro echoed the inexperience factor but gave Sarah high marks for her ability to connect with voters locally. "It will be interesting to see if that recipe works for her on the national stage," he told the *Anchorage Daily News*.

Sen. Ted Stevens also was supportive. He called her "bright and energetic" and said that if elected, she would bring the same qualities to the vice presidency. "I share in the pride of all Alaskans."

Meanwhile, Lyda Green, the Republican state Senate president who supported Sarah in her first mayor's race but later had a falling out over the oil-tax increase and the award of a $500-million incentive to a Canadian firm to build the natural-gas pipeline, said Sarah wasn't prepared to be governor, so how could she be prepared to be vice president? "Look at what she's done to this state. What would she do to the nation?" Green told the *Daily News*.

Former House speaker Gail Phillips, a Republican who finished behind Sarah in the 2002 lieutenant governor's race, was in close contact with Sens. Ted Stevens and Lisa Murkowski and raised a red flag—as far as she knew, McCain's advance team had not vetted Sarah's history. "This can't be happening, because his advance team hasn't come to Alaska to check her out," she told a reporter.

Phillips and other Palin critics wondered if McCain had the whole picture. In a matter of hours, Palin stories were filling cyberspace with details of Sarah's political and personal life. There were thought-out criticisms by such Sarah critics as Anne Kilkenny, who wrote an insider's letter on Sarah's life and career in Wasilla from her own perspective as a city gadfly. She sent the letter to a few friends before it circulated on the Internet, reaching tens of thousands of readers and leading to a page-one profile in the *Los Angeles Times*—"Wasilla Gadfly Swirls in a Storm . . ." Journalists used it as a tip sheet to generate countless features and investigative stories on the governor.

"Dear friends," it began. "So many people have asked me about what I know about Sarah Palin in the last two days that I decided to write something . . . basically Sarah Palin and Hillary Clinton have only two things in common: their gender and their good looks." There were positive observations of Sarah: "She is enormously popular . . . she is energetic . . . hardworking . . . smart . . . savvy . . . a babe," but the letter also raised questions about her controversial management of the city of Wasilla. "[Her] acceptance of pork from Senator Ted Stevens for Wasilla building and infrastructure projects . . . her failure to support her stepmother-in-law when Faye Palin ran for mayor in 2002." "The first thing I thought was, 'Poor Todd,' " Kilkenny said.

"Do not post it on any Web sites," Kilkenny asked her friends, "as there are too many kooks out there." But it was too late. By the end of September, the eleven-page August 31 letter had generated 538,000 Google hits.

McCain's announcement immediately sparked crazy rumors. Oldest son Track was portrayed in tabloids as a party boy and a discipline problem. The bigger rumor was that Trig Palin was Bristol's baby, not Sarah's. Tabloid reporters, bloggers, and some Wasilla residents were convinced that Trig had to be Bristol's. They pointed to how Sarah managed to keep her pregnancy a secret from staffers and barely looked pregnant for a woman who was eight months along when she gave birth. Critics also wondered why Bristol suddenly dropped out of Wasilla High in December and transferred to a high school in Anchorage. They claimed if Sarah were pregnant, she never would have flown to Texas five weeks before her due date to give a speech at the Republican Governors Association, nor would she have flown back after her water broke.

McCain's camp squelched that rumor with a personal revelation that McCain himself knew only hours before he invited Sarah to join him on the GOP ticket:

Daughter Bristol, seventeen, was five months pregnant, and she was going to marry the father, who was just eighteen. McCain said it didn't eliminate Sarah from being his running mate.

A statement followed from Sarah and Todd that announced that Bristol planned on keeping the baby and marrying the unnamed father, who turned out to be Levi Johnston. "Our beautiful daughter Bristol came to us with news that as parents we knew would make her grow up faster than we had ever planned. We are proud of Bristol's decision to have her baby and even prouder to become grandparents," they wrote. "Bristol and the young man she will marry are going to realize very quickly the difficulties of raising a child, which is why they will have the love and support of our entire family," they said. On the same day, they released information about Todd's 1986 DUI. There was also an erroneous report of Sarah's old membership with the secession-promoting Alaska Independence Party, though it turned out the affiliation was Todd's and not Sarah's.

Sarah announced, too, that she had hired an attorney to represent her in the legislative investigation of her firing of Walt Monegan and whether she had abused her power when she dismissed the public safety commissioner. Monegan claimed he was fired because he

wouldn't fire trooper Michael Wooten, who was involved in a custody battle with Sarah's sister, Molly Mc-
Cann.

In a separate development, the day after Sarah was
announced as McCain's running mate, Faye Palin was
reached at her home in Wasilla by a reporter from the
New York Daily News. Faye reportedly said she liked Barack Obama's acceptance speech and hadn't decided
whom she was going to vote for in the general election.
Her husband, Jim Palin, later said she was misquoted.
"She voted for Sarah," he said in October. "We both
did." He explained that the couple mailed in their ballots
in the last days of the election before joining Sarah on
the campaign trail in Nevada, speaking to men's groups
and senior citizens. Faye, however, was asked by the
McCain campaign to refrain from any future interviews.

And this was only Monday—seventy-two hours
after the selection of Sarah to the GOP ticket.

By Tuesday, media outlets were questioning the Mc-
Cain campaign about how closely the Arizona senator had
looked into Sarah's past before placing her on the ticket:
"Palin Disclosures Spotlight McCain's Screening Process" the headline read in the *New York Times*. The vetting
began in earnest the week after Sarah joined the campaign
trail. Meanwhile, there was the matter of the Republican

National Convention, scheduled to begin that week in Minnesota. Rumors were already circulating that Sarah might be dropped from the ticket, but McCain squelched them. Still, questions remained about his judgment and whether her selection had been a hurried decision. Media reports indicated that McCain's first two choices favored abortion rights and were unacceptable to the Republican conservatives. Palin filled the conservative void but really wasn't in the running until the week before she was announced as his running mate.

Both Lyda Green and Gail Phillips told the *New York Times* that McCain's people did not quiz Alaska legislators or business leaders about Sarah, though McCain advisers said lawyers working for McCain did interview the Alaska governor. However, the campaign's priority may have been to keep the pick as a surprise, thus restricting the number of contacts with information.

Meanwhile, Sarah had to get ready for the biggest political challenge of her life, her acceptance speech at the Republican Convention, just two days away. But rather than discussing McCain's heroism, Sarah's pro-life values, or her reputation as a reformer, people were preoccupied with what kind of mother she was. After the announcement about Bristol, Janet Kincaid, a Palin family friend, said she knew of the pregnancy in early August from someone who knew Levi. "I just thought, 'Poor Sarah, there is always one that knocks the socks off you and keeps you humble, just when you think you're the greatest mom,' " she told the *New York Times*. Another friend said the Palins hold onto their children very tightly, and they don't let the kids run wild. Sarah has said she has always been a proponent of both abstinence and contraception, though she supports the former over the latter. "Ideally abstinence," she told *People* magazine. "But we have not been ones to say that students should not know what preventative measures are. I've always been a proponent of making sure kids understand—even in schools—they'd better take preventative measures so they don't find themselves in these less-than-ideal circumstances. Perhaps Bristol could be an example that life happens and preventative measures are, first and foremost, an option that should be considered."

In a show of support for the young couple, the campaign invited Levi to join the Palin family at the convention in Minnesota. Levi needed a suit, said Chuck Heath, Sarah's father. "He was a little embarrassed about that," he added. Sarah was already there, ensconced in a hotel room receiving some coaching before her Wednesday night speech. She still hadn't spoken to a reporter since her *People* interview the previous Friday, and it was clear that the campaign wanted more time with her before they let her out on her own. In St. Paul, campaign aides and advisers focused on the speech—debriefing her on McCain's political positions on the economy, energy, and Iraq. They also discussed how Sarah should broach the subject of Bristol's pregnancy, which they could not skate around, since the eighteen-year-old hockey-player boyfriend was en route to the convention. If Sarah was feeling any uncertainty, she certainly didn't show it to the extended family that had gathered to witness her big moment. A few hours before her speech, Sarah gathered with relatives at her hotel.

"Are you nervous?" her aunt, Katie Johnson, asked.

"Nervous?" replied Sarah. "I'm not nervous. Seems kind of exciting, doesn't it?"

Back in Wasilla, the bars and restaurants were jammed with Palin supporters. At the Tailgater family restaurant, friends from Sarah's church organized an event and gathered all the McCain memorabilia they could find on short notice and even manufactured a giant McCain-Palin placard for folks to sign. Supporters like Kathy Chapoton, a retired schoolteacher, dug out their old red "Palin for Governor" buttons and displayed them proudly on caps and shirts. "Tonight we will hear the real Sarah," she told a reporter. "It has been terrible hearing all those awful things in the media."

When Sarah stepped out to the podium, the crowd chanted, "Sarah! Sarah!" When the camera panned over to Levi Johnston, looking sharp in his new suit, Kathy's husband, Martin, a Palin friend and a champion Iditarod racer, said, "That Levi, he dresses up pretty good!" Rally organizer and Wasilla Chamber of Commerce executive director Cheryl Metiva said, "Levi's attending shows they're a united family."

After a week of sticky questions and negative publicity for the campaign, Sarah's speech enthralled the convention crowd and turned around the McCain campaign. She needled Barack Obama, calling him a distant elitist, and drew cheers when she said she put Frank Murkowski's jet up for sale on eBay. She billed herself as a small-town hockey mom and PTA member and reminded the crowd that the only difference between a hockey mom and a pit bull is lipstick, borrowing the phrase she coined in her open letter to Murkowski that called him out for possible ethics violations. She talked about being mayor of Wasilla. "Since our opponents in the presidential election seem to look down on that experience, let me explain to them what the job involves," she said. "I guess a small-town mayor is sort of like a community organizer, except that you have actual responsibilities. . . . I took on the old politics as usual in Juneau . . . when I stood up to the special interests, the lobbyists, big oil companies, and the good-old-boys network." At the end of the speech, the Palin family got up onstage, including Levi, who held hands with Bristol as the crowd cheered.

Sarah was running on adrenaline for the rest of the night. Late in the evening, she was relaxing with family in her hotel room when a campaign staffer came by and asked if she wanted to go meet Robert McFarland and Marlon Fitzwater. "They were asking for her," Johnson recalled. "I could tell the Secret Service wanted her to stay in her room because of all the people, but she insisted on going downstairs to meet them. She dragged them downstairs, and we all went with her."

The lift from Sarah's speech was just what the McCain campaign needed. All night long, family gathered around the TV set to listen to the glowing reviews. The media organizations that had previously been scrutinizing her qualifications praised her delivery. The headline in the *Anchorage Daily News* raved, "Palin Electrifies GOP." George Stephanopoulos gave her an A and said, "The crowd loved every minute of her speech." NBC's Tom Brokaw called her "winning and engaging." CNN's Anderson Cooper said she was "a force to be reckoned with." The *Washington Post* said it was "an impressive debut on a national stage," and Meredith Vieira said "she showed she could throw some pretty good punches of her own."

The Alaska delegates at the convention weren't surprised. Randy Ruedrich, still the chairman of Alaska's Republican Party, said, "We're finally relevant," signaling that the icy relationship between the Republican delegation and its governor was starting to thaw. "It is just a unique ability to communicate. The only person I have seen who has done it better is Ronald Reagan."

"It's an absolutely historic moment," said Sen. Lisa Murkowski, whose father had suffered a bitter defeat at the hands of Palin in the 2006 governor's race. "People here are excited about Sarah, our Sarah."

But not every fact in her speech was accurate, and on a closer examination, some remarks were downright misleading. Some skeptics thought she misled people with the eBay reference, implying that she sold the jet on the Web site, when, in reality, it was sold through a broker after failing to sell on eBay four times. On her campaign stops, she kept repeating the line that garnered big cheers in St. Paul and elsewhere, about telling Congress "Thanks, but no thanks" to the Bridge to Nowhere, when in truth she initially supported the $400-million Ketchikan bridge. She only changed her mind after Washington dropped the financing.

A speech she gave in June 2008 to a youth group at her old church, the Wasilla Assembly of God, was posted in cyberspace during her first days of the campaign, and critics raised questions about the governor's religious beliefs and the appropriateness of asking young people to pray for the completion of a $30-billion natural-gas pipeline or for political leaders to say they are sending soldiers overseas "out on a task that is from God."

Sarah may have been tailoring that speech to her audience, as she had gotten high marks for distinguishing between her personal religious beliefs and public policy. The McCain campaign said that while Sarah was deeply religious, she didn't mix faith and government affairs. Later, Sarah clarified these comments, explaining in her interview with ABC's Charlie Gibson, "I would never presume to know God's will or speak God's words."

After the speech, Sarah hit the campaign trail, usually with Todd, Trig, and one or two of the girls in tow. Bristol, in her fifth month of pregnancy, returned home to Wasilla to take correspondence courses and work toward earning a high school diploma. According to Chuck Heath, Todd and Sarah also hired a full-time live-in nanny, a local girl from Wasilla, to help out with the caretaking duties at home for Trig and the girls.

On September 5, Palin began the hardscrabble campaigning she was known for, though this time the stakes were a bit higher than a seat on the Wasilla city council. She stopped in a Wisconsin ice cream shop and ordered moose-track ice cream in a waffle cone, shaking hands and greeting customers. A man approached Palin and said, "There's a big groundswell for Piper for president." Sarah replied, "Oh, she would be the one." Mothers with disabled children sought her out in particular. It was a natural fit for the governor but one that wouldn't be taken full advantage of by the campaign until much later, when Sarah promised families with special-needs kids the flexibility to enroll their kids in private schools using taxpayers' dollars. One Wisconsin mom, Carolyn Rehfeldt, brought her eight-year-old daughter who has Down syndrome to see Sarah. Rehfeldt said she was thinking of voting for McCain, but Palin's addition to the ticket "sealed it for me."

From there, Sarah and McCain moved on to Detroit, Michigan, where they spoke to police union members, after earning an endorsement from the 328,000-member National Fraternal Order of Police. McCain spoke to the crowd, lauding the "excitement and enthusiasm that our vice-presidential nominee has had, and I hope you welcome a woman whose husband is a member of the United Steelworkers Union."

But while Sarah was allowed to interact with voters, the media were kept at a distance until she sat down with Charles Gibson for a series of one-on-one interviews. The Gibson interviews went relatively smoothly, as Mc-Cain's advisers had taken special care to make sure she was prepared. Unfortunately that wasn't the case in her series of interviews with CBS anchor Katie Couric. Critics said Sarah stumbled badly and was "wobbly" and that some of her answers were nonsensical, what old foe Andrew Halcro had once labeled "Palin gibberish." One especially embarrassing moment was Palin's insistence to Couric that she had foreign-policy experience because of Alaska's maritime border with Russia. The exchange was mocked later by Tina Fey in her impersonation of Sarah on *Saturday Night Live*.

In its postmortem of the McCain campaign, the *New York Times* reported she did not have the time or focus to prepare for Couric. "She did not say, 'I will not prepare,'" a McCain adviser said. "She just didn't have the bandwidth to do a mock interview the way we had prepared before [for Gibson]. She was just overloaded."

Preparation had also been an issue during her gubernatorial campaign in 2006. After a particularly dreadful performance at a political forum where she showed little knowledge of Alaskan affairs, aides became frustrated by her "limited attention span" for digesting issues for debate preparation, the *Los Angeles Times* reported. Thirty minutes couldn't pass without Sarah being distracted by a phone call or a family matter. "We were always fighting for her attention," one aide told the *Times*. But to her credit, she got better and outdueled her opponents with what one former gubernatorial opponent called a "Reagan-like ability to win over audiences," despite her penchant for ignoring facts and questions.

The unmitigated disaster that was the Couric interview led to scathing critiques not only from liberals but also from conservative voices like columnist Kathleen Parker, a Sarah advocate at the outset who reversed her support and asked Sarah to step aside to "save McCain, her party, and the country she loves." "Quick study or not, she doesn't know enough about economics and foreign policy to make Americans comfortable with a President Palin, should conditions warrant her promotion," Parker reported in the *National Review*. Parker even went so far as to offer Sarah face-saving ways to return home, such as spending more time with her children.

If jabs by late-night hosts like Jay Leno and David Letterman weren't damaging enough at this stage (Letterman said her meetings with foreign leaders at the United Nations resembled "Take your daughter to work day"), Tina Fey started making regular appearances on *Saturday Night Live*, imitating Palin at her most awkward. Sarah, to her credit, showed a remarkable ability to laugh at herself and even made an appearance on the show, chatting up Alec Baldwin and taking Fey's place at a pseudo-press-conference lectern, as if to say, "Step aside, the real Sarah Palin has arrived." Critics questioned whether the timing of the appearance in October undermined the GOP's attempt to have her taken seriously as a candidate.

Still, leading up to the vice-presidential debate, Sarah's base of support—evangelical Christians and social conservatives who support her anti-abortion position—remained loyal. These voters were swayed by her decision to keep Trig, when most mothers in the same position might choose the abortion route. They were also impressed by her love and support for her pregnant daughter, who also "chose life," as the governor was apt to say. Crowds poured into her campaign stops, and she was drawing better crowds than McCain himself. Buoyed by her popularity, he campaigned with her after the convention. In public, he remained steadfast in his support, telling audiences that she remained his partner and would be on his team reforming everything that was wrong in Washington. If anything, Republicans felt that perhaps McCain should loosen the reins and let Palin have more contact with the press and the public.

Mitt Romney, who was defeated by McCain in the primaries and was under consideration as a running mate, said the McCain campaign needed to "let Sarah Palin be Sarah Palin. Let her talk to the media, let her talk to people," he told MSNBC. Campbell Brown of CNN ripped into McCain, calling him sexist and chauvinistic for shielding Sarah from the media. "Stop treating Sarah Palin like she's a delicate flower that will wilt at any moment," she said. "This woman is from Alaska, for crying out loud; she's strong, she's tough, she's confident. Free Sarah Palin. Free her from the chauvinistic chain you are binding her with."

As the vice-presidential debate approached, the Sarah bounce diminished in the face of the faltering economy and the stock-market meltdown. McCain and Palin had no control over the economy, and it was about to make their job tougher. Obama surged ahead four points, 48–44, after McCain had drawn within a couple of points in days following Sarah's well-received convention speech, according to the RealClearPolitics survey of polls. A *Washington Post*–ABC News poll that came out on the day of the October 2 debate showed six in ten voters said Sarah lacked the proper experience to be an effective president. McCain also had to be nervous that Sarah wasn't attracting women voters as he had hoped. White women voters favored McCain by just two points over Obama, compared with the fourteen-point advantage George Bush enjoyed in 2004. While the Couric interview was damaging, it wasn't fatal. However, Sarah's support was also wilting in her home state, largely because of Troopergate, and her approval rating dropped to sixty-eight percent from a high of eighty-two percent.

Of the political attacks, McCain campaign spokeswoman Meghan Stapleton said, "I think after weeks and weeks of vile partisan attacks, her approval rating is still quite strong, and they would naturally fall when you're dealing with constant attacks and falsehoods and miscommunications."

Still, as one Alaska lawmaker who has watched Sarah's political career ascend in Alaska observed, "The political landscape here is littered with people who have underestimated Sarah Palin." So said Sarah's old ally in the Frank Murkowski ethics scandal, Eric Croft, a former Democratic lawmaker who ran for governor in 2006 and participated with Sarah in several candidates' forums.

Palin's debate skills improved over time in the 2006 governor's race as she employed her skills as a former sportscaster and looked relaxed and confident onstage.

Halcro, who lost to Palin badly in the general election (he ran as an independent), explained that audiences loved her. And "her biting comments give you a sense of how competitive she is. Anybody who doesn't take her seriously does so at their own peril."

On the day of the debate, Sarah got a much-needed surprise. Track, whom she had seen off in September when he left for Iraq from Alaska's Fort Wainwright and who had already spoken to his girlfriend but not his mother, called from the Middle East to say hello. "It was so wonderful because it was the first call since they were deployed over there, and it was like a burden lifted even when I heard his voice," she told columnist William Kristol. When his mother told him she had a debate coming up, Track replied, "Yeah, I heard, Mom. Have you been studying?" Sarah said, " 'Yeah, I have,' and he goes, 'OK, well, I'll be praying.' I'm like, total role reversal here, that's what I've been telling him for nineteen years."

The debate turned out to be one of the most-watched political events in history, with 69.9 million viewers tuning in. For Sarah, it was all positive. She hustled onstage and shook hands with Joseph Biden. "Hey, can I call you Joe?" she asked. Critics complimented her performance, calling it a return to her form in her Republican Convention speech. Her folksy demeanor came through as she peppered her talking points with chummy expressions like "betcha," "maverick," "doggone it," "Washington outsider," and "Say it ain't so, Joe." She was open to viewers up front, telling them, "I may not answer the questions you or the moderator want to hear," she said, referring to Joe Biden and the moderator, Gwen Ifill. "I'm going to talk directly to the people." She also dropped a few G's.

Biden was impressive; his answers were steady, thoughtful, leaving viewers with the sense he was more intellectually gifted than his opponent, but Palin's shout-out to a third-grade class back in her home state and her moxie, including a wink to the audience as the debate was winding down, probably won the night for her. Biden didn't come across as arrogant, which was a victory for him. Righting past wrongs, she appeared more solid than previously on foreign-policy references and attempted to recast her botched interviews as a liberal setup. "This is going to help stop the bleeding," observed Todd Harris, a Republican consultant who had previously worked with McCain. "But this alone won't change the trend line, particularly in some battleground states."

The battle was still going to be a struggle. The day of the debate, McCain pulled out of Michigan, a move Sarah would later criticize. But the numbers didn't lie.

McCain was starting to lose ground in traditional Republican states, and the stock market continued to worsen. Harris said the terrible economy turned the Republican strategy on its head, from a "referendum on Obama to a referendum on who can get us out of this mess." But Sarah held up her end by not repeating the mistakes she made with Katie Couric and by holding her own with Biden.

Encouraged by her performance and with so much ground to make up in the polls, Sarah was given more leeway out on the campaign trail. She told the *New York Times* after the debate that she felt liberated by the contest with Biden and that she was looking forward to continuing the race, "getting to speak directly to the folks."

Meanwhile, Sarah went back to work, drawing enthusiastic crowds and even answering impromptu questions from the media. She suggested that her running mate "take the gloves off" and take the battle to Obama. Conservative pundits were now pinning their hopes on Sarah to take the fight to the Democrats, complaining that McCain somehow didn't seem up to it. "She reenergized the conservative base," said Nelson Warfield, a conservative Republican consultant.

Sarah's first task was to go after Obama for his association with Sixties radical Bill Ayers, a founder of the radical Weather Underground. To supportive crowds, Sarah described Obama as someone "palling around with terrorists" who "doesn't see America as you and I see it." She cited a *New York Times* story that suggested that Obama had been less than forthcoming about his relationship with Ayers. While Sarah did the heavy lifting, campaign spinners said her questions were fair and reasonable. Obama countered, calling the accusations "swift boat" jibes on his character, charging the Republican ticket would rather "tear our campaign down than lift this country up."

Though the offensive was criticized for its mean-spirited tenor, with the continued crash of the economy, few were paying attention. On a day when the stock market dropped 679 points, Sarah focused her talk at a rally in Ohio on Ayers and his ties to Obama. Her base loved the speeches, but the media were harsh. The *San Francisco Chronicle* labeled the drive a "desperate attempt" to "distract voters from the economic disaster that's unfolding" and called the attacks "irrelevant." McCain, the paper said, was in danger of tainting his legacy. Eventually, McCain called off the attacks and tried to steer voters' attention to his economic solutions for the stock-market crash.

On the night of the second presidential debate, October 7, Sarah seemed in high spirits. Asked to reflect on her first month on the campaign trail, she said that the ticket had some work to do. "I've been an underdog quite often in my life—and so has John McCain. And we both have come out victorious," she told the *Washington Post*. After speaking at East Carolina University in Greenville, North Carolina, she led her staff to a pizzeria to watch the debate and relaxed with diners, posed for cell-phone pictures, and knocked back a few diet Red Bulls.

When a male patron named Dana Corey handed Sarah his cell phone and asked her to say hello to his wife, the governor, in a playful mood, relayed into the cell, "Libby, why is your husband here drinking beer without you?" Palin sat down at a table with the state's Republican senators, Elizabeth Dole and Richard Burr, and studied the debate, taking notes and evaluating the commentary. Later on, reporters were invited over, and Sarah gave her analysis. "I think Barack was even less candid than usual, but McCain has fought on and sounded very energized," she said. "It's gonna be a great twenty-eight days to go."

Following her campaign stops, Sarah was dogged by issues back home, including the revelation that she was accepting a sixty-dollar per diem for the three-hundred-plus days she stayed at her own home in Wasilla since she was elected governor. She also was charging taxpayers for her children's plane tickets when they traveled with her on state business. The *Washington Post* also looked into her public-disclosure records and found that since she took office in late 2006, she had accepted forty-one gifts totaling more than $25,000 from municipalities and private citizens, some even as she was pushing her ethics-reform bill that limited gift giving to politicians. However, Sarah said the gifts had no undue influence on her, and the attorney general's office said there were no ethical violations.

Then there was also the Pebble mine controversy, involving a proposed copper-and-gold mine of gigantic proportions that would bring one thousand jobs to a depressed region. Environmentalists argue that it might threaten Alaska's greatest salmon-spawning ground, Bristol Bay. Opponents of the mine created a clean-water ballot measure that would prevent giant mines, like the one proposed at Pebble, from contaminating salmon streams. Sarah was thought to be neutral, but in August, she spoke out against the initiative, leading to its defeat.

Sarah's mantra about being an average middle-class hockey mom took a hit when her disclosure statements showed the Palins' assets and income topped $1 million in 2007. Certainly this didn't compare to the wealth of John and Cindy McCain, both multimillionaires, but the Palins' combined income did reach $230,000 that year, making them better off than most working Americans.

In mid-October, the Trooper Wooten case reached a head when a bipartisan Alaska legislative panel ruled that Sarah had abused her power by pushing for the removal of Wooten, but she was within her rights to fire public safety commissioner Walt Monegan. "I'm very pleased to be cleared of any legal wrongdoing," Sarah said, despite the findings that determined she had violated state ethics laws in pressing for Wooten's termination. Sarah disagreed with that conclusion. "Not at all, and I'll tell ya," she said, "I think you're always going to ruffle feathers as you do what you believe is in the best interest of the people whom you are serving." The Alaska Personnel Board, in a separate investigation, contradicted the panel's finding, saying the governor did not apply improper pressure to have the trooper fired or violate state ethics laws in firing Monegan, and it vindicated her on election eve. It claimed the earlier panel had based its findings on an incorrect interpretation of the state ethics laws, according to the *New York Times*. Wooten also apologized for the actions he was disciplined for, including the use of the Taser and the moose kill. "I was young and made mistakes," he told CNN. "I want to be the best dad I can be to my children and be the best trooper I can be." Since his suspension in 2006, Wooten remained a trooper in good standing, officials said.

At the same time, Todd's role in the governor's office came under scrutiny, with voters wondering if he would become an activist spouse like Hillary Clinton if his wife were elected vice president. In his report on Troopergate, independent legislative investigator Stephen Branchflower detailed Todd's "frequent and intimate presence in the day-to-day workings of his wife's administration," the *Los Angeles Times* reported. The *Times* found he attended cabinet meetings closed to the public, was copied on high-level government correspondence, and, according to a member of Sarah's security detail, spent about half his time in Sarah's office. Todd responded in written testimony to Branchflower: "I have heard criticism that I am too involved with my wife's administration. My wife and I are very close. We are each other's best friend. I have helped her at every stage in her career the best I can, and she has helped me." A spokesman for the McCain campaign said Todd received e-mails at home so he could print them out there, allowing his wife to review them at night. He also came into the office to help care for Trig.

But with less than two weeks to go before the election, Politico.com may have done serious damage to the McCain-Palin campaign when it was revealed that the Republican National Committee spent $150,000 on designer clothes and accessories for Sarah and her family shortly after she was named to the ticket. The figure included shopping sprees at Neiman Marcus and Saks Fifth Avenue. Sarah's traveling makeup stylist, Amy Strozzi, who works on the reality TV show *So You Think You Can Dance*, billed the campaign $22,800 for parts of September and October. Strozzi and Sarah's hairstylist, Angela Lew, who both worked full-time during the two-month-long campaign, charged the RNC a combined $110,625 for their services. These aren't unusual fees for top-echelon Hollywood hair and makeup stylists, but the exorbitant sums derailed McCain's effort to bill Sarah as a middle-class American. On the campaign trail, both McCain and Sarah emphasized that the clothes didn't belong to her and that the $75,062 in items bought at Neiman Marcus and the $49,425 spent for clothes at Saks would be donated to charity. "Those clothes are not my property. We had three days of using clothes that the RNC purchased," Sarah told Fox News. "If people knew how Todd and I and our kids shop so frugally. My favorite shop is a consignment shop in Anchorage. And my shoe store is called Shoe Fly in Juneau, Alaska. . . . It's not, you know, Fifth Avenue–type shopping." Even McCain was forced to make a statement to quell the story. "She needed clothes at the time, and they'll be donated to charity," he said on a Florida campaign stop.

More details would come out after the election. Unidentified McCain aides unleashed a torrent of negative publicity about his running mate in an obvious attempt to deflect their own candidate's failure. One unnamed source described Palin and her family as "Wasilla hillbillies looting Neiman Marcus from coast to coast."

But Sarah's press adviser during the presidential campaign, Meghan Stapleton, laid the responsibility of the lavish spending at the feet of campaign staffers.

"The news reports concerning purchases of services and accessories are disappointing, considering Governor Palin did not authorize the expenditures made on behalf of the vice-presidential campaign," she said. "The governor was not consulted about these immaterial and inconsequential decisions, as she was focusing on the substantive areas of the campaign and running the state of Alaska. The decisions reflected in this disclosure are financially poor decisions made by campaign staffers hired by the campaign and not the governor. The governor expected judicious decisions to be made, and they weren't. She is absolutely appalled at the news and the amount of money reportedly spent on the vice-presidential campaign. To this day, the governor has not seen a list of expenses for the campaign and its staff, and she does not know who benefited from all the expenditures reported."

What clothing remained Sarah did return, and she denied forcing anyone to buy her anything. The RNC is currently doing an inventory to account for the items.

Sarah went on the *Today Show* and *Larry King Live* to defend herself. "I think that was the most ridiculous part of the campaign was the whole clothes story," she told King. "They weren't my clothes. They aren't my clothes. I don't have the clothes. I don't think it was $150,000 worth of clothes, anyway. It was for eight people—everybody in my family plus a couple of others that arrived at the convention with our overnight bags. There was a wardrobe there, just like there was staging and lighting and all the other effects of a national—a multi-, multimillion-dollar convention.

"I borrowed the clothes along the campaign trail, wore them once in a while, and they are back in the RNC's hands, where they were going to be all the way."

Sarah felt the Democratic ticket never did give a satisfactory explanation of who was dressing them and doing their makeup. "Kind of a double standard there, Larry," she said.

One friend, Judy Patrick, came to her defense, saying that Sarah is not a clotheshorse and is usually so busy that friends and family often pick clothing items up for her. Patrick, who works near Sarah's favorite consignment shop in Anchorage, was in there over the summer and picked up a few things for Sarah. "If I see something she likes and I know her size, I buy it, and she writes me a check, and if she doesn't want it, I take it back," Patrick said.

Before Sarah left for Minnesota, Patrick spoke to her and asked if she needed any clothes. Sarah requested blazers, so Patrick bought a few and had Sally Heath take them to her. "She kept one item, an eighty-dollar blazer," she said.

Reports also surfaced later that clothes for Todd exceeded $30,000. That kind of spending for the "First Dude" seemed out of character. In general, "Todd doesn't like to spend money on clothes," said Patrick. Sarah does have designer tastes, however. Back in June, she showed up for a *People* interview in Franco Sarto boots and Kazuo Kawasaki eyeglasses. Sarah also uses a personal shopper at Nordstrom. The shopper wouldn't comment, but Heather Bruce explained the process this way. "Sarah does not love to shop. I remember wandering into one of the nicer parts of Nordstrom, and I met the personal shopper, and she said she knew Sarah. She said, 'I know what size she is—she tells me what she needs, and she trusts me.'" In fact, Bruce said the woman already had an outfit for Sarah to look at when she returned from the campaign, but the shopper suggested she put it aside for Bruce so she could give it to Sarah as a Christmas present. "I don't know how she shops for the campaign," Bruce said. "But she looks good in anything."

As the campaign entered its final week, Sarah's family rallied to her side for final stops in Nevada. She weathered one last embarrassment as her campaign was hoodwinked by a Canadian comedian posing as the president of France, who got Sarah to admit she wanted to be president one day, "maybe in eight years." This revelation upset McCain, who preferred a running mate who kept her ambitions in check. It was also another example of Sarah's decision to take a more independent course from McCain, dubbed "going rogue" by one of McCain's advisers. In addition, Sarah also came out publicly against the campaign's decision to pull out of Michigan and criticized McCain's robo-calls to voters. Her side said Sarah was just trying to distance herself from a poorly managed campaign.

For the campaign's final days, Jim and Faye Palin, along with Chuck and Sally Heath, flew to Nevada to campaign with Sarah. The Palins and the Heaths traveled to Las Vegas, Henderson, Reno, and Elko. "In Carson City, Faye and I walked in a parade and shook hands with voters," Jim Palin said. "The support they showed for Sarah was amazing. We caught up with Todd and

Sarah in Reno and flew with them to Elko. We had a rally in a high school gym, and it was amazing. It was their final rally of the campaign, and the place was packed, and the people were going crazy. She introduced Todd—she always has a huge smile on her face when she introduces him—and she said, 'This reminds me of the time in high school when Todd and I played basketball together.' "

After the rally, the Palins and the Heaths drove to Salt Lake City to catch a plane to Phoenix, while Todd and Sarah flew home on a campaign jet to Wasilla to cast their votes on election day. When they returned to Phoenix for the election returns, they brought the kids with them, Jim said. "We are all so proud of her," Jim said. The family, he said, was sad when the results came back, but it wasn't totally unexpected. Obama captured fifty-two percent of the popular vote to McCain's forty-six percent. With ninety-eight percent of the precincts reporting, Obama amassed 349 electoral votes to McCain's 162. As Todd Palin might say, it was tough sledding from the outset.

McCain's obstacles included a faltering economy and a weak campaign budget. On election night, after exit polling showed Pennsylvania, Ohio, and Florida all going to Obama, the election was effectively over.

Some pundits debated whether McCain's choice of

a running mate amplified his issues concerning his age and health. That sentiment was buttressed when reports surfaced that Sarah, bucking protocol, had asked McCain if she could give her own farewell speech on a night traditionally reserved for the presidential candidates. Sarah's father, Chuck Heath, said Sarah's plea to speak on election night was motivated by her desire to pay homage to McCain.

"I was disappointed she didn't get to speak," Chuck said. "The campaign managers told her she was not to say anything. She had written two speeches—one if they won and one if they lost. And her plan was to introduce [McCain] and compliment him and talk about their friendship, which had been mischaracterized in the media. John is a very humble guy, and Sarah had some kind and flattering things to say about him."

Instead, it was McCain paying the compliments to her. During his gracious concession speech from Phoenix, he sincerely thanked Sarah, who tearfully nodded in appreciation. He also told a national television audience that he was impressed with Sarah's tenacious stumping over the last week of the campaign. The audience got the message that McCain felt he had made the right choice all along in selecting the Alaska governor as his running mate. McCain also recognized the historic nature of the moment—America had elected its first African-American president. Quelling boos from the crowd, he asked his supporters to get behind the new president and show full support, just as he planned to do.

"There was a lot of disappointment," said Chuck. "We were expecting it to be a lot closer, but it's not the end of the world, and you'll see Sarah again somewhere."

The next morning, Jim and Faye visited Todd and Sarah in their hotel suite to say good-bye. The elder Palins were flying back early, while Sarah, Todd, and the kids were expected to take a campaign jet home later in the day. "It was eight thirty a.m., and they were already awake, having breakfast with the kids," Jim said. "I'm so proud of her. Sure, she had some bumps in the road, but she just got better."

When this author reached Todd on his cell phone later in the day, he was busy getting ready to fly back to Wasilla with his wife and family and said he would pass along my request for an interview to his wife. "How are you doing?" I asked. Laid-back as ever, Todd replied, "We're doing good."

EPILOGUE

I'm sorry, you guys. I know you didn't ask for this, and I hope things are OK. It's all new to me, too," said Sarah Palin, calling her sister Heather from the campaign trail after another negative story.

The good news for the Palin and Heath families was that they got Sarah Palin back after the loss. "During the campaign, I thought, if she wins, our kids get to see her make history, and it would be nice to be a part of that," Heather said. "If she loses, we get her back, and she steps back into her old role of Aunt Sarah, sister, and governor of Alaska. She has learned so much, and she will be a better governor for it."

In an interview with CNN before departing Phoenix, Sarah said, "Right now, I can't even imagine running for national office in 2012. [It] sounds so far off I can't even imagine what I'd be doing then," she said, while carrying her infant son, Trig, and standing next to her seven-year-old daughter, Piper. "We will be enrolling him in kindergarten. She'll be headed to what? About fifth grade, sixth grade, by then."

If Sarah wanted to reenter the national scene, she would have some repair work to do. Surveys of voters from the presidential election reported that sixty percent believed she was unqualified for the presidency. Anonymous McCain aides were ruthless, saying Sarah didn't know Africa was a continent and that she could not name the three countries in the North American Free Trade Agreement—the United States, Canada, and Mexico. In her defense, Sarah said, "I consider it cowardly" that they wouldn't allow their names to be used. She said any comments she made during her debate prep about Africa and NAFTA "were taken out of context. That's cruel. It's mean-spirited. It's immature. Those guys are jerks if they came away with it, taking things out of context, and then tried to spread something on national news. It's not fair, and it's not right."

Republican consultant Todd Harris told *USA Today* that Sarah's future outside Alaska would be contingent upon how she improves her credentials and counters comments from McCain aides that she was a "diva" and a "whack job." But at her rallies, supporters were wearing homemade shirts declaring "Palin in 2012." And by "going rogue" on the campaign trail, expressing her opinions, and speaking candidly with journalists, she at least distinguished herself from McCain's losing campaign.

Ed Rollins, a former political director for Ronald Reagan, said after the election, "She definitely is going to be the most popular Republican in this country when this thing is over."

"If there's a role for me in national politics, it won't be so much partisan," Sarah told the *Chicago Tribune* while waiting in line for coffee at a Wasilla café. "It will certainly be a unifier type of role."

Sarah seemed to be in rescue mode in December when she hit the campaign trail for Sen. Saxby Chambliss of Georgia. Chambliss was in a run-off with Democratic challenger Jim Martin for a coveted seat in the U.S. Senate. A victory for Martin would have meant the Democrats would have been one vote closer to the sixty needed to stop Republican filibusters. Chambliss won easily, and he was thrilled to have Sarah touting his conservative record promoting gun rights and opposing abortion. Crowds in Augusta, Savannah, Gwinnett County, and metro Atlanta wore pink "Palin 2012" T-shirts and "Palin for President: You Go Girl" buttons, greeting the Alaska governor with chants of "Sa-rah!"

"Losing an election doesn't mean we have lost our way," she told an excited crowd of 2,500 in Perry, Georgia. Chambliss told Fox News that Sarah "truly is a rock star. I mean, she came into town to help us electrify our base, make sure that these folks get fired up and turn out tomorrow, and she did exactly that."

Now that the national election was over, at least Sarah wouldn't have to worry about Tina Fey impersonations on *Saturday Night Live*. The actress told *Entertainment Weekly* that she was hanging up her beehive wig to focus on her day job on *30 Rock*. While Sarah complimented Fey's impersonation, Fey was annoyed by critics who called her Palin portrayal mean and sexist.

"What made me super-mad about it was that it seemed very sexist toward me and her," Fey told *Vanity Fair*. "The implication was that she's so fragile, which she is not. She's a strong woman. And then, also, it was sexist because, like, who would ever go on the news and say, 'Well, I thought it was sort of mean to Richard Nixon when Dan Aykroyd played him,' and 'That seemed awful mean to George Bush when Will Ferrell did it.' And it's like, 'No, that's not the thing. This is a comedy sketch on a comedy show.' 'Mean,' we agreed, was a word that tends to get used on women who do satirical humor and, as she says, 'gay guys.' " Fey added, "I feel clean about it. All these jokes were fair hits."

The reaction in Alaska could be chilly for a while. Alaska Democrats criticized Sarah's decision to leave the state to campaign for Chambliss in Georgia, though her spokesman said the governor had been absent only five of the then twenty-seven days since the presidential election.

Community activist Chris Whittington-Evans, who lives in Palmer, Wasilla's sister town, said he believes "her carte blanche in Alaska has run out, but it's still a red state with conservative, independent, and libertarian roots. She has been exposed a bit, but if she can keep gasoline inexpensive and get the potholes filled, she will be rewarded for it. If she gets the natural-gas line built, she'll get rewarded for it."

Much of her success could depend on the price of oil. If the price keeps dropping, it could pose problems for Sarah, since the revenue for state services is directly tied to oil profits. If that happens, she may be forced to exercise unpopular program cuts.

If politics isn't in the crystal ball, a future in Hollywood might be. The entertainment industry has taken note of Sarah's unique appeal and the excitement she generated during public appearances. Her popularity could translate nicely into a career as a talk-show host or political analyst on cable news. Speaking to Reuters, morning-show producer Steve Friedman observed that "any television person who sees the numbers when she appears on anything would say Sarah Palin would be great," referring to the huge ratings numbers she garnered on *Saturday Night Live* and the *CBS Evening News* for her interview with Katie Couric. "The passion she has on each side, love and hate, makes television people say, 'Wow, imagine the viewership.' "

An autobiography or biopic TV movie also would seem natural, given her rich life story. "Sarah Palin is the hottest property in media. Producers and agents all over showbiz are trying to figure out what to do with her. One serious possibility could be an Oprah-style talk show," said Hollywood publicist and media expert Michael Levine. "I think she's a perfect fit as a TV host because she stirs passions on both sides."

Chuck Heath said the support for his daughter has been overwhelming, with more than 100,000 letters delivered to Anchorage and Wasilla since Sarah hit the national stage on August 29. "We're getting several hundred letters a day now, and we read them all," he said, adding that they've set up an office to handle the influx of mail. "We have people answering the letters, and where appropriate, we're sending many on to the governor. Many of the letters that have come after the election offered their condolences, and almost all of them have said the media is a bunch of SOBs. People are asking if they're going to see her out there again because they want another chance to vote for her."

In the short term, Sarah had two other new titles to preoccupy herself with: grandmother and mother-in-law. Bristol, who turned eighteen on October 18, gave birth to a son, Tripp Easton Mitchell Johnston, on December 27, 2008, and the wedding to the baby's father, Levi Johnston, had been expected in the summer of 2009, though Sarah wished it to be earlier. "Hopefully before that," she told *People*. "Bristol turns eighteen in a few days [October 18]. That's what we wanted her to wait for: eighteen, and a decision on her own about how she's going to go forward, her and Levi, at this point."

Sarah will be forging ahead, too, and she's giving hints of what's to come. She said she wants to keep representing working women in a positive manner. "I'm not going to let women down," she said. She said she also wants to be an advocate to the millions of families with special-needs children across the country. "You have a friend," she told them on the campaign trail. Already in Alaska, Sarah increased spending for programs for special-needs children and bolstered state funding to fight fetal alcohol syndrome and aid adult mental-health services and faith-based social services.

Sarah may indeed run for the U.S. Senate one day, but as of this writing, she was concentrating on the governors' races of 2010. "The future for us is not the 2012 presidential race," she said in her November speech to the Republican Governors Association. "It's next year and our next budget, and the next reforms in our states, and in 2010, we're going to have thirty-six governors' positions open across the U.S. That's what we're focused on."

Palin also reminded her GOP peers not to let "obsessive, extreme partisanship" get in the way of "doing what's right."

"We're in the minority, but let's not be negative," she urged. "Losing the election does not mean losing our way."

SOURCES

Adams, Chris. "Palin Approval Rating Drops in Alaska." *Anchorage Daily News*, October 1, 2008.

Anonymous. "Any Excuse to Run a Picture of Sarah Palin [Corruption in Alaska]." Wonkette blog, November 12, 2007.

Ayres, Sabra. "Alaska's Governor Tops the Charts; 89–93 Polls Ratings: Palin Has Pleased Most Voters by Sticking to Her Promises." *Anchorage Daily News*, May 30, 2007.

Becker, Jo. "Once Elected, Palin Hired Friends and Lashed Foes." *New York Times*, September 14, 2008.

Bell, Tom. "Alaskans Line Up for a Whiff of Ivana." *Anchorage Daily News*, April 3, 1996.

Benet, Lorenzo. "Sarah Palin Sees Her Son Off to Iraq." People.com, http://www.people.com/people/article/0,,

SOURCES

20225153,00.html?xid=rss-fullcontentcnn, September 11, 2008.

Bernton, Hal. "Palin Heartily Embraced Earmarks; Regular Requests to Congress As Mayor, Alaska Governor—Running Mate McCain Opposes Common Practice As 'Disgraceful.' " *Seattle Times*, September 3, 2008.

Blackledge, Brett G. "AP Investigation: Palin Got Zoning Aid, Gifts." Associated Press, September 28, 2008.

———. "Alaska Funded Palin Kids' Travel." Associated Press, October 21, 2008.

———. "Palin Office Defends Charging for State Travel." Associated Press, October 22, 2008.

Braun, Stephen. "Underestimate Palin at Your Own Risk, Former Rivals Say." *Los Angeles Times*, October 1, 2008.

Bumiller, Elisabeth. "Internal Battles Divided McCain Palin Camps." *New York Times,* November 6, 2008.

"Campbell Brown Rips McCain's Sexist Treatment of Palin." *Huffington Post*, September 23, 2008.

Carlton, Jim. "Ethics Adviser Warned Palin about Trooper Issue." *Wall Street Journal*, September 11, 2008.

SOURCES

Chambers, Mike. "Gov. Murkowski Appoints Daughter to fill Senate Seat." *Associated Press*, December 20, 2002.

Cockerham, Sean. "Lieutenant Governor Candidates Speak Out; GOP: Crowded Field of Hopefuls Try to Distance Themselves from the Pack." *Anchorage Daily News*, July 25, 2002.

———. "Fink Touts Palin for Lieutenant Governor; Campaign: Gail Phillips Touts Her Own Qualifications for Job." *Anchorage Daily News*, July 28, 2002.

———. "The Race for No. 2; GOP Lieutenant Governor Candidates Offer Answers to Key Question." *Anchorage Daily News*, August 21, 2002.

———. "Fund-Raiser E-Mail Haunts GOP Leader; Ruedrich: Message Raises 'Serious Ethical Questions,' Critic Says." *Anchorage Daily News*, November 4, 2003.

———. "Ruedrich Resigns Post as Regulator of State Oil and Gas Commission; Conflict: Alaska GOP Chairman Made Decision After Meeting with Governor." *Anchorage Daily News*, November 9, 2003.

———. "Groups Call for 3-Part Fiscal Fix; Letter to Governor: Leaders Push Cuts, Taxes, Tapping Fund." *Anchorage Daily News*, November 11, 2003.

SOURCES

———. "Frustrated, Palin to Quit Oil Panel Job; Ethics Law: Ex-Mayor Wants to Talk about Ruedrich's Stepping Down." *Anchorage Daily News*, January 17, 2004.

———. "Embattled Renkes Resigns; State Attorney General Blames News Media, Political Attacks." *Anchorage Daily News*, February 6, 2005.

———. "Election Chances Difficult to Judge; Governor: Alaska Pollsters Say Much Depends on the Field." *Anchorage Daily News*, December 11, 2005.

———. "Count Binkley in for GOP Race; Governor: Fairbanks Republican Would Keep Murkowski Substance but Not His Style." *Anchorage Daily News*, December 20, 2005.

———. "Choice Stuns State Politicians." *Anchorage Daily News*, August 30, 2008.

———. "Palin Electrifies GOP." *Anchorage Daily News*, September 4, 2008.

Cohen, Jon. "Skepticism of Palin Growing, Poll Finds." *Washington Post*, October 2, 2008.

Davey, Monica. "Palin Pregnancy Interrupts GOP Convention Script." *New York Times*, September 2, 2008.

SOURCES

Demer, Lisa. "Baby Has Down Syndrome." *Anchorage Daily News*, April 22, 2008.

———. "Is Wooten a Good Trooper? Palin's Ex-Brother-in-Law: Union Says Yes, but Investigation Found Serious Concerns." *Anchorage Daily News*, July 27, 2008.

DeVaughn, Melissa. "Natural First Parents; Chuck and Sally Heath's Lives Emphasize an Affinity with Wilderness." *Anchorage Daily News*, November 18, 2007.

Dilanian, Ken. "Palin Backed Bridge to Nowhere in 2006." *USA Today*, August 31, 2008.

Ditzler, Joseph. "Palin Is Ready for Return to the Public Arena and Service; Q&A." *Anchorage Daily News*, June 8, 2005.

———. "Palin Makes Race Official; For Governor: GOP Vet Backs All-Alaska Pipeline, Aid to Schools." *Anchorage Daily News*, October 19, 2005.

Dobbyn, Paula. "Bipartisan Duo Seeks Formal Ethics Probe of Governor, Renkes; Conflict: Palin, Croft Question Investigation's Credibility." *Anchorage Daily News*, December 11, 2004.

Halpin, James. "Palin Signs Ethics Reforms; Law Closes

Loopholes, Stipulates Bans as Legislative Cleanup Begins." *Anchorage Daily News*, July 10, 2007.

Hoffman, Jan. "The Buzz About Palin Started Here." *New York Times*, September 14, 2008.

Holmes, Elizabeth. "Palin Heads Home, Says 2012 Is a Long Way Off." *Wall Street Journal*, November 5, 2008.

Hopkins, Kyle. "Same-Sex Unions, Drugs Get Little Play; Governor's Race: Gas Line Leaves No Room to Talk on Other Hot Issues." *Anchorage Daily News*, August 6, 2006.

———. "Knowles Brings Abortion into Debate; Governor: Palin Has Disputed the Issue's Relevance to the Election." *Anchorage Daily News*, September 20, 2006.

———. "It's Governor Palin; Candidate of Change Resonated with Voters." *Anchorage Daily News*, November 8, 2006.

———. "Inaugural Eye; With Campaign Over, Palin Government Takes Shape." *Anchorage Daily News*, December 3, 2006.

———. "Palin Tries New Tactic to Unload Hated Jet; Aircraft Broker: Turbo North Aviation Takes Stab at Murkowski Albatross." *Anchorage Daily News*, April 22, 2007.

Hunter, Don. "Partisan Politics Put Aside by Palin; Governor's Race: GOP Candidate Talks to Democratic Club." *Anchorage Daily News*, January 27, 2006.

Jenkins, Sally. "Palin's Strengths Rooted in Alaska; Family and Friends Hope She'll Show Trademark Confidence during Debate." *Washington Post*, October 2, 2008.

Johnson, Kaylene. *Sarah*. Kenmore, WA: Epicenter Press, 2008.

Johnson, Kirk. "In Palin's Worship and Politics, a Call to Follow the Will of God." *New York Times*, September 6, 2008.

Johnson, Rebecca. "Sarah Palin: An Alaskan Straight Shooter Is Determined to Fight Corruption." *Vogue*, February 2008.

Joling, Dan. "Alaska GOP Head Has No Plans to Resign after Ethics Settlement." Associated Press, June 23, 2004.

———. "Palin Picks AG, Commerce, Health Commissioner." Associated Press, December 14, 2006.

Kaye, Randi. "McCain Criticized Wasilla Earmarks in 2001." www.cnn.com, September 10, 2008.

Kizzia, Tom. " 'Fresh Face' Launched, Carries Palin's Career; Rising Star: Wasilla Mayor Was Groomed from an Early Political Age." *Anchorage Daily News*, October 23, 2006.

SOURCES

————. "Rebel Status Has Fueled Front-Runner's Success Election 2006; Palin: Her Reputation as a Crusader Has Had Perfect Timing." *Anchorage Daily News*, October 24, 2006.

————. " 'Creation Science' Enters the Race; Governor: Palin Is Only Candidate to Suggest It Should Be Discussed in Schools." *Anchorage Daily News*, October 27, 2006.

————. "Appeal Came from Being an Outsider and a Fresh Face." *Anchorage Daily News*, November 9, 2006.

————. "Commute and Current Job Work for Palin; Q&A Part Three of Three." *Anchorage Daily News*, September 4, 2007.

Komarnitsky, S. J. "Palin Wins Wasilla Mayor's Job; Nolfi, Hartrick Capture Borough Assembly Seats." *Anchorage Daily News*, October 2, 1996.

————. "New Wasilla Mayor Asks City's Managers to Resign in Loyalty Test." *Anchorage Daily News*, October 26, 1996.

————. "Wasilla Mayor Fires Police, Library Chiefs." *Anchorage Daily News*, January 31, 1997.

————. "Museum Staff Quits in Anger." *Anchorage Daily News*, August 6, 1997.

SOURCES

————. "Palin Wins Re-Election in Wasilla; Mat-Su Rejects Zoning as 17% Cast Ballots." *Anchorage Daily News*, October 6, 1999.

————. "Judge Backs Chief's Firing; Wasilla Mayor within Rights." *Anchorage Daily News*, March 1, 2000.

————. "Wasilla Elections Low-Key; Apathy: Few Residents Seem Overly Interested in Local Politics." *Anchorage Daily News*, September 28, 2002.

Kovaleski, Serge F. "Palins Repeatedly Pressed Case against Trooper." *New York Times*, October 10, 2008.

Kristol, William. "The Wright Stuff." *New York Times*, October 6, 2008.

"Locals Abuzz over Candidate's Idaho Roots; Palin Was Born in Sandpoint and Attended Both NIC, UI." *Spokesman Review*, August 30, 2008.

MacGillis, Alec. "As Mayor of Wasilla, Palin Cut Own Duties, Left Trail of Bad Blood." *Washington Post*, September 14, 2008.

————. " 'First Dude' Todd Palin Illustrates Alaska's Blend of Private and Public." *Washington Post*, September 22, 2008.

SOURCES

Mauer, Richard. "Palin to Back Miller for U.S. Senate; Decision: Former Wasilla Mayor Will Not Run, Says Lisa Murkowski, Knowles Too Alike." *Anchorage Daily News*, April 24, 2004.

———. "GOP Chief Settles, Is Fined; Randy Ruedrich: Party Boss Admits Violations, to Pay $12,000." *Anchorage Daily News*, June 23, 2004.

———. "Palin Explains Her Actions in Ruedrich Case; Ethics: Former Oil and Gas Commissioner's Missteps Went beyond His Partisan Work." *Anchorage Daily News*, September 19, 2004.

Mendoza, Martha. "Palin: More and Less Than She Seems." Associated Press, September 6, 2008.

Morain, Dan. "Trig's Story Is Safe Ground for GOP." *Los Angeles Times*, September 8, 2008.

Murphy, Kim. "Sarah Palin's Husband Todd Was a Fixture at Governor's Office." *Los Angeles Times*, October 12, 2008.

Myers, Steven. "Obama Calls Attacks on Him Out of Touch." *New York Times*, October 6, 2008.

Nagourney, Adam. "In Debate, GOP Ticket Survives a Test." *New York Times*, October 3, 2008.

SOURCES

"Opinion." *Anchorage Daily News*, September 25, 2004.

"Palin Daughter Pregnant." Commercial Appeal, Press Service, September 2, 2008.

"Palin Decides to Reside in Wasilla; No Mansion: Governor Won't Move to Juneau Until the Legislature Starts Up." Associated Press, August 30, 2007.

"Palin Flies High As Reformer; Gov. Palin: Higher Tax on Oil, Bids for a Gas Line Help Develop National Attention." *Anchorage Daily News*, December 27, 2007.

Parker, Ashley. "Alaska to the Fore." *New York Times*, September 4, 2008.

Parker, Kathleen. "Palin Problem." *National Review*, September 26, 2008.

Pesznecker, Katie. "Iron Dog Unleashed; Governor Starts the Longest Snowmachine Race and Cheers for Husband." *Anchorage Daily News*, February 12, 2007.

Popkey, Dan. "Idaho Claims Palin As One of Its Own." *Idaho Statesman*, September 13, 2008.

Powell, Michael. "Palin's Hand Seen in Battle over Mine in Alaska." *New York Times*, October 22, 2008.

Ruskin, Liz. "Mum's the Word from Murkowski; Rumors

SOURCES

Rule; Across the Nation, State, Theories Abound on Who the Next Senator Will Be." *Anchorage Daily News*, December 4, 2002.

Scheiber, Noam. "Barracuda." *New Republic*, October 22, 2008.

Smith, Ben. "Documents Detail Palin's Political Life." Yahoo.com,http://news.yahoo.com/s/politico/20080902/pl_politico/13084/print;_ylt=AhtOjambUkr9_41HBpn3t C_Cw5R4, September 2, 2008.

Smolowe, Jill. "Sarah & Todd Palin: Alaska's Multitaskers." *People*, September 22, 2008.

"State Studies Potential Fred Meyer Impact on Lake Wasilla." Associated Press, December 25, 1998.

Szep, Jason. "Palin's Troubles Mount for McCain in White House." Reuters, September 29, 2008.

Thornburgh, Nathan. "Call of the Wild." *Time*, September 15, 2008.

Volz, Matt. "Prop. 4 Takes Long, Windy Road to Ballot; Senate Vacancies: Alaskans Will Decide If Governor Can Fill Seat." *Anchorage Daily News*, October 23, 2004.

Wallenstein, Andrew. "Sarah Palin May Have Brighter

SOURCES

Future in Hollywood." Reuters, October 24, 2008.

Wellner, Andrew. "Wasilla's Police Force Marks 15 Years' Growth." *Mat-Su Valley Frontiersman*, June 1, 2008.

Westfall, Sandra. "The Palins." *People*, November 11, 2008.

Wilmot, Ron. "2,000 Miles Full Throttle; Punch It: Snow-machiners Go from Wasilla to Nome and Back with $75,000 at Stake." *Anchorage Daily News*, February 12, 2005.

Yardley, William. "Governor Finishes Third in Alaska G.O.P. Primary." *New York Times*, August 24, 2006.

————. "Palin Start: Politics Not As Usual." *New York Times*, September 3, 2008.